THE
DILMUN
TEMPLE
AT SAAR

The publication of this book has been supported by
the National Bank of Bahrain

London–Bahrain Archaeological Expedition: Saar Excavation Reports I

Contributors

David Cutler, Shahina Farid, Charles French
Emily Glover, Marlies Heinz, Brian Irving, Martin Jones
Timothy Lawrence, Roger Matthews, Wendy Matthews
Dominique de Moulins, Robyn Stocks

Illustrations

Photography: Marcus Woodburn
Colour artwork: Robert Britton
Finds illustrations: Duncan Woodburn

THE
DILMUN
TEMPLE
AT SAAR

Bahrain and its Archaeological Inheritance

Edited by

Harriet Crawford, Robert Killick, Jane Moon

KEGAN PAUL INTERNATIONAL
London and New York

in association with

The London–Bahrain Archaeological Expedition
The Institute of Archaeology, University College London
The Ministry of Cabinet Affairs and Information, State of Bahrain

First published in 1997 by
Kegan Paul International
UK: P.O. Box 256, London WC1B 3SW, England
Tel: (0171) 580 5511 Fax: (0171) 436 0899
E-mail: books@keganpau.demon.co.uk
Internet: http://www.demon.co.uk/keganpaul/
USA: 562 West 113th Street, New York, NY, 10025, USA
Tel: (212) 666 1000 Fax: (212) 316 3100

Distributed by
John Wiley & Sons Ltd
Southern Cross Trading Estate
1 Oldlands Way, Bognor Regis
West Sussex, PO22 9SA, England
Tel: (01243) 779 777   Fax: (01243) 820 250

Columbia University Press
562 West 113th Street
New York, NY 10025. USA
Tel: (212) 666 1000   Fax: (212) 316 3100

Set in Garamond
Printed in Great Britain

British Library Cataloguing in Publication Data
Crawford, Harriet
DilmunTemple at Saar : Bahrain and Its
Archaeological Inheritence
1. Title
939.49
ISBN 0-7103-0487-0

Library of Congress Cataloging-in-Publication Data
The Dilmun Temple at Saar : Bahrain and its archaeological
inheritance / Harriet Crawford, Robert Killick, and Jane Moon.
148 p. 276 cm.
Includes bibliographical references and index.
ISBN 0-7103-0487-0
1. Sar Site (Bahrain)   2. Temples--Bahrain--Sar Site.
3. Excavations (Archaeology)--Bahrain--Sar Site.   I. Killick, R.G.
II. Moon, Jane.   III. Title.
DS247.B23C73 1995
939'.49--dc20
95-15529
CIP

Dedicated with permission
to

His Highness Shaikh Isa Bin Salman Al-Khalifa
Amir of the State of Bahrain

Patron of the London–Bahrain Archaeological Expedition

Contributors

Harriet Crawford
Institute of Archaeology
University College London
31–34 Gordon Square
London WC1H 0PY

David Cutler
Jodrell Laboratory
Royal Botanic Gardens
Kew, Richmond
Surrey

Shahina Farid
Pre-Construct Archaeology
Creekside Wharf
The Stowage
Deptford
London SE8 3DF

Charles French
The McDonald Institute for Archaeological
Research
University of Cambridge
Downing Street
Cambridge CB2 3ER

Emily Glover
Institute of Archaeology
University College London
31-34 Gordon Square
London WC1H 0PY

Marlies Heinz
Orientalisches Seminar
Albert-Ludwigs-Universität Freiburg
Postfach
D–79085 Freiburg

Brian Irving
Environmental Archaeology Unit
University of York
Heslington
York Y01 5DD

Martin Jones
The McDonald Institute for Archaeological
Research
University of Cambridge
Downing Street
Cambridge CB2 3ER

Robert Killick
Institute of Archaeology
University College London
31–34 Gordon Square
London WC1H 0PY

Timothy Lawrence
Jodrell Laboratory
Royal Botanic Gardens
Kew, Richmond
Surrey

Roger Matthews
British Institute of Archaeology at Ankara
24 Tahran Caddesi
Ankara
Turkey

Wendy Matthews
McDonald Institute for Archaeological
Research
University of Cambridge
Downing Street
Cambridge CB2 3ER

Jane Moon
McDonald Institute for Archaeological
Research
University of Cambridge
Downing Street
Cambridge CB2 3ER

Dominique de Moulins
Ancient Monuments Laboratory
English Heritage
23 Savile Row
London W1X 1AB

Robyn Stocks
School of Archaeology,
Classics and Ancient History
University of Sydney
NSW 2006
Australia

Contents

Foreword

For many years scholars and archaeologists have been hard at work investigating the origins and growth of Bahrain's earliest civilization. Their efforts have been rewarded by the uncovering of many new archaeological sites on Bahrain.

The London–Bahrain Archaeological Expedition began excavations at Saar in 1990. The research has focused on the excavation of a Dilmun settlement dating to the Early Dilmun period, around 2000 BC. The discovery and excavation of this settlement and its associated temple represent important additions to the archaeological heritage of Bahrain, and complement earlier discoveries at Barbar, Diraz, and Umm As-Sejjur.

This book contains a full account of the excavation and finds from the Dilmun Temple at Saar. It discusses in detail the design and construction of the temple and provides invaluable new information about daily life, social customs and religious beliefs of the period.

The Ministry of Cabinet Affairs and Information encourages scientific publications such as this one and is aware of the contribution they make towards revealing the significant role played by Bahrain throughout its long history.

The results achieved by the The London–Bahrain Archaeological Expedition are of immense importance, providing a significant increase in our knowledge of Ancient Dilmun society as well as enhancing our onjoyment of archaeology by improving our historical perspective of the distant past.

I would like to extend my thanks and appreciation to all members of the The London–Bahrain Archaeological Expedition, and particularly to the editors of the volume, Drs. Harriet Crawford, Robert Killick, and Jane Moon. I would also like to pay tribute to the role of the Arab Mission and to its leader, Dr. Hussein Kandil, who first excavated the site in 1983.

This book, I believe, will make an excellent addition to scholarly works on the history of Bahrain's past civilizations, and I am sure that researchers and all other interested parties will find it a valuable source of historical information. Finally, I hope that the programme of research at Saar will continue and that it will result in further publications in the near future.

Mohammed Ebrahim Al-Mutawa
Minister of Cabinet Affairs and Information

Acknowledgements

Six years of excavating on Bahrain have passed by all too quickly. During that time, the Expedition has grown from fairly modest beginnings in 1990 into a major archaeological endeavour. The results of this work can be seen at Saar itself, where much of the ancient town now lies open to visitors, and in the breadth and number of our publications. None of this would have happened without the help of the individuals mentioned below and on the following pages. By responding so generously to our many requests for financial and logistical support they ensured that the Expedition not only survived but prospered, and that Ancient Saar is no longer under threat of redevelopment, but a potential national monument to be proud of.

HH Shaikh Isa bin Salman Al-Khalifa, Amir of the State of Bahrain, kindly agreed to become our patron. We also received an immense amount of help and support from the Ministry of Cabinet Affairs and Information (formerly the Ministry of Information).

In particular, we would like to thank the following: HE The Minister, Mohammed Al-Mutawa; Dr. Abdulla Yateem, Assistant Under Secretary for Culture and National Heritage; Dr. Kadhim Rajab, Assistant Under Secretary for Tourism; Shaikha Nayla Al-Khalifa, Director of the National Museum; Mr. Khaled Al-Sendi, Curator of Antiquities; and Mr. Abdul Aziz Soweileh, Superintendent of Archaeology. We also owe a great debt to the former Minister of Information, Mr. Tariq Almoayed.

In the creation of the Expedition Mr. John Shepherd, former HBM Ambassador to Bahrain, and Mr. Michael Rice played crucial roles. The British Council, under Mr. John Wright, provided the funding for our exploratory first visit to Bahrain. Mr. Yousif Al Shirawi proved himself a formidable ally in championing our cause, and we have also been the recipients of many kindnesses from Shaikh Mohammed bin Salman Al-Khalifa on whose land much of Ancient Saar sits. Mr. John Samuels provided major financial support during the early years as well as hosting many Expedition events in his splendidly-restored wind-tower house.

We must also thank those companies and institutions which have consistently supported the research work at Saar. We would particularly like to acknowledge our major supporters: Al Ahli Commercial Bank, Aluminium Bahrain, Bahrain Petroleum Company, Ministry of Cabinet Affairs and Information and Philip Morris. Bapco has been especially generous in providing free accommodation and transport for the Expedition as well as a host of other services, maintaining a tradition of support for archaeological work that goes back to Geoffrey Bibby.

Major financial support has also been received from The British Academy, while the programme of environmental archaeology was funded largely by grants from the National Geographic Society.

Finally, we must offer thanks to our professional staff of archaeologists for their commitment to the project, displayed particularly during the second season which corresponded with the Gulf War of 1991; to our unpaid volunteers who *inter alia* eradicated the Expedition's entire backlog of unsorted flotation residues and to our Bahraini workforce from Saar village who adapted well to the demands and rigours of archaeological excavation. It is a pleasure to acknowledge here our debt to them all.

Robert Killick, Jane Moon, Harriet Crawford
December 1995

10

SUPPORTERS

Aluminium Bahrain
A. Latif Al-Aujan Group
AJM Kooheji & Sons
ABN Amro Bank N.V.
Adel Fakhro Enterprises
ad-shop
Aeradio Technical Services
African & Eastern (Bahrain)
Airmech Eastern
Al Ahli Commercial Bank
Al Ahlia Insurance Company
Al Hilal Group
Al Jazira Cold Store Company
Al Ubaf Arab International Bank
Al Zamil Group
American Women's Association
Arab British Chamber of
    Commerce
Ashrafs
AT & T
Australian Meat & Livestock
    Corp.
Awal Plastics
Bahrain Airport Services
Bahrain Centre for Studies &
    Research
Bahrain Fibreglass
Bahrain Financing Co.
Bahrain Flour Mills Company
Bahrain Insurance Co.
Bahrain International Bank
Bahrain Jewellery Centre
Bahrain–Kuwait Insurance Co.
Bahrain Maritime & Mercantile
    International (BMMI)
Bahrain Technical & Trading Co.
    (BTTC)
Bank of Bahrain & Kuwait
Banque National de Paris
Bapco
Banagas
Banz
Basrec
Batelco
British Academy
British Aerospace
British Bank of the Middle East
British School of Archaeology in
    Iraq
Brown and Root
Budget Rent-A-Car
Buehler International
Business International
Caltex (Bahrain)
Cathay Pacific Airways
Charlotte Bonham Carter
    Memorial Trust

Chemical Bank
Citibank
Clifford Chance
Credit Suisse
Deborah Services
Denis Buxton Trust
Diplomat Hotel
Ernst & Young
Fakhro Electronics
FAM Supermarket
Flemings
Fortune Promoseven
Garmco
GPIC
Global One
G.P. Zachariades (Overseas) Ltd
Gulf Air
Gulf Business Machines
Gulf Colour Laboratories
Gulf Daily News
Halliburton Worldwide Ltd
Hasan Mansouri
Hempel Marine Paints
Inchcape Middle East
Intergraph
International Agencies Co. Ltd
Investcorp
Jalal Costain
Jardines Insurance Brokers
Jashanmals
Kazerooni Contracting
Kimberly-Clark Regional Services
    (Bahrain)
Kodak (Near East) Incorporated
KPMG Fakhro
Linacre Associates (Overseas) Ltd
Lloyds Register of Shipping
Mansouri McInerney
McDonald Institute for
    Archaeological Research
Memac
Merrill Lynch
Ministry of Foreign Affairs,
    Germany
Ministry of Cabinet Affairs &
    Information, State of Bahrain
Mohammed Jalal & Sons
Morrison International Ltd
National Bank of Bahrain
National Geographic Society
National Imports and Exports Co.
National Insurance Co.
NCR Corporation
Oriental Press
Palmer Cowen
Philip Morris
Quantas Airways
Saad Investments

Sanwa Bank Ltd
Scotpac International
Serco-IAL Ltd
Standard Chartered Bank
Swiss Bank Corporation
Tele-Gulf Directory Publications
The British Council
Thomas Cook
Thomas De La Rue & Co. Ltd
Tourism Projects Co.
UCO Marine Contracting
Unitag
United Energy Ltd
United Gulf Bank
United Gulf Industries
    Corporation
United Insurance Co.
Yaqubi Stores
Yateem Brothers
YBA Kanoo
Yousuf Mahmood Husain
Zamil Aluminium

ROLL OF HONOUR

Salman Abassi
Abdul Ghaffar Abdulla
Irene Abu Hamad
Kamelia Ahmed
Deyana Ahmadi
Mohamed G. Akhtarzadeh
Sameer Alwazzan
Abdul Rahman Ali Al Wazzan
Lynne Al Wazzan
Hussain Al-Ansari
Mohammed Al-Ansari
Abdul Latif K. Al-Aujan
Wajeeha Al-Baharna
Saad Al-Hooti
Samar Al-Gailani
Sh. Dana Al-Khalifah
Sh. Haya Ali Al-Khalifah
Sh. Salman bin Hamad bin Isa Al-
    Khalifah
Fawzi Al-Jaber
Mahmoud Al-Mahmoud
Mohammed A. Al-Mannai
Abdulla Al-Moajil
Salman Al-Moosawi
Abdulla Al-Muqla
Yousif Al-Nashaba
Abdulnabi Al-Sho'ala
Mohammed Al-Shroogi
Hala Al-Umran
Shamsan Al-Waswasi
Mohammed Al-Zamil
Walid Al-Zamil
Mohamed Issa Al-Zeera

Fatima Alireza
Y.K.A. AlMoayed
Nabil AlMoayyed
Ismail Amin
Y.Ando
Eric Arnaud
Alex & Margaret Askew
Beshara Ayyash
Mohammed Bahman Ali
Gordon Bailey
Arvind Baliga
John Bartley
Bisharah G. Baroudi
Phil Basson
Bill Beckett
Vinay Benjamin
Ian Best
Lou & Val Best
Geoffrey Bibby
James Black
Rainer Boehmer
Abdullah Buhindi
Pat Brown
Gunter & Uschi Buhr
Alison Bywater
Mavis Callanan
Peter Callenfels
Elizabeth Carter
Paul Carty
Richard Chalkeley
Diane Chapman
Yan Chew
Kathy Chouai
Angela Clarke
Eric Cockerill
Jeremy Cooper
Colin Craig
Jonathan & Eileen Crosse
Basil Dandan
Alan Davies
Brian Davis
Gordon Davis
Sadiq Dawani
Tony Dawes
Harry Dawkins
Mahmoud Daylami
Paul & Lucy Dean
Iqbal Dhanse
Neil Dinan
Carol Dunk
Stephen Egerton
Joy & Cyrus Elliot
Otilie English
Ebrahim Eshaq
Jan-Peter Faberij de Jonge
Adel Fakhro
Jamal Fakhro
Malcolm Faren

Mohamed A. Ferhan
Louise Foster
Steven Fullenkamp
Michael Fuller
Peter Gartrell
Tony Gillett
Patrick Grant
Steven Green
Hussein Haider
Jamil Hajjar
Per Halberg
Jonathan Hann
Christine Hänzi
Mohammed Haroon
David Harris
Nicholas A. Harrison
Chris Hart
Abdulrazak Hassan
Andrew Hearn
Don Hepburn
Graham Honeybill
Martina Horan Al-Akber
Les Horton
Ridha Hourani
Wim Huidekoper
Flemming Højlund
Mahmood Hussein
Patrick Irwin
Steven Jackson
Clive Jacques
AbdulRahman Jaffer
Mohammed Jalal
Rodney James
Tony & Diane James
Abdul-Rahman Jamsheer
Bharat Jashanmal
Fadel Jassim
Clarke John-Cox
Peter Johnson
Eric Jenkinson
John Jones
Roger Jordan
Abdullah Juma
Hassan Juma
George E. Karam
Abdul-Latif Kanoo
Adrine Katchadurian
George Khamis
Corinne and Bill Khouri
Howard King
Nemir Kirdar
Sam Knight
David Knights
Mahmood Kooheji
Keith Levers
Ian Lewty
Graeme Lindsay
Jeremy Long

Kevin Lovegrove
Paul & Liz Lovell
Frances Luff
Edward Lutley
Ewan Macmillan
Mark Mansour
Karim Mansouri
Suhail Habib Matlub
D. Marpole
Rob McEwen
Christopher McGonigal
Robin McIlvenny
Dave and Marthe Merrey
Ronnie Middleton
Akram Miknas
Geoffrey Milne
Ishu Mirchandani
Peter Moon
Roger Moorey
Abdulla Rahman Morshed
George Morton
Eddie Moutrand
Khamis Muqla
Paul Nevin
Ebrahim Nonoo
John Pastorel
Bas Payne
Kay Patience
Brian Pickering
Kae & Danny Pratt
Chris Preece
Brian Prosser
Mohammed Redha
John Riddick
Peter Rooke
Barry Rowe
Mustafa Rugibani
Kerim Salimi
Jalil Samaheji
Jaime Samour
John Samuels
Sirvat Sakr
Malik Sarwar
Chris Scarre
Alan Schofield
May Seikalay
Mohammed Shehabi
Tracey Shiels
John Shorter
Peter Smith
Peter Spink
Sreekumar
David Stephenson
Peter F. Stevenson
Ginny Stigter
Peter Taylor
Tim Thom
John Tidy

Godwin Tofte
Wendy Toorani
Hugh Tunnell
Toni Underwood
Krishna Vasdev
Jamil Wafa
John Weir
Mel White
David Wilkie
Alan & Elspeth Wright
Henry Wright
Peter Wynne
Hussain Ali Yateem
Mohammed Yateem
Colin Young
Jalil Zainal
Khalil Zaman

TEAM MEMBERS

Daoud Yusuf Ahmed
Khalil Yusuf Al Faraj
Adele Arthur
Daniel Barrett
David Bartlett
Ben Bellefroid
Sarah Blakeney
Amanda Brady
Dominique de Moulins
Keith Dobney
Shahina Farid
Kate Flavin
Rowena Gale
Jonathan Gillian
Hilu Ginger
Emily Glover
Neil Gorsuch
Amanda Haughey
Maria Heinz
Alison Hicks
Martin Hicks
Brian Irving
Mohammed Jaffar Isa
Abdul Kerim Jasim
Deborah Jaques
Yvonne Jenkins
David Jennings
Ali Ibrahim Kadhim
Jennifer Kiely
Idunn Kvalo
Alan Lupton
Catharine Maclaughlin
Wendy Matthews
Bill Moffat
Saleh Ali Mohammed
Rebecca Montague
Wendy Murphy
Mark Nesbitt

Kirsty Norman
Abbas Ahmed Salman
Mustafa Ibrahim Salman
Lewis Somers
Robyn Stocks
Jaffer Jawad Tahar
David Underwood
Alex Wasse
Duncan Woodburn
Marcus Woodburn
Abdulla Hasan Yahir
Ali Omran Yusuf

VOLUNTEERS

Fred Adkins
Nabil Al Shaikh
Christopher Appel
Marie Appel
Robert Bradley
Jan Cumming
Claire Dallimore
Disa & Ruri Fedorowicz
Steven Green
Traudel Halangk
Dale Halderman
Izzaladin A. Al Hassan
Juliet Hutchinson
Sophie Jalal
Helen Jones
Shelagh Jordan
Corinne Khouri
Renate de Kleine Stephenson
Jill Leonard
Liz Lovell
Jill Markham
Suzanne Martinchalk
Dee Mills
Carol McCoy
Chris Meritzis
George Morton
Lauren Mendeck
Meg Mendeck
Aida Mendez
Dee Mills
Brigitte Opitz
Kae Pratt
Fiona Price
Helen Raymont
Edwina Riddell
Dale Rose
June Seddon
Sue Stankevicius
Chantelle Wadingham
Anita Walker
Sandy Warringer
Eriko Yoshino
Roseanne Zaziski

Chapter 1. Early Dilmun and the Saar Settlement

The Early History of Dilmun

The Early Dilmun culture flourished in the Arabian Gulf more than four thousand years ago, from the middle of the third millennium to about 1700 BC. Its origins lie in the Arabian Peninsula, but during its most important and prosperous period, from about 2000 BC - the time of the Saar temple, it was Bahrain which became the centre of an innovative and independent trading nation. As such, it played a crucial role in the international commerce linking southern Iraq (ancient Mesopotamia) with the Oman Peninsula and the Indus Valley, the home of the Harappan culture [1].

The Dilmun people themselves have not left us any written records, but there are many references to the country in the cuneiform documents of Mesopotamia. In fact, the name Dilmun appears in some of the oldest written documents in the world, dating to about 3200 BC (Nissen 1985). The term may originally have applied to the whole area south of Mesopotamia, but gradually became more specific as the region became better known. By the end of the third millennium it came to mean the area now covered by the Eastern Province of Saudi Arabia and the island of Bahrain, and then Failaka too. By the beginning of the second millennium, Bahrain had become the political and economic focus of the area.

Dilmun's overseas connections

Contacts between Mesopotamia and the Gulf began even earlier than this, and date back to the 'Ubaid period of the late fifth and early fourth millennia BC. The first sailors would have some difficulty in recognizing the region today [90]. Minor climatic fluctuations occurred, but there is no agreement yet about the details. The region has, however, been getting dryer since about AD 1300 (Larsen 1983, 170). Coastlines have definitely fluctuated, but the situation is complex, with many apparently very local variations

(Potts 1990a, 19–21). Small 'Ubaid habitation sites such as al-Markh, where much fish and shell-fish was obviously consumed, are today well inland, which is evidence for the sea being higher around Bahrain during the fourth millennium (Roaf 1974). It no doubt contained even more edible creatures than its now over-exploited waters can support. Wind patterns, on the other hand, were probably much the same, so that the ancient sailors would have followed routes similar to those taken by sailing boats in modern times.

Dilmun lay across one of the major trade routes of the time, linking the Indus valley (ancient Meluhha, in modern Pakistan) and Oman (ancient Magan), each rich in raw materials, with the highly-developed but resource-starved Mesopotamia. Especially vital was the supply of Omani copper for tools and weapons. Bahrain was particularly strategically placed between the head of the Gulf and the straits of Hormuz, and offered safe anchorage and plentiful fresh water to the sailors and traders who transported the vital supplies of copper and hard woods from the Indus Valley and Oman up to Mesopotamia. More exotic luxury goods such as ivory, semi-precious stones and strange birds were also traded along the same route (Ratnagar 1981). Textiles and foodstuffs, both archaeologically invisible, are thought to have travelled from Mesopotamia in the other direction (Crawford 1973), and many of these goods were bought and sold in the markets of Dilmun, bringing with them great prosperity for its people.

As well as being a major international stop-over and market place for merchants involved in these transactions, much as Bahrain is today, Dilmun also seemed to have a merchant navy of its own. In addition to carrying goods for other people, it exported a limited range of its own garden produce. Documents from Mesopotamia mention onions (or garlic) and dates (Potts 1990a, 183). Records of about 2600 BC refer to the ships of Dilmun bringing timber to build new temples in the southern

Mesopotamian city of Lagash (Sollberger and Kupper 1971, 46). In the 24th century ships from Dilmun were known to have moored at the quays of Agade, capital city of the Akkadian Empire (Englund 1983, 87). Other texts of various periods refer to the superior size of Dilmun dates (Kramer 1963), which were much sought after. Written evidence referring to trade during the early second millennium - the period during which the Saar temple was built and used - is not extensive. However, we are lucky in having the business records of one merchant called Ea-Nasir who was based in the southern Mesopotamian city of Ur and who traded with Dilmun on behalf of a local syndicate. His main business was in copper, and his business methods seem to have left much to be desired (Potts 1988, 121–2).

In these circumstances it is unsurprising that the archaeology and material culture of Dilmun shows evidence for contacts with all its major trading partners. These contacts enrich the local culture, but never overwhelm it. Both Mesopotamian barrel weights and Indus cube weights have been found in Early Dilmun contexts in Bahrain (Højlund and Andersen 1994, 395–397) [91]. The earliest seals from Bahrain show evidence for close links with the Indus Valley. Like the Indus ones they are stamp seals, though they are round not square, and in some cases Indus Valley writing occurs on them. The humped bull which is a central motif on the Harappan seal is also very popular on the early 'Persian Gulf' seals, as they are called. A little later, the Indus Valley influence seems to have become of less importance and motifs from Mesopotamia, like the god in a horned hat, begin to appear. The shape of the seal changes: it becomes larger and flatter. The back is also decorated with a characteristic design of three incised lines and four dotted circles [92]. These changes in fashion reflect changing patterns of trade, and seem to indicate that ties with the Indus Valley became of less importance during the first quarter of the second millennium, while those with Mesopotamia became closer. This change is also reflected in the Mesopotamian texts of the early second millennium, which deal exclusively with trade between Dilmun and Mesopotamia, with no mention of Magan or of the Indus. The period between about 2000 BC and 1700 BC marks the height of Dilmun's importance as an independent political and economic power.

Dilmun was an urban civilization, with major centres. The earliest of these identified to date is the settlement of Tarut in the Eastern Province. Also dating back to the third millennium is the greatest Dilmun city, Qala'at al-Bahrain, which was enlarged and walled around 2000 BC, and remained the most important place on Bahrain into Islamic times. Settlement on the island of Failaka, off Kuwait, did not start until the early second millennium (Højlund 1987, 157).

A unifying feature of Dilmun urban centres is the well-built stone architecture which has no parallels in either Mesopotamia or the Indus valley, for in both these areas mudbrick was the main building material. Tarut remains unexcavated, but preliminary survey showed massive blocks of worked masonry (Bibby 1970, 388). At Qala'at al-Bahrain there is a massive stone town wall complete with gateways. The skill in masonry which is demonstrated here and at some of the other important sites on Bahrain may have been learned from the builders of the fine masonry tombs typical of the Oman peninsula during the slightly earlier Umm an-Nar period (2500 BC). For example, at the Barbar temple, the main religious complex on Bahrain, the method of jointing some of the stones is matched at the Umm an-Nar tombs at Hili in Abu Dhabi (Doe 1986) [93]. On the other hand, the plans of the temples on Bahrain have no parallels outside the island, and show a wide variety of forms.

Religion

That the people of Dilmun believed in an afterlife is apparent from the large number of tombs found on Bahrain, but details about their religion are lacking as yet. It has been suggested that water played an important part in the mythology of Ancient Dilmun (Bibby 1986, 194), but only at the Barbar temple has a well actually been found *inside* a temple enclave. The variety of temple plans suggests that a number of different gods and goddesses were worshipped, each with their own ritual and own style of temple. One of them may have been a water god, perhaps even the Mesopotamian god Ea, or a local counterpart. Various myths and stories refer to this deity's special relationship with Dilmun (al Nashef 1986). The only Dilmun god we know by name is Inzak, described as god of Dilmun (*ibid*, 341) but nothing is known about his attributes. He was not just a local figure, because a temple was also dedicated to him in the city of Susa, capital of Elam (south-western Iran). The name of another deity, Meshkilak, perhaps the wife of Inzak, also appears in the cuneiform record.

Other scraps of information about the religion of Dilmun can be gleaned from the stamp seals characteristic

[1] The Gulf and its neighbours
This map, with east at the top, highlights the advantageous geographical position of Bahrain which
enabled it to control trade up and down the coast between Oman and southern Iraq.

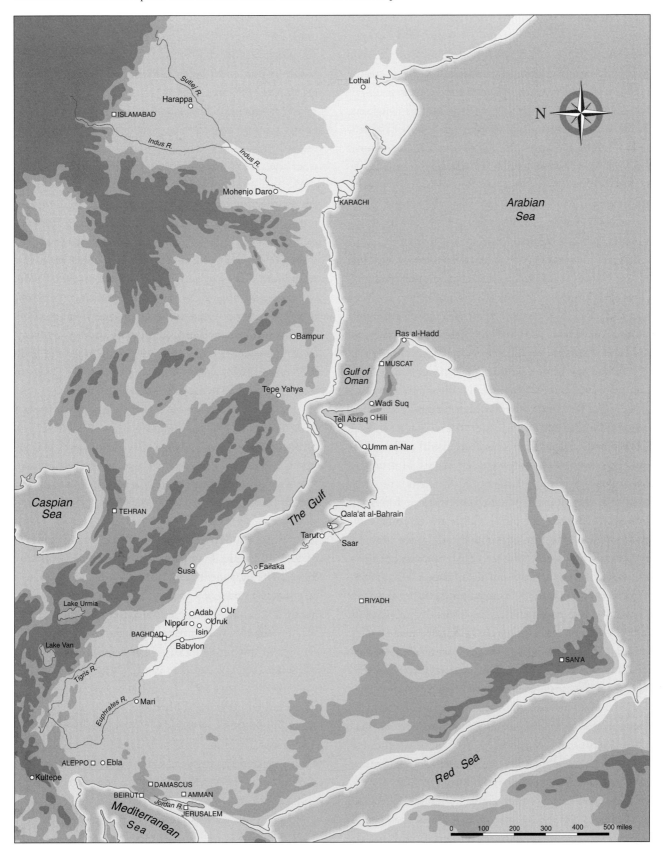

of the Dilmun culture. They sometimes show offerings being made to altars and divine symbols [94]. A seal found at Saar appears to show a dramatic murder scene from Dilmun mythology, though sadly we cannot attribute it to any particular god. One of the Mesopotamian creation myths describes Dilmun as a fertile and beautiful place where many plants were created as the result of various complicated and incestuous unions between the great Sumerian god Enki and his daughters. These hints mark the limit of our knowledge of the religion of Dilmun, though the skill lavished on the temples and their prominence among the buildings in the settlements they served indicates how important they were to the inhabitants.

Graves, politics and society

The great mound-fields of Bahrain were among the first of the island's antiquities to attract attention from travellers with an archaeological bent (Potts 1990a, 209). As late as 1947, however, their date and significance were poorly understood, and Geoffrey Bibby was probably not the only visitor to be told they were Portuguese (1970, 25). Once the most significant feature of the Bahrain landscape, the mound-fields have all but disappeared, though the few small groups which remain continue to exercise fascination over visitors to the island. Indeed, from photographs taken when one could still become quite lost in these seemingly endless 'forests' of tumuli, it is easy to sympathize with the early researchers who imagined that they must represent the graves of foreigners brought to Bahrain for burial: there seemed to be more than an island the size of Bahrain could have provided corpses to fill (Potts 1990a, 214–215). Estimates of actual numbers vary, but a figure which has gained recent acceptance is that of 172,000 mounds, of which perhaps 78% are single adult interments (Larsen 1983, 45; Potts 1990a, 215). Other types are discussed below. Some recent research has suggested that a population of no more than 18,000 souls could easily require so many tombs over a five hundred year period (Frohlich 1983, 60 and Table 6; Larsen 1983, 45–47). As research into Early Dilmun artefacts progresses, it becomes increasingly obvious that, with occasional exceptions, there is nothing 'foreign' about the material found in these graves. On the contrary, they represent a single material culture.

Nearly all Early Dilmun graves on Bahrain have been robbed in antiquity, so complete groups of grave-goods are almost unknown. Whatever the structure of the tomb, the body was usually laid on its side, with its knees bent. Typical finds are simple jewellery, occasional seals, pottery, metal artefacts and bitumen-covered baskets. Preservation of skeletal material is generally poor, but surviving teeth point unmistakably towards a very high incidence of dental caries, no doubt exacerbated by the consumption of Dilmun's famous dates (Højgaard 1986, 66).

While social differentiation on the basis of grave-goods cannot be affirmed from the current state of research, differences in size of tomb are apparent. There were one or two particularly high mounds among those of the Saar mound-field, and at A'ali, in the centre of the island, there still survives a large group of monumental mounds, up to 12 m in height [95]. Some have been excavated (Frifelt 1986), and although they have inevitably been robbed, these graves must once have been magnificent. They have two-storey chambers with a floor and ceiling of huge slabs of stone, and the contents were probably rich too: pieces of decorated ivory, perhaps from furniture or containers, painted pottery, and a gold bead of quadruple spirals were among the scraps recovered [96]. The A'ali tombs obviously represent an elite group of some description (Reade and Burleigh 1978).

The presence of monumental buildings in the form of both tombs and temples indicates a considerable level of prosperity, and also the ability on someone's part to organize large and expensive public projects. There is at least a case for supposing that the early second millennium saw the formation of a state in Dilmun. Apart from monumental tombs, there is a single reference to a king, in a letter written at Mari, a city in Syria. It concerns a present of fine oil for the king ('Lugal') of Dilmun (Groneberg 1992). The settlement at Qala'at al-Bahrain seems to have acquired the status of a capital about this time: it grew to about 15 ha, and a wall was built around it. Pottery-making ceased to reflect the influence of Mesopotamia to any great extent, and developed indigenous styles (Højlund 1992).

The demise of Early Dilmun

Early Dilmun's independence was not to last, however. The major political changes in Mesopotamia and Syria which characterize the period around 1700 BC also had profound effects on the trade routes down the Arabian Gulf. South Mesopotamia was systematically devastated in acts of political retaliation by the kings of Babylon. This devastation included the destruction of the main port of Ur, through which goods had entered the Mesopotamian market from the south. The same kings of Babylon also extended their power northwards into Syria to include the important trading city of Mari, which controlled much of the traffic up and down the middle Euphrates to the Anatolian highlands. The highland area is rich in the same raw materials, copper and timber, that had previously been supplied via the Gulf. The new political conditions made it feasible to bring such heavy goods down-river to Babylonia direct from their sources in central and eastern Anatolia. The last extant reference to Dilmun copper also mentions for the first time copper from the country of 'Alashiya', modern Cyprus (Potts 1990a, 226). The market for Dilmun copper was drying up, and there seem to have been problems in the Harappan cities too. Many Dilmun settlements were abandoned. Qala'at al-Bahrain continued to be occupied, but by the mid-second millennium BC it had lost its independence, and had a governor appointed by the king of Babylon (Potts 1990a, 310).

Dilmun Settlement on Bahrain

Aquifers of stored Pleistocene rainwater are present near the ground surface in Bahrain, and this water is available in certain locations, mainly near the north coast, from natural springs or from wells. Settlement has therefore always concentrated in the northern part of the island.

The major excavated Early Dilmun settlement sites on Bahrain are Qala'at al-Bahrain, Barbar, Diraz and Saar [97]. There is also an unexcavated settlement just south of Saar and another inside the confines of the Al-Areen wildlife park near Zallaq, on the west coast. Surveys (such as Larsen 1983) indicate others, but it is hard to be sure whether sherd scatters really indicate settlement, as reworking of land for agriculture and building has resulted in much redeposition. It is highly likely, however, that there was a significant settlement in the A'ali region.

Qala'at Al-Bahrain

Qala'at al-Bahrain (Bahrain Fort, or Ra's al-Qala'a), the island's most important site in antiquity, is on the seashore 6 km to the NE, and visible from Saar on a clear day [98]. Here the Danish Expedition which began work in 1953 sampled the superimposed levels of periods ranging from the mid-third millennium BC to the time of the Portuguese. The earliest occupation of the site was

dubbed 'City I', and the succeeding level 'City II', divided in the latest, revised consideration of the excavations, into a, b, and c (Højlund and Andersen 1994, 464). The Kassite period begins with City III, before which Saar was already abandoned.

Early Dilmun levels at Bahrain Fort lie for the most part very deep, and were only reached in certain places, with no large exposure of coherent architecture. City I levels, for instance, were only clearly represented in a sounding to the north of the fort, and this is where the 'chain-ridge' pottery was identified as characteristic of the archaeology of City I (Bibby 1970, 159). An important feature of the City II occupation, which is contemporary with the main exposure at Saar, was the great wall constructed around the Bahrain Fort settlement. Remains of houses, and a seal workshop were found near the north part of the wall. In City II the 'chain-ridge' pottery disappears, to be replaced by a similar type, also easily recognizable, with plain ridges. Other aspects of the material culture are also paralleled at Saar.

Although little can yet be said of the architectural nature of the Dilmun remains at Bahrain Fort, there can be little doubt that they represent a large and important settlement, which may have housed perhaps 3,000 people (Højlund 1989).

Barbar

The Barbar Temple, to the north of Saar, was discovered in 1954, or rather 'rediscovered' as Captain E.L. Durand had noticed a pierced limestone block protruding from the crest of the mound in 1879 [99]. Excavations (by Helmut Andersen and Peder Mortensen of the Danish Expedition) continued until 1962, by which time three superimposed temples had been investigated. The earliest dates to the end of Bahrain Fort City I. Its successor, of City II date, is the more impressive, with a massive oval platform of ashlar blocks, and an upper terrace with a pair of enigmatic semicircular structures on top. Other features of this upper terrace were three upright subrectangular stone blocks on the south side, each with a hole through. These have been variously interpreted as tethering posts for sacrificial animals (Glob 1955, 192) and as votive stone anchors (Mortensen 1986, 184). To the north of the semicircular structures were two socketstones, one of which, sticking through the surface, had caught Durand's eye. The third temple, of which little remains, included a large, square platform, and is probably of late City II date.

The temple was built to include the site of a fresh-water spring on its western edge, around which a well was constructed, with steps down to it, and channels leading off from the bottom. This has led to much speculation as to whether the temple cult was centred on the *abzu,* the underground sweet-water sea of Mesopotamian myth, which is in the charge of the god Enki (Potts 1990a, 204). Several unusual finds were made at Barbar, such as fine alabaster vessels, lapis beads and copper objects, including the well-known copper bull's head, which has Central Asian affinities (Lombard and Kervran 1989, 30) [100].

Although it looms in apparent isolation today, sherd scatters in the vicinity suggest that the Barbar Temple was surrounded by other occupation.

Diraz

About 3 km NW of Saar, and less than 2 km from Barbar, were the remains of a considerable settlement, much of it of Dilmun date, just east of the modern village of Diraz [101]. Badly disturbed by later activities, most of it is now beyond archaeological intervention. At the south end, however, the fragmentary remains of a temple were excavated in 1973 by a British team (McNicoll and Roaf, 1975; Roaf 1976a). The use of circular stone structures, perhaps offering tables, outside the Diraz Temple provides a striking parallel with Saar.

Umm al-Sujur

At the opposite end of the Diraz settlement to the temple, on the northern edge, the Danish Expedition excavated next to a spring known as 'Ain Umm al-Sujur [102]. On the spoil-heaps around it were strewn large blocks of dressed limestone. Local legend tells of a well at Diraz destroyed in the 7th century AD on the orders of a caliph, as a punishment for an attempted reversion to idolatry on the part of the locals. The excavations revealed a stone staircase leading down to a well and, on the staircase, two decapitated stone animal statuettes, discoveries which seemed to echo the story. Eight years later, however, the pottery was re-examined and recognized to be, in fact, of City II date (Bibby 1970, 81–85).

In 1993, a second investigation was made at Umm al-Sujur (Konishi 1994). No more could be made of the undated stone blocks or the great spoil heaps around the modern well, but another staircase with a well-head was discovered adjacent to the first, as well as irrigation channels leading off from both. The remains of other structures in the vicinity were fragmentary and incoherent, but a finely carved 'altar' of stone, with curved top, was found on the stairs to the second well. Given the presence of cult objects - perhaps the animals were to 'protect' the well - it would not be too imaginative to see offerings being made at the settlement's vital water supply, whether or not connected to a temple now vanished.

The great limestone blocks remain unexplained, but their presence has given rise to the assumption that a temple stood nearby, and the stone rams and 'altar', if contemporary with them, could be taken to support the view that the wells had some cultic connection.

Archaeological Remains in the Saar Area

The Early Dilmun settlement

The archaeological site of Saar is named after the modern village of the same name which lies in the NW part of the main island of Bahrain, on the northern edge of a large ancient burial field. The village has in fact given its name to various excavations carried out around and about the area. In 1954, Peter Glob excavated under the modern village and found walls and Islamic pottery over three metres below the surface under drift sand (Bibby 1970, 67). Islamic pottery can also be found on the surface to the SE of the village, indicating a sizeable settlement in this area. To the west and south of Saar village stretched the extremely large mound field, and just off its eastern flank, 1 km south of the modern village, is the Early Dilmun settlement of which we write [103].

The settlement was first discovered by Dr. Moawiyah Ibrahim and colleagues (Ibrahim 1982, 3). When the proposed route of the causeway which now links Bahrain with Saudi Arabia was found to cut through the middle of the Saar burial field, rescue excavations were undertaken, starting in 1977. Burial mounds along the route of the causeway in an area designated Sar el-Jisr were excavated by an Arab expedition and a complex of interconnecting graves discovered, called here the Southern Burial Complex (Ibrahim 1982, Mughal 1983). It was while excavating these burial mounds and cemetery that the surrounding area was examined in the hope of finding associated settlement, and Ancient Saar was duly discovered. It is half-a-kilometre to the north of the cemetery.

The settlement was subsequently sampled between 1983 and 1985 by an Arab team led by Dr. Hussein

Kandil. The results of some of this work exist in manuscript form but are not yet published (Kandil n.d.). Bahraini archaeologists also identified a second burial complex lying between the first one and the Early Dilmun settlement, referred to here as the Northern Burial Complex, which remains largely unexcavated.

The Saar mound-field

The Saar mound-field contained perhaps 15,000 mounds, now mostly cleared, which have been the subject of intermittent rescue archaeology. In addition to the excavations of Ibrahim and Mughal already mentioned, a large section of the mound-field west of the settlement was excavated recently by the Bahrain Directorate of Antiquities [104]. Altogether it is clear that most of these tombs were approximately contemporary with the settlement at Saar. They probably also served the unexcavated settlement south of the causeway road. There is also the possibility that other, undiscovered, Early Dilmun settlements contributed to their numbers.

Similar to many others of comparable date, the essential mound burial on the Saar field consisted of a rectangular, stone-built tomb, capped with one or more large stones, and surrounded by a ring-wall. Variations include more than one tomb inside a ring-wall, and subsidiary ring-walls added on, with more interments within. The area inside the ring-wall was deliberately filled with earth and stone chippings, but the characteristic humped shape, still so familiar four thousand years later, resulted from the eventual collapse of the ring-wall from the internal pressure of its earth fill. Originally, many of these structures resembled free-standing circular towers, or short cylinders (Mackay *et al.* 1929, 5) [105].

Southern Burial Complex

Another cemetery associated with Saar is the Southern Burial Complex - the so-called 'Honeycomb Cemetery' - which was excavated between 1979 and 1982 by archaeologists working on mounds to be destroyed by construction of the Saudi causeway. This cemetery was not made up of individual burial mounds. Instead, the graves were interlocking. Each one consisted of a rectangular chamber, usually enclosed by an arc of outer walling tacked on to the side of earlier cells, so that graves multiply outwards from the original single cell at the centre [106].

Most of the artefacts found in this cemetery can be dated to the early second millennium BC, again contem-

porary with the main phase of settlement at Saar. A few pieces can be dated earlier, specifically seals of 'Persian Gulf' type, and steatite vessels of the 'série récente' style (Ibrahim 1982, 25; Mughal 1983, 9–10, 30). Whether these pieces should be considered heirlooms or not is debatable (Potts 1990a, 177), but in either case they still fall within the time range of the Saar settlement.

Northern Burial Complex

The Northern Burial Complex is located on the eastern edge of the limestone ridge and covers an approximate area of 100x60 m [107]. It is only a few metres away from the Southern Burial Complex, and perhaps it is merely an extension. It was found by Bahraini archaeologists who exposed the tops of many of the graves but did not actually open them. A sample of ten graves was excavated by the London–Bahrain Expedition in 1991, but otherwise the cemetery remains unexplored. The following comments should, therefore, be considered provisional.

The cemetery seems to be another of the 'honeycomb' type. The graves again interlock with one another and are built in the same fashion: a stone-built tomb capped with large stones and surrounded by an arc of stone wall. Along the eastern edge of the cemetery there appears to be an area reserved for child burials, while along the northern limit there are several examples of 'stand-alone' burial mounds.

The ten excavated graves produced few surprises. All were robbed and contained very little human bone. In fact, on closer inspection it could be seen that the entire cemetery had been robbed systematically. Most graves had a capstone missing, while holes in the outer walls of others showed where the robbers had burrowed through into the neighbouring burial. This suggests that the robbers knew where to go and that the grave robbing occurred quite soon after the construction of the graves.

The few finds recovered show that at least the excavated graves are contemporary with the settlement and with the Southern Burial Complex [108].

A neighbouring Early Dilmun settlement

The nearest settlement of the same date as Ancient Saar lies just 250 m SW of the Southern Burial Complex across the other side of the highway to Saudi Arabia. It is in fact nearer to that complex than is our own settlement. This one is unexcavated, but there is a sherd scatter and ruin-field extending over an estimated 40,000 square metres, making it perhaps twice the size of the Saar settlement. Early Dilmun pottery of City IIB and City IIC date has been found on the surface, as well as masonry and plasterwork, so it is clearly contemporary with Saar.

Late Dilmun/Tylos building

In the SW corner of the Northern Burial Complex, there are the remains of a rectangular building which was constructed directly on top of the Early Dilmun graves [109]. Finds by the Bahraini team who excavated the building are said to include a silver coin from the reign of Kavad I, the Sassanian monarch who ruled from AD 488–531 (Vine 1993, 74). Thought by some to be a fire temple, the purpose and function of this building in fact remains uncertain.

The Settlement at Ancient Saar

Location

The Early Dilmun settlement occupies a favoured spot on the eastern slope of the limestone ridge which runs parallel to the west coast [110]. The advantages of building a settlement here are first of all that there would have been an ample supply of fresh water, as evidenced by a well discovered on the edge of the settlement during the 1995 excavations. Secondly, in a flat, intensely hot and humid landscape, the slight elevation of the ridge (about 13 m) catches any available breeze. A third reason, as yet unproven, is that there was probably easy access to the eastern seaboard. This may seem surprising, given that today the west coast is much closer to the settlement than the east (3.7 km as opposed to 7 km). However, the study of historical and geomorphological maps of Bahrain shows that even quite recently there was an inlet stretching inland from the east coast to within 3.6 km of Saar. Furthermore, examination of the archaeobotanical and faunal remains from the settlement show that the economy of the town was heavily biased towards the exploitation of marine resources (Dobney & Jaques 1994, 107; Glover 1995) which suggests relatively easy access to the sea.

Settlement size and layout

The maximum estimated size of Ancient Saar is 22,500 square metres (2.25 ha). To the west and south of the central part of the site the edge of settlement is delimited by bedrock appearing on the surface. Northwards, towards the Later Islamic settlements, a resistivity survey

carried out in 1995 and followed up by selective excavation showed that the town appears to end abruptly only some 30 m north of the temple. On the eastern flank, preliminary excavations around the well suggest an equally abrupt end to the buildings. The site is thus smaller and far more compact than our original guess (Killick *et al.* 1991, 110). It is strung out along the side of the limestone ridge for a distance of approximately 250 m, whereas its maximum width across the ridge is only 100 m, and in most places considerably less [111].

The main characteristics of the town are: a wide street with subsidiary alleyways running off approximately at right angles; a temple on the highest point; housing blocks sometimes arranged around an open square; and two- and three-roomed houses with regular suites of domestic installations [112, 113].

The main artery of the settlement, labelled 'Main Street', leads from the southern limit of the town up the light rise on which the temple is sited, and on towards the northern boundary. Where it passes the temple entrance another road, 'Temple Road', leads off to the NE, narrowing as it proceeds down the hill into the plain towards the hypothetical sea inlet. There is a well in the same vicinity [114]. Two small alleyways lead along either side of the temple, both of which, as we now know, open out into small public squares with houses grouped around.

Housing blocks

Houses were usually built in blocks, consisting of three or more separate dwellings [115]. Each house in a block displays a marked uniformity of ground plan. With one or two exceptions, the basic dwelling unit consists of an outer rectangle, with an inner rectangle built into one corner, providing an L-shaped outer area and a single inner room, on average about 35 square metres altogether [116]. Several houses have a further open area behind. Ceiling debris found in House 100 suggests that the inner room was roofed, but evidence for covering of other areas is not yet forthcoming. The state of the floors suggests that they were at least partly open to the weather. Experience of the climate, however, would strongly indicate some shade or covering during the hot season.

The space inside the houses was certainly exploited in different ways, but many of the domestic features such as hearths, basins, benches and bins show a regularity of construction as well as position. Typically, there is a basin just inside the door, built of stone and lined with plaster [117]. Next to it is a jar stand of similar construction (in

House 206 the jar was still *in situ*), the two providing a washing or water-cooling area. Cooking was done in the L-shaped courtyard. There are some simple hearths, but many houses have a sophisticated 'kitchen range' built against a wall [118]. This consists of a semicircular hearth at ground level, made of ashy paste, and next to it a set of tripod legs of plastered stones, just the right size for an average round-bellied Dilmun cooking pot. A bread-oven, identical to the modern *tannur* of the Near East, may be adjacent or separate. Other kitchen equipment often found in a house includes a large quern, and usually several grindstones and pounders.

It will be evident that most of the population lived in the same sorts of houses, used the same kinds of domestic equipment, and used it in much the same way.

Non-domestic areas

There are, of course, exceptions to the standard housing pattern. The most notable of these are: the area immediately NW of House 3 which included a large storage tank, an oven and a plastered pit; House 56 which in its final form had a group of tiny rooms, some of them coated with a hard gypsum plaster; and House 53, unusual for its size and the range of storerooms and enclosed courtyard at the rear.

House 56 may have been connected with the processing of dates. This is suggested by the presence of a quantity of charred date-stones in one of the small rooms and by an analysis of the plaster of the same room which has been shown to be impregnated with date juice. Other interpretations of room function cannot, however, be ruled out.

Across Main Street, the occupant of House 53 seems to have needed a lot more storage space than his neighbours to carry out his business, whatever that might have been [119]. One of the few clues we have is the presence of an unusual number of copper fragments found in one of the rooms (Moon & Killick 1995).

Otherwise, there is a remarkable lack of evidence for public and administrative buildings, or for craft-specific or industrial activities within the town. The ubiquity of casting slag suggests, however, that copper objects were being fashioned at Saar in spite of a current lack of other evidence to support this assumption.

The Development of the Settlement

The earliest settlement at Saar seems to have been confined to an area beneath the temple and its surrounding houses. Excavations below House 202, in

Test Pit 1 of the temple, and east of House 222, have all produced examples of 'chain-ridge' pottery which predates the main phase of the settlement. It is the area around the temple which has the greatest build-up of archaeological deposits (5.45 m). Further out, by Houses 1–4 and Houses 100–111, the deposits are much shallower, and this early phase does not seem to exist.

The subsequent main phase of the settlement, as represented by all the houses shown on the site plan, seems to have lasted for some time, long enough for several floor levels to have built up inside most houses, and for modifications to have been made to the architecture in many places. Some of these modifications are minor, such as a blocked doorway indicating a change in circulation within a house. Others reflect more major changes, perhaps in ownership, where, for example, two originally separate houses in the same block are remodelled as one.

In other cases, there had clearly been time for demolition and reconstruction. House 52, for example, was abandoned prior to the construction of House 53, and House 102 also predates its neighbours. Three houses along the main street (Houses 53, 56 and 100) have porches outside their front doors, and these have been added at a time when the street level had risen far above the lowest floors in those houses. The people in House 210 had refashioned their threshold several times to keep up with the changing level of the road outside.

At some point, the settlement began to contract again until it was eventually abandoned entirely. All the signs point to this being a gradual planned event rather than a hurried departure. There is no evidence for destruction: no burning, and none of the disorder which results from looting. Three houses (Houses 53, 203 and 57) had their main entrances blocked with stones, the original wooden doors having presumably been removed. This suggests not only that the householders left in no hurry, but also that they removed to a location not too far distant. There is further evidence that the abandonment was piece-meal. Those houses with porches appear to have been occupied after the neighbouring ones had fallen into ruin and the temple itself seems to have remained in use longer than most other buildings in the town.

Date of the Settlement

Comparison of the material assemblage from the houses at Saar with Qala'at al-Bahrain, Failaka and with sites in the

Lower Gulf suggests a date for the main phase of the town of around 1900 BC. Any estimate of the length of occupation represented by this phase remains subjective, but given the evidence for long use of the houses we would estimate that it is between one and two hundred years.

The initial occupation of the site dates back much earlier: on the evidence of carbon 14 dates, to as early as 2300 BC [38]. One would assume continuity of occupation from this time all the way through to the final abandonment of the settlement.

Chapter 2. The Architectural History of the Temple

The temple was built on the highest part of the settlement mound, at the junction of the two main streets. For much of its life it was a stand-alone building, fronting onto the junction of Main Street and Temple Road, and separated from adjacent buildings by two small alleyways (labelled North and South Alley) [120]. Buildings to the north and south were terraced down from the temple [121]. The temple is trapezoidal in shape, with a curious loop of wall in one corner. A single entrance in the NE side gave access to the main room, some 16.30 m long [122]. In the NW corner, a second doorway led into a small storeroom.

The temple was built of rough uncoursed limestone, quarried locally, and the walls were bonded with a mortar of small stone chippings, gypsum and sand. Three thickenings in the long walls and one each in the centre of the short wall indicate where the main roof beams were placed, at least from Phase 3 onwards. These were also supported by the three central columns. No roofing material was recovered from the temple, but excavation of the houses has shown that layers of palm frond were laid on the roof over beams and poles, and presumably sealed with a mud or gypsum-based plaster.

The exterior of the temple originally had a hard, smooth coat of plaster, of which a single fragment remained adhering to the front wall near the doorway. Internally, some crimson-painted plaster fragments were found collapsed in the NE corner.

The building was excavated by the previous expedition down to what we believe was the highest surviving floor. Subsequently we excavated in certain areas to the base of the walls, establishing six architectural phases (Phases 1–6) and one pre-temple phase (Phase 0). The temple was completely excavated down to the highest floor of Phase 2. Earlier deposits were excavated selectively in a series of Test Pits, and this should be borne in mind when comparing these phases with the later ones.

Each of the architectural phases corresponds to raised internal floor levels and modifications to the building, sometimes major, sometimes minor. These phases are labelled as follows:

0   Pre-temple remains
1   Construction and first use
2   Minor additions
3   A major rebuild
4   Modifications
5   Adding a room
6   External renovations and abandonment

The schematic phase-by-phase plan highlights the changes between each phase [124]. The major event within the life of the temple was the demolition and rebuilding which separated Phase 2 from Phase 3. This was accompanied by the construction of a second altar and an additional plinth in the NE corner. Other significant events were the construction of a storeroom in the SW corner in Phase 5 and the addition of five offering tables in the street in Phase 6.

Phase 0: Pre-Temple Remains

The contours of the Saar ridge and the heights of the surrounding houses always suggested that the temple visible on the surface of the mound was only the latest in a series of buildings to have been erected on this spot. It seemed likely that, if we were to excavate below the floors and walls of the temple, earlier buildings would be found below it. To test this hypothesis, a test pit was excavated inside the temple, down through the consecutive floors of the building (Test Pit 1) [123]. We were surprised, nevertheless, at the amount of underlying archaeological material: below the earliest floor of the temple was a further 3 m of archaeological remains before undisturbed soil was reached. There can be no doubt that the settlement had a considerable history even before the temple under investigation was built [125].

This excavation within the temple was necessarily confined in order not to disturb the integrity of the building. Further test pits within and outside the building were undertaken mainly to recover details about the initial construction of the temple but some of these too provided additional pieces of information about the pre-temple history of the site. Although the earliest history of the area underneath the temple will never adequately be understood, these excavations, taken together, do allow some tentative observations to be made about the nature of the occupation.

Above the bedrock found in Test Pit 1 were some 50 cm of deposits characterized as wind-blown sands with occasional ashy horizons, and including a small amount of fish-bone, pottery and charred date seeds (Phase 0.1). At best we can detect intermittent human activity in this area, such as the lighting of fires, though this does not preclude a permanent presence elsewhere. The absence of well-defined floor horizons is a further indicator that, at the very least, this area was not within a building. Carbon dating of the charred date stones found in these layers means that we can even provide a time range for this first occupation: 2375–2370 BC (or earlier; BM 2873) [126]. This interference increases as we proceed up the section: in the next half metre a substantial hearth appears with an associated floor and finds include worked stone, a pearl, and slag from metalworking (Phase 0.2). Bits of mortar and plaster, the debris from building activity, also appear for the first time. Carbonized date stones provide one date of 2290–2035 BC for this phase (BM 2872), and a second date with parameters too wide to be of much use (BM 2870).

Sitting above these deposits is the wall of the earliest building (or buildings) identified in Test Pit 1 (Phase 0.3) [127]. It lies directly under the levelling associated with the initial construction of the temple (Phase 0.4), and can be connected with fragments of walls found further west in Test Pits 2, 3 and 4 [128]. The plan is fragmentary and there are few clues as to function but the deposits which characterize the inside of the temple, such as laminated plastered floors, were not observed anywhere in association with this lower building. Our conclusion is, therefore, that these walls represent the remains of a pre-temple building which was non-religious in nature.

Phase 1: Construction and First Use

The construction phase of the temple was investigated only within the limited areas of the test pits. Investigation of the Phase 1 temple was also circumscribed: we were able to determine the ground-plan and the flooring sequence, but the actual floors associated with this first phase were not excavated in their entirety [130].

Prior to the construction of the temple, the existing buildings on the site were demolished. Some of the stone was presumably used for the new building, while other debris was spread out over the site to level it. In Test Pit 2, it was clear that an earlier Phase 0.3 wall was partly incorporated into the temple [129].

On the surface from which the builders began construction, traces of their activities could still be detected. A shallow depression in the main chamber, lined with plaster, was probably used for mixing up mortar [131]. That it dates to the time of the temple's construction, and not to the time when the building was in use, is proven by the fact that one of the temple columns was built directly on top of it. Similar plastered pits have been found in the construction horizon of houses in the settlement (Woodburn & Crawford 1994, 94).

In constructing the temple, the builders seem to have considered foundation trenches unnecessary. No foundation material was found under the temple walls in any of the test pits, in spite of detailed examination. Most of the walls were simply built directly on top of pre-temple occupation horizons and floors.

The wall alignment of the Phase 1 temple is poor: while the short walls are reasonably true, the long walls have appreciable curves and kinks in them. The worst piece of construction is where the looping section of the west wall rejoins the straight section, or rather fails to rejoin it. There is no doubt that this is an original piece of construction and not, as was first hypothesized, a later rebuild (Killick et al. 1991, 114).

A single shallow buttress was built into each of the short walls to carry the load of the main roof beams. There appeared to be only a single buttress in the long walls, located on the SE wall. The roof was also supported on three columns running down the centre of the temple, a circular one at the eastern end near the doorway and, further in, two rectangular columns.

Within the temple, there was a single altar along the SE wall and a suite of installations in the NE corner. The altar belonging to the earliest phase of the temple had been partly destroyed during the subsequent rebuilding. The front, however, was still preserved, and was a low rectangular table. Like its later, better preserved, counterpart, it seems to have had a back, perhaps with a curved device attached, though only a small fragment of lipped plaster was left to suggest this [132].

Built into the NE corner of the temple, directly to the right of the temple entrance, was a high bench or podium, of a long rectangular shape. It was approached by two low steps. Next to this high bench, constructed along the north wall, was a low long bench, with a smaller one adjacent to it [133].

The high bench was utilized throughout the life of the temple, replastered in Phase 2, and rebuilt and plastered again in Phase 3. Integral to the construction of this bench were the two low steps. Both steps were replastered several times and the upper one was particularly well worn.

The adjacent long bench was built against the NW wall [134, 135]. During the excavation of Test Pit 7, we could observe that it was a primary furnishing of the temple, as the earliest Phase 1 floors ran up to it. The long bench had a stone core, and remnants of a white gypsum plaster could be observed adhering to the Phase 1 stonework. We assume that the other installations in this corner also originated in Phase 1 though we did not dig underneath or through them to establish this for certain.

The temple floors in Phase 1 were recorded only in the test pits [136]. In composition and nature they seem to have been no different from the excavated ones of the later phases, that is, accumulated lenses of plaster, sand and occasional ash, many of which were very localized. Rather oddly, no evidence was found of a good, solid, primary floor to go with the actual construction of the temple, but rather pockets of flooring levelling out the uneven surface left by the construction debris in the temple. There was one good floor horizon which ran through all of Test Pit 7, but it was not picked up towards the western end of the temple. Notably, too, in Test Pit 7, three plastered depressions were recorded in the sections through the Phase 1 floors, similar to those found at the back of the temple in Phase 2.

Within the storeroom, the floors of Phase 1 were partially excavated. A plastered circular depression was found in the room, as well as a pivot stone inside the doorway on the north side. This was made up of a piece of limestone with a circular groove in the centre, and had been wedged in place with a large pottery sherd [137].

Outside the temple, excavation stopped at the base of the two stone columns or offering tables which are dated to Phase 2. It is not known, therefore, whether similar structures existed in Phase 1 or whether they were a novel introduction in Phase 2.

The plan of Phase 1 also shows the limits of the neighbouring buildings. It should be pointed out that these buildings, shown in outline, belong to Phase 3 and upwards. However, sufficient excavation has been carried out below the Phase 3 levels of these buildings to show that the street pattern around the temple remained much the same throughout the life of the temple. Limited excavation in Houses 203, 200, and next to House 220 in Main Street showed earlier buildings retaining the same line. Where earlier buildings have been investigated elsewhere within the settlement, it has generally been the case that later buildings have respected the line and orientation of underlying houses.

Phase 2: Minor Additions

Various minor additions and modifications were made to the temple after its construction in Phase 1 and prior to the major rebuild which characterizes Phase 3 [140]. Internally, these modifications comprise the addition of a narrow buttress to the mid-section of the NW wall, and the construction of a possible shelf along the back wall [141]. Phase 2 is also the earliest phase for which we were able to excavate an entire floor inside the temple, as well as associated external surfaces and features [138].

The reason for the construction of the buttress is not clear. It may have served to reinforce the roof, its narrow width of only 20 cm representing a trade-off between providing structural support and encroaching upon the internal space of the building. The measure apparently achieved only temporary success as it was this central section of wall which was subsequently entirely demolished.

The main floor of the temple (Floor 1) was traced across all of the inside of the temple. It was an undulating and worn horizon of compact sand and plaster with grit and ash inclusions. Ash layers were particularly concentrated around the base of the altar [139]. The eastern side of the altar and adjacent wall were scorched, perhaps from the heat of the burnt debris of food offerings shovelled off the top of the altar, an event documented by the micro-morphological study of the Phase 3 altars.

At the back of the temple nine circular depressions had been made in the floor [142]. These varied in diameter from 65 to 96 cm and in depth from 18 to 50 cm. Two contained some small stones at the bottom. Our interpretation is that these, and subsequent depressions found scattered across the temple, were settings for storage jars, with the small stones being used to wedge the vessels upright.

Beside the wall of the storeroom was an area of collapsed stone debris. Once this was cleared away, two low stone walls were uncovered: one wall abutted the back wall of the temple and the other ran parallel, between the column and the corner of the storeroom. These two walls may have served as the support for a shelf, or for some other superstructure. Their construction would have cut off circulation around the back of the column.

Floor 1 was also traced into the storeroom but here it was truncated by the demolition and reconstruction of Phase 3.

The latest area of floor associated with Phase 2 was a plastered patch confined to the eastern end of the temple (Floor 2). Impressions of bare feet were found in the plaster, a child's footprints south of the circular column and adult ones by the benches and east of the central column [143]. Also south of the circular column were very faint linear impressions which may have been made by matting. Micromorphological analysis has also provided some evidence for floor coverings in the NE corner.

At this latest horizon of Phase 2, the benches and altar had been replastered with a fine mortar composition which lipped on to Floor 2. This gives an indication of the extant heights of these features during their use in Phase 2: the altar stood 35 cm above the final floor, the high bench to a height of 139 cm, the long bench 34 cm and the small bench 20 cm. Although the steps showed signs of wear, the bench surfaces were in a relatively crisp condition. From impressions found in the plaster on top of one of these benches, it would seem that at least one square container had been placed there before the plaster had time to dry properly, or perhaps the container was sufficiently heavy, or had stayed there long enough, to create the indentations.

The thresholds associated with the doorway of Phases 1–2 remained unexcavated but could be seen in section [144]. Obstructing the street in front of the temple in

Phase 2 were two stone-built bases, one circular and the other with a square end [145]. Whether they had antecedents in Phase 1 is not known, as the relevant street levels remain unexcavated. Both bases survived to less than 1 m in height. Their function is unknown, but they seem to have no structural relationship to the temple and may have been low tables set outside for some public function. The street deposits around the bases were clean wind-blown sands, providing no further clue about function.

Against the front wall of the temple in the street was a small, rectangular stone feature with a circular depression in the top [146]. It may represent a setting for a post, or perhaps a support for a standard such as can be seen on the seals. This feature was not replicated in subsequent phases.

One of the last events that took place in the temple before the remodelling of Phase 3 was the excavation of an irregular-shaped pit next to the altar. The debris from this operation had been dumped next to the pit on the temple floor. This curious phenomenon requires explanation. Possibly there was an installation adjacent to the altar which needed to be dug out and resited when the temple was renovated, but the amount of dumped spoil argues against this. Or perhaps the pit represents an excavation to locate something which had previously been buried (or thought to have been buried) in the temple, perhaps as a ritual deposit.

Phase 3: A Major Rebuild

A major remodelling of the temple took place after Phase 2: the central section of the NW wall and practically the entire length of the SE wall were dismantled. The internal floor level was raised by as much as 1 m in places. Two altars replaced the single one of Phase 3 and a new bench was constructed in the NE corner [149].

The process of demolition was well-documented archaeologically, and it would appear that the dismantling of the walls was done quite carefully. Whereas the rubble and mortar debris from the two walls making up the possible shelf support at the back of the temple were left in a heap, the rest of the temple area was relatively clean of any demolition debris and the installations of Phase 2 were buried in pristine condition. Certainly at some point, and perhaps first of all, sand was brought in to the main room and laid down to a depth of 60–100 cm in order to raise the floor level and provide easier access from the street

[148]. This sand layer also protected the Phase 2 installations from any damage. The equivalent deposit in Area 220 was an homogenous and compact layer of mortar which contained some broken pottery vessels [147].

Foundation packing was then laid down in those areas where the line of the new walls did not sit exactly over the Phase 2 alignments. In particular, the opportunity was taken to straighten up the SE wall, resulting in the mid-section being pulled in by some 30 cm over the line of the earlier wall [152].

The NW and SE sections of walling were rebuilt to the same width but three internal buttresses were incorporated into each wall. These are only marginally thicker than the main wall and some 70 cm wide on average. Because they are roughly aligned with the columns they were probably constructed to provide additional support for the main load-bearing roof beams. Obviously, the builders would have had to add additional courses of stonework to the short walls of the temple at the same time, though we could not spot this in the existing stonework, and the same applies to the internal columns. Within the storeroom, however, there is a possible horizon on the internal wall where additional stonework may have been added, and, in particular, the southern door-jamb shows a corresponding slight offset.

This remodelling of the temple appears to relate to structural weaknesses in the Phase 2 building, in particular the inability of the walls as constructed to provide adequate support for the ceiling. A second consideration may have been the difficulties of access caused by the continual deposition of wind-blown sand outside in the street.

The building of new installations shows evidence for both continuity and change in cultic practices in the temple. Above the Phase 2 altar, a new, slightly smaller version was constructed. The front of the altar was a low, rectangular table built with a stone surround and with an inner fill of soft sand scorched from fires. The altar back was crescent-shaped and constructed of one thickness of small stones covered with fine plaster and fashioned into a crescent-shaped moulding [150].

As the temple floors were repaired and replastered in subsequent phases, extra courses of stone and plaster were also added to the front and sides of the altar table. Ash deposits on the altar table continually built up, interspersed with replastering. Micromorphological analysis of part of the altar recorded 16 layers of surviving plaster.

A major innovation in Phase 3 was the construction of a second altar against the central column, roughly on the same alignment as its counterpart and facing the same direction. This has not been dismantled so its construction is assumed to be the same as the southern altar. The plaster over the moulded back was a brittle gypsum rendering with at least two layers visible [151].

The two low benches in the NE corner wall were replaced by a single bench in Phase 3 [153]. Rather curiously, the high bench in the NE was not raised during renovation but merely replastered, so that in Phase 2 its height was effectively reduced by half. Because of this, the steps that led up to the high bench were no longer required.

Investigation of the top of the high bench revealed some tantalizing clues to its function. The latest plaster layer was only partly preserved. Beneath it, earlier plaster was also in fragmentary condition, but nevertheless could be seen in three places to have clearly lipped up to an object (or objects) that had been positioned on top [154].

The inference is inescapable that one or more objects, probably with rectangular or square bases, had been set upon the top of the bench prior to its being plastered. Furthermore, these objects must have been of major cultic significance: they were originally placed in an elevated position, they were frequently approached (as indicated by the worn treads of the steps), and they were serviced by subsidiary temple fixtures in the form of adjacent benches. The high bench is the only feature in the temple to have survived intact through the lifetime of the building, and an unwillingness perhaps to remove the objects on top might provide an explanation as to why it was not rebuilt to its full height in this phase.

Another new addition to the cultic installations in the temple was the construction of a square plinth adjoining the south end of the high bench and 15 cm higher. The plaster on the sides of this plinth was one continuous rendering so that its original height is preserved (74 cm). Part of the top was raised higher and had some plaster ridging, again indicating that some immovable object had sat on top [156].

Two small, upright stones were set in the temple floor immediately SE of this plinth, forming, with the side of the plinth and adjacent temple wall, a small rectangular cavity, perhaps a setting for a post or standard.

Due to the location of one of the test pits of the earlier expedition much of the information about the area next to the temple doorway is incomplete. The threshold for Phase 3 was preserved: it was constructed of an edging of small stones set against what might have been a plank and mortared over [155]. On the inside, the threshold had a 6 cm step down to floor level where the mortar lips out, but any further trace of it was removed by the previous excavations. Externally, this mortar spread in a continuous layer outward from the threshold, up the sides of the stone bases which survived the transition from Phase 2 to Phase 3, and beyond, covering an area approximately 10 m north to south by 7 m. It followed a gentle slope from the temple entrance down towards the east on a 1:4 gradient. It thus provides one of the very few clear stratigraphic links between the street area and the internal temple sequence [157].

As with Phase 1, no neatly-laid primary surface extending across the entire temple was identified for Phase 3. Instead, the flooring consisted of many localized laminations and plaster lenses (Floor 1). In front of the central altar, for example, twice as many floor plasterings were observed in the microstratigraphic section as at the side of the altar.

At the eastern end of the temple, Floor 1 was hard and mortar-like, while around the altars the deposits were much more ashy, and at the back of the temple there was a relatively large amount of occupation debris, pot sherds, bone and shell. Some fragments of plum-coloured painted plaster were found lying on top of the floor by the western end of the low bench.

The floor had been cut through just west of the low bench. This linear cut (Feature F) was quite difficult to define. Similar cuts, each time a little further to the west, were identified in the succeeding phases 4 and 5. Their function is not clear.

Floor 2 in this sequence was traceable across most of the temple, although there were worn patches to the east around the entrance, around the circular column and between the central and western column. In the immediate area of the bench, was an area of very hard gypsum flooring. The same material was used to plaster the installations. Many fragments of gypsum plaster from the installations had collapsed onto the floor between repairs, showing that the benches and plinths in this area were in a continual state of disrepair and probably needed constant renovations.

Further plastered depressions were found in Phase 3, similar to those of the preceding phase, but their distribution appears more random, with no particular concentration in any one part of the temple. The two largest depressions were in the storeroom.

Phase 4: Modifications

Phase 4 is defined by minor modifications within the temple: the table of the central altar was lengthened, the low bench of Phase 2 in the NE corner was replaced by a similar one, and a new threshold was built [161]. All the internal floors which ran up to the new altar table but were cut by the construction of the Phase 5 room were assigned to this phase. Externally, a house was constructed attached to the SW wall of the temple, where previously there had been unobstructed passage around the back of the temple. During the construction of this house a door-jamb was inserted into the back wall of the temple.

The table of the central altar was extended by 17 cm with the addition of a single row of stones to the front of the altar. Its original height was 30 cm, which provides also a minimum height for the Phase 4 altar table. By the end of Phase 5, both had been much reduced by rising floor levels.

The Phase 4 bench was built directly over the Phase 3 example and stood to a height of 50 cm. It was originally built of a core of small stones and faced with larger ones. One small fragment of very brittle gypsum plaster survived, adhering to the short SW face of the bench, indicating that originally the bench would have been so plastered [158].

A new threshold made up of horizontally-laid stones replaced that of Phase 3. There was no pivot stone, but this may have been removed in the earlier series of excavations.

During Phase 4, House 206 was constructed abutting House 207 to the SW and the back temple wall [159]. It conformed to the standard house plan of a rectangular block with a small internal room surrounded by an L-shaped outer area. During construction of the house, the overlapping end of the curving section of the back wall of the temple was dismantled, and a door-jamb for the house inserted. A similar event may have taken place at the south eastern entrance to the house, but in this area Phase 5 and 6 additions to the outside of the temple wall masked the Phase 4 sequence.

The floors of Phase 4 have been divided as excavated, into five. They are notable for containing superimposed plastered depressions which were concentrated in the storeroom and the SW corner of the temple [160, 162]. The earliest floor, made up of a compacted grey brown sand and plaster with randomly spread remains of calcified plant material, was present in the central area of the temple and through into the storeroom. Accumulated ash deposits and fish-bone fragments were present next to both altars. Towards the storeroom, the composition changed to a more plastery horizon and within the storeroom it became a dense smooth plaster floor, very worn and uneven.

Floor 2 existed only in the SW corner. It was present as a compact smooth plaster in the corner and contained more sand and ash next to the southern altar. The next floor up in the sequence, Floor 3, was a patchy and worn floor stretching from the bench in the north east corner across most of the room, though it was not traced through into the storeroom. Signs of burning and scorching were visible on this floor next to the buttress on the SE wall closest to the temple entrance. To find traces of burning in the temple, apart from around the altars, is unusual.

The fourth floor in the sequence was very patchy. Next to the installations in the NE corner, the floor was a hard, compact, sand and gypsum plaster with fragments of collapsed gypsum plaster. Around the altars the floor was, as usual, more ashy, and within the storeroom it was made up of several laminations of very hard uneven plaster. The final floor in this sequence, Floor 5, was confined to the west end of the temple and to the storeroom. On top of this floor, immediately around the altar, were deposits rich in ash and calcified plant material. Towards the entrance to the storeroom, the floor became compacted, with laminations of sand and plaster.

Phase 5: Adding a Room

Throughout the life of the temple we have seen a tendency for material to be stored at the back of the temple and in the storeroom in the NW corner. In Phase 5 a second internal room was added to the temple, constructed inside the angle of the SW corner [167]. Part of the reason for adding internal walls may have been to provide additional support for the roof. Simultaneously, the central column which had by now acquired a significant lean to the south, was also strengthened by the addition of a stone skirt around the base. Masonry skirts were also added along the entire external length of both the SE and SW walls [163, 164 & 166].

The walls of the additional room (Area 221) were built with foundation trenches, and abutted the main walls of the temple. The doorway was formed by adding a

skin of stones to part of the existing buttress in the SE wall, an unsatisfactory procedure which resulted in the door-jamb dropping away from the wall.

Rising internal floor levels again forced some adjustments to the height of the altar tables. An additional course of stones was added to the table of the southern altar raising it by 28 cm, and the back of the altar, with its curved shape, was also rebuilt and replastered. The same may have happened to the central altar but as it was not dismantled it is not possible to be certain. Certainly the square column which the central altar abutted was strengthened at this time by adding a collar or skirt to the three unobstructed sides. This was intact, and stood to a height of 1.26 m. At the bottom it had a maximum thickness of 24 cm, and was tapered so that at the top it was almost flush with the column sides [165, 168 & 169].

A single floor horizon was dated to Phase 5. The floor, containing several laminations of dense plaster, was located in the area east of the two altars. It disappeared towards the SW column but was traced through the doorway of the new room where it had a fine grey skim on top. On a patch of this floor located north east of the entrance to the new room was a child's footprint. Concentrated around the base of the altars were deposits of ash, a scattering of calcified plant material, and fragments of bone. The temple threshold was raised once more by the addition of rather large stones in the doorway. Again, as in Phase 4, the associated pivot stone was probably removed prior to the start of our excavations.

Externally, the SE and SW walls were strengthened by the addition of buttresses along their entire length [172]. For whatever reason, probably to do with the vagaries of the wind, sand had accumulated in greatest depth at the front of the temple so that the buttress against the SE wall stood far higher at the front of the temple than at the back. That this addition post-dated House 206 of Phase 5 is shown by the fact that the buttresses were built through the doorway of the house.

Phase 6: External Renovations and Abandonment

In Phase 6, two further modifications were made to the external walls of the temple and the two bases in front of the temple were replaced by five [175]. Although there is no direct stratigraphic link between these external changes and the internal floor sequence of the temple, we have made the assumption that they are contemporary with the final plastering of the temple floor prior to abandonment. This floor had been excavated by the previous expedition and had thus been exposed to the elements for several years before being re-examined [171]. It is difficult for us to say much about its original composition, but according to the excavators (Kandil n.d.), it was made up of reddish clay, and on and around the central altar was a thick deposit of ash containing fish-bone, animal bone, shell and burnt date palm. Three circular pits were identified in the floor SW of the central altar and it is recorded that fish-bone mixed with shell was present in each of these pits. It is not clear if these features represent true pits or are further examples of plastered depressions.

In Phase 6 an additional skin of stone was added on to the SW corner of the temple. It ran along the SW wall, around the corner, and up South Alley for a distance of 2.30 m [170]. By this time, South Alley had just about filled up with sand, covering much of the support skin that had been added to the SE wall of the temple in Phase 5. Sitting on this sand was a raft of pink mortar, which had been ramped up to the SE wall of the temple. This mortar deposit also ran over the walls of House 200 on the other side of South Alley demonstrating that by the last phase of the temple the neighbouring buildings to the south had fallen into disuse. It was on top of this mortar that the Phase 6 buttress had been constructed [177].

Initially, the mortar deposit was thought to represent wash off the walls, or perhaps plaster left over from reno-

vations of the temple, but it appears too thick and solid for either of these. It may, perhaps, have been another rather clumsy attempt to stabilize the temple wall. Finally, a small buttress was added to the SE corner of the temple [173].

In front of the temple, the two stone bases of Phase 5 were replaced by five circular ones arranged in two rows. The first row was set some 2.5 m away from the temple façade, with the second row a metre further away to the NE [174]. These bases were built very high up in the deposits of wind-blown sand that had accumulated in the street, and associated with them on the north side of Temple Road were the fragmentary remains of a late house, House 220, built over the top of the earlier houses on the same site [176].

House 222 on the south side of Temple Road also seems to have been abandoned before the construction of the five bases, as its entrance is way down in the sand upon which the bases sat. While erosion and destruction may mean that we have lost some late buildings in this area contemporary with Phase 6 of the temple, our impression is that some of the buildings in the immediate vicinity of the temple had fallen into disuse at the end of Phase 5.

The temple was subsequently abandoned, as recorded in the notes of the previous expedition. The doorway was deliberately blocked with stones and then nature took its course, the wind filling up the interior with sand prior to the collapse of the building. Sand up to 110 cm thick was recorded above the latest floor.

Chapter 3. Activities Inside the Temple: The Evidence of Microstratigraphy

Introduction

Background

The sequences of floors and occupation deposits which accumulated during the use of the temple have been analysed both in the field and in large thin-sections under the microscope, in order to provide new evidence for the activities which took place in different areas of the temple. This is the first analysis of the microstratigraphy and micromorphology of archaeological deposits in the Gulf. The sequences of floors and occupation deposits within the temple are being compared to sequences within domestic houses, unroofed areas and streets at Saar, in order to study differences in the formation of deposits and the use of space in ritual and domestic contexts. These analyses are part of a three year research project at The McDonald Institute for Archaeological research, University of Cambridge, supported by the Natural Environment Research Council. The objective of this project is to develop the application of thin-section analysis to the study of occupation sequences and the use of space within early urban sites in the Near East. The depositional sequences at Saar will be compared to those from the other sites in the project, namely Tell Brak in NE Syria in levels dating to 3,600–1,600 BC, and Çatalhöyük in central Turkey in levels dating to 6,200–5,500 BC.

It has long been recognized in studies of traditional life in the Near East that the types of floors and occupation deposits vary according to the use of space. Kramer recorded that:

"The floor of each area within a house compound is peculiar to that kind of area and therefore diagnostic of primary function...It is likely that an excavator could readily discriminate between roof and unroofed areas, [and] identify stables, storerooms, kitchens and living rooms...by evaluating variations in floors." (Kramer 1979, 148–49)

Geoarchaeologists have also observed that, in modern urban sites from a wide range of geographical contexts: *"The rate and type of build-up differ on living floors, in streets and alleys, or in and around community structures, such as civic buildings, walls, terraces, and drainage systems."* (Butzer and Freeman quoted in Rosen 1986, xiii) Other archaeological research has suggested that it is the smaller artefactual remains which are *"more likely to become primary refuse"* even in areas which are periodically cleaned (Schiffer 1987).

It is now possible to study the nature and deposition of these smaller artefactual residues - and the sediments, organic remains and floors of which archaeological sites are mainly composed - with greater sensitivity, not only in the field, but also under the microscope, as large thin-sections of undisturbed, resin-impregnated block samples (Courty *et al.* 1989; Courty *et al.* 1994; Matthews 1992).

Analytical techniques and methods

The method we have applied is designed to integrate analysis in the field with analysis in thin-section. In the field, one metre wide sequences of floors and occupation deposits from excavated sections were photographed, drawn at 1:5, and described in detail, using soil science descriptions which have been adapted for use in archaeology (Courty *et al.* 1989; Hodgson 1976; Limbrey 1975; Matthews 1993). Blocks of deposits, 13.5x6.5x8 cm, were then cut out of the section with a knife and wrapped tightly in tissue and tape. These samples were exported to the laboratory in Cambridge in wooden boxes, with the kind permission of the Bahrain Department of Antiquities and Heritage. In Cambridge the blocks were consolidated by impregnating them under vacuum with an unsaturated crystic polyester resin which takes six weeks to harden. Once hardened, the block was cut, ground and polished into large thin-sections 13.5x6.5 cm, 20–30 μm thick. The thin-sections were analysed under large field and optical polarizing microscopes at magnifications of x5–x400.

Sample no.	Context	Phase	Microstratigraphic Unit
Sr93.1	Test Pit 1	0.1	0
Sr93.2	Test Pit 1	0.1	1–4
Sr93.11	Test Pit 1		bedrock
Sr93.3	Southern altar, front	3–5	7–10
Sr93.4	Southern altar, E side	3–5	6.1–11.2
Sr93.79	Southern altar, top, Series 2	3–5	18–32
Sr93.84	Southern altar, top, Series 1	3–5	1–18
Sr93.13	Central altar, front	3–5	4–12
Sr93.14	Central altar, side	3–5	9–13.6
Sr93.85	Area 220, scoop	1–7	
Sr93.86	Area 200, NE corner	3–5	1–12

[2] **Thin-section samples**

One hundred and eighteen microstratigraphic units from the temple were studied and described in thin-section, following the internationally standardized format and terminology which has been adapted to applications in archaeology (Bullock *et al.* 1985; Courty *et al.* 1989; Matthews 1995). The abundance of the different components in deposits has been quantified and is presented as a percentage of the total area of a deposit in thin-section. These percentages have been assessed with the aid of a visual percentage chart (Bullock *et al.* 1985, 24–25). Quantification using computerised image analysis techniques has yet to be refined in its application to heterogeneous settlement deposits.

In the temple at Saar we have analysed and sampled sequences of floors and occupation deposits from vertical sections in the following areas of excavation:

Area 200
NE corner close to the benches
Southern Altar, top, front and eastern side
Central Altar, front and western side

Area 220
Depressions in NW storeroom

Test Pit 1
Phase 0.1 Sand and intermittent occupation above bedrock

The top of the altars had been excavated by the previous expedition. The sequences studied in this research, therefore, are likely to have been slightly higher originally.

Presentation of results

This report is divided into four parts. The first outlines the nature of the research and the layout of the report. The four major sets of characteristics which have been analysed in order to study depositional processes are discussed as well as the evidence for activities in different areas of the temple. The third part is a contextual analysis of the character of floors and occupation deposits in each of the areas studied. In conclusion, the sequences from different areas of the temple are compared and examined in relation to other evidence for ritual activity elsewhere.

Lists of the thin-section samples from the temple and of the deposit types referred to in the report are included here [2–4]. Major groups of deposit types have been assigned a number, from 100–126, which refers to readily recognizable types of floors and occupation deposits. Thus deposit Type 104 refers to all packing and levelling materials, deposit Type 105 refers to all fine plaster floors, and deposit Type 112 refers to all deposits with more than 40% plant remains. These major groups of deposit types have been subdivided on the basis of a range of significant attributes. The term *occupation deposit(s)* is used loosely to refer to depositional units which accumulated during the use of the temple, to distinguish these as a general group from deliberately laid structural materials.

Type No.	Description
101	stone
102	mortar
103	wall plaster
104	packing/levelling material
105	fine plaster
106	medium plaster with 5–25% carbonate rock fragments
107	gritty plaster with 30–40% carbonate rock fragments
108	gypsum and other plasters
109	matting
110	occupation deposits with less than 5% plant remains
111	occupation deposits with 5–40% plant remains
112	occupation deposits with more than 40% plant remains
113	occupation deposits with organic staining
114	industrial debris
115	fire-installation structure
116	fire-installation *in situ* fuel
117	architectural collapse
118	silt lens associated with use of mats
119	sand lens associated with use of mats
120	naturally laid deposits: water
121	naturally laid deposits: wind
122	naturally laid deposits: other
123	features: structural materials
124	features: activity residues/fill
125	miscellaneous
126	indeterminate

[3] **Major deposit types**

[90] Fertile Bahrain
Despite the rapidly falling water table, parts of Bahrain still contain very lush and fertile gardens. In ancient times, the natural fertility of Bahrain, supported by natural springs, must have seemed in marked contrast to Babylonia, where extensive irrigation networks were required to harness the water of the Euphrates and Tigris Rivers.

[91] Weights found at Saar, for use with different systems
Cubical weights, usually of banded chert, are the same as those used in the Indus. This one (5019:01) weighs 6.7 gm and measures 1.2x1.5 cm. The barrel-shaped examples, on the other hand (F18:10:06, 3.9 cm long; I14:16:16, 3.3 cm long) fit into the system based on the Mesopotamian shekel of 8.3 gm.

[92] The back of a Dilmun seal from Saar
The typical Dilmun seal has a domed boss bisected by three parallel lines at right angles to the perforation holes and ornamented by four dot-and-circle patterns. This is in contrast to earlier Gulf seals which are without such decoration. Diameter: 2.12 cm.

[93] Stone-jointing detail in the Barbar temple
Some of the stones at the Barbar temple are jointed by fitting the bottom right-hand corner of one stone exactly into a recess cut into the top left-hand corner of the one below it, just as with Umm an-Nar tombs at Hili.

[95]'Royal' tombs at A'ali.
One of the giant mounds which conceal monumental stone-built burial chambers.

[94] Seal from Saar with mythological scene
A seated figure is identified as a deity by his horned hat, similar to those worn by gods in Mesopotamian art. He is shown apparently being stabbed by a naked man standing in front of him with a sword. Another naked human looks on in horror. (5168:01. Diameter: 2.54 cm.)

[96] Painted goblets from A'ali
These rather clumsy chalices with black-painted decoration are typical of Dilmun funerary wares.

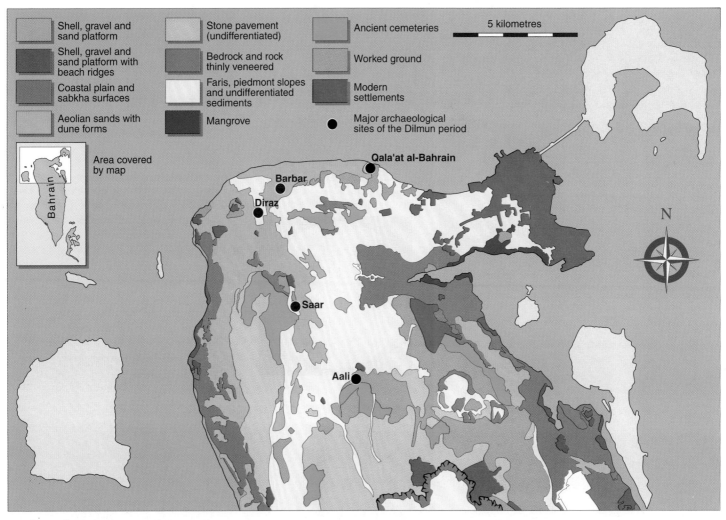

[97] The geomorphology of northern Bahrain

The map (simplified from Doornkamp *et al.* 1980, Map 2) shows the major geophysical characteristics of the northern part of Bahrain prior to the most recent expansion of villages. North of Saar, extending up to Diraz, stretched the largest sand-dune formation to be found on Bahrain, left over from when the island was linked by a land bridge to Saudi Arabia about 6,000 years ago. Eastwards, an area of coastal plain and sabkha marks the limit of what might have been a saltwater inlet in Early Dilmun times.

Legend:
- Shell, gravel and sand platform
- Shell, gravel and sand platform with beach ridges
- Coastal plain and sabkha surfaces
- Aeolian sands with dune forms
- Stone pavement (undifferentiated)
- Bedrock and rock thinly veneered
- Faris, piedmont slopes and undifferentiated sediments
- Mangrove
- Ancient cemeteries
- Worked ground
- Modern settlements
- Major archaeological sites of the Dilmun period

Area covered by map

5 kilometres

Bahrain

Qala'at al-Bahrain
Barbar
Diraz
Saar
Aali

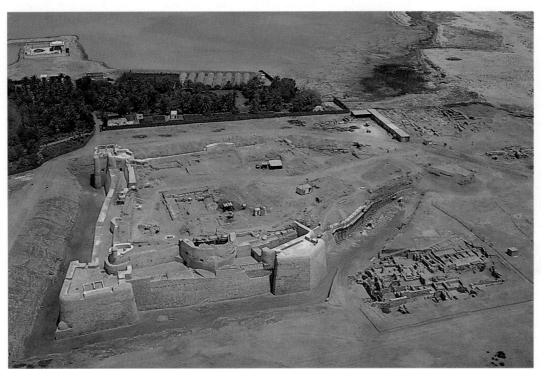

[98] Bahrain Fort

The moated fortress which now dominates Bahrain's principal historical site is Portuguese, but its predecessors date back to the 14th century AD. Beneath and around it are remains of most periods of Bahrain's history. In the right foreground are the excavations begun by the original Danish Expedition from Moesgaard Museum and currently continued by a French team from Maison de l'Orient, Lyon. It was here that large public buildings of the Kassite and Assyrian periods were found. Above right, by the shore, are the Danish excavations which revealed the earliest levels, dating back to the third millennium BC.

[99] The Barbar temple, looking south
All three phases of the monumental Barbar temple are still partly visible, which makes for a rather confusing aerial view. The well which characterized this impressive place of worship from at least Phase 2 is at the top right. Three of the 'altar stones', or 'anchors' still stand in a row on the Phase 2 platform. They are about 80 cm high.

[100] Bull's head from the Barbar temple
This bull's head, cast in copper or bronze by the lost wax process, remains the best known *objet d'art* of the Dilmun period. The eyes were probably originally inlaid. Height: 18 cm.

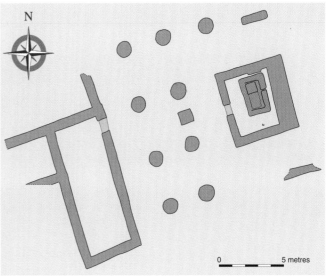

[101] Reconstructed remains (looking east) and plan of the Diraz temple
As reconstructed, the temple had a small rectangular *cella* with a low platform (Roaf 1976a). Outside, a series of possible offering tables, mostly circular, ran around two sides. These tables were 1.10–1.20 m wide and preserved to a maximum height of 0.6 m. The nature and function of the building to the west is uncertain.

[102] Umm al-Sujur, looking south
Seen below is the well and staircase found by Geoffrey Bibby in 1954. That seen above and next to it was discovered by the Japanese team in 1993. They also found the channel attached to each well and leading off to the left. The proximity of the water table is evident from the dark discoloration of the soil. The stairs are about 1.0 m wide in both cases.

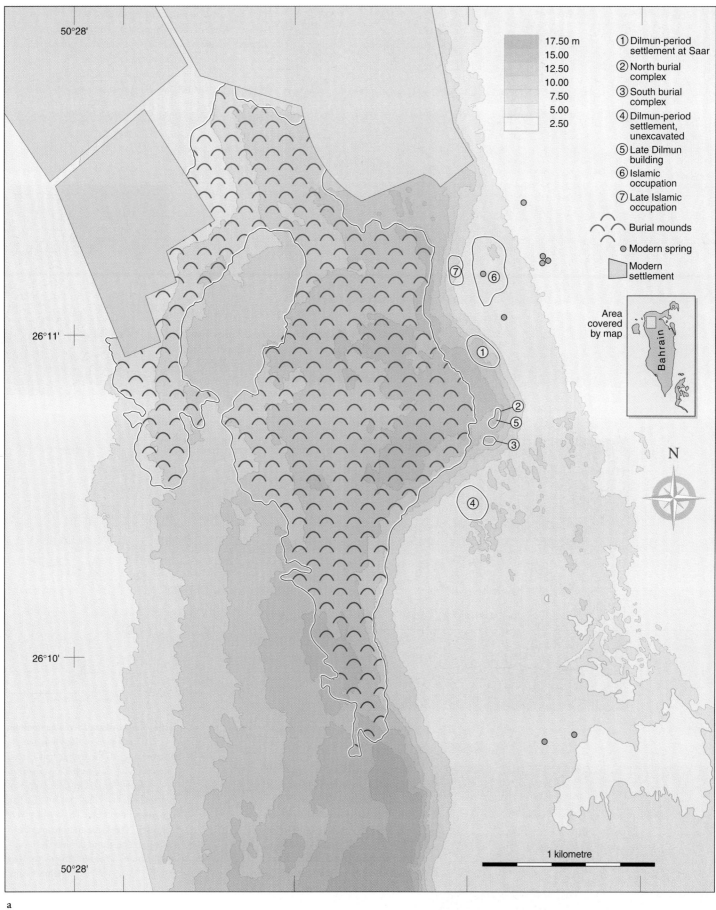

50°28'

17.50 m
15.00
12.50
10.00
7.50
5.00
2.50

① Dilmun-period settlement at Saar
② North burial complex
③ South burial complex
④ Dilmun-period settlement, unexcavated
⑤ Late Dilmun building
⑥ Islamic occupation
⑦ Late Islamic occupation

⌣⌣ Burial mounds
● Modern spring
▱ Modern settlement

Area covered by map

Bahrain

N

26°11'

26°10'

50°28'

1 kilometre

a

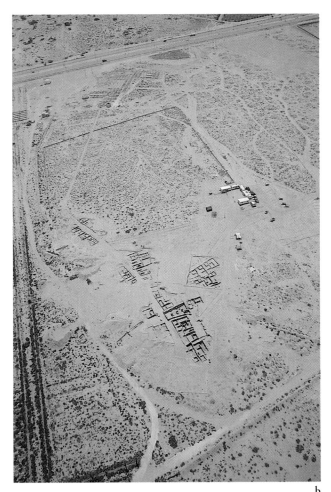

b

[103] **Archaeological remains in the Saar area**
The Southern Burial complex (no. 3 on map) lies at the very top of
the photograph, cut by the line of the modern road to Saudi Arabia.
Below it a grid of archaeological squares marks the area of the
Northern Burial Complex (no. 2). The white buildings are the
Expedition's camp, and the large enclosure wall is modern. The
excavated part of the settlement is in the foreground, just above the
junction of the modern tracks.

[105] **A Dilmun burial mound**
A circular tomb with four shaft burials lying on the northern edge of the Northern
Burial Complex was restored in 1993. The stones in the ring-wall had tumbled
outwards and were lying on the ancient ground surface, a clear indication that the
tomb was an above ground structure, rather than a burial tumulus. The apertures in
the wall are modern, left so that visitors can see into the shaft burials.

[106] **The Southern Burial Complex**
The graves in this 'honeycomb' cemetery
were built of rough limestone and were
generally between 1 and 3.5 m long, and
0.5 to 1 m wide, usually with a small
alcove on one side.

[104] **Saar burial field, looking north-east**
The Saar Burial Field once covered 7 square
kilometres. Much of the northern half was cleared
for development in 1992, as shown by the flat areas.
Some original burial mounds can be seen along the
right-hand side, though these too have subsequently
been demolished.

[108] **Jar from Northern Burial Complex**
Red-painted jars of this type are commonly found in Early Dilmun graves. This one came from Grave 5 of the Northern Complex (Gr 5:01:01), and is 16.8 cm high. The irregular knife-cut grooves under the rim are typical.

[107] **The Northern Burial Complex and Late Dilmun/Tylos building**
The ring-walls and capstones of unopened graves can be seen within the archaeological grid, with the rectilinear walls of the Late Dilmun/Tylos building sitting directly on top. Towards the top of the picture (looking SE) is the Southern Burial Complex.

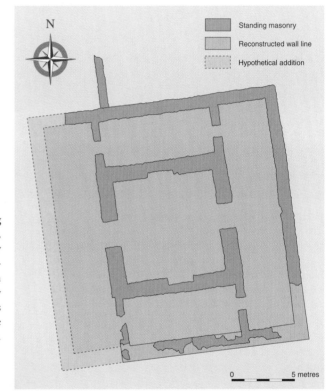

N

Standing masonry
Reconstructed wall line
Hypothetical addition

0   5 metres

[109] **Late Dilmun/Tylos building**
The plan shows a central square room, 7.70 m across, surrounded on three sides, and perhaps on the fourth, by a single long chamber. A fragment of wall running further north suggests that there might originally have been additional parts to the building, but these have now eroded completely. The central room is notable for its two opposed niches and for the aligned doorways on the other two walls.

[110] **The plain to the east of Saar**
Only 30 years ago much of this area was covered with date-palm plantations but modern buildings and massive reworking of the soils have combined to render invisible the ancient landscape.

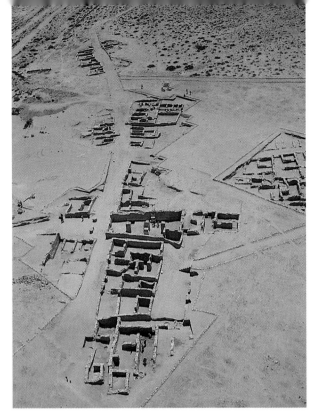

[111] The Saar settlement from the air
Looking SE, Main Street can be seen running through the settlement up to the temple in the middle of the picture. The east side of the street (left as viewed) is clearly visible, though not so many of its buildings had been exposed at this stage. The houses in the far distance, to either side of Main Street, mark the limit of settlement to the south, and the block on the right-hand edge of the frame must be close to the western edge.

[113] Buildings around the temple
Viewed from the east, the temple is in mid-frame, with House 200 to the left and the first houses of the block to the north (Houses 202 and 203) on the right. The intersection of Temple Road with Main Street is in the foreground, with the corner of House 222 showing along the bottom.

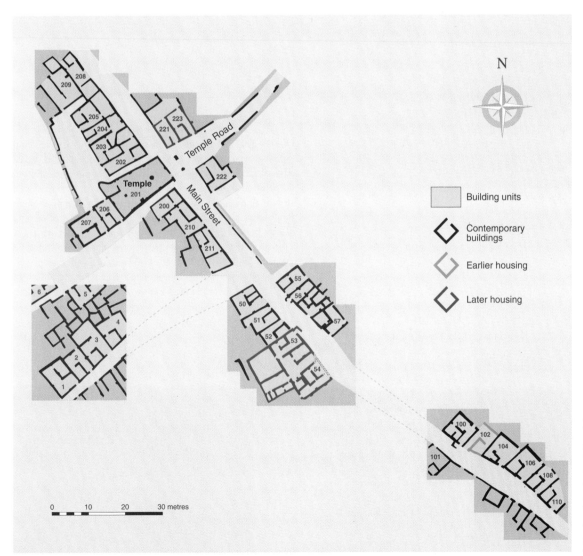

[112] Schematic plan of the Early Dilmun town
The plan shows the main phase of the settlement as excavated by the end of the 1994 season. Building phases within and between the various buildings have been simplified on this plan and only unequivocal instances of earlier and later houses are shown.

[114] **The well on the eastern flank**
The well predates the main phase of the settlement. It was lined with uncoursed stone to a depth of approximately 2.5 m and then cut through bedrock for a further 1.5 m. An associated surface and channel was at 7.07 m above sea level, while bedrock was cut down to 3.66 m. This suggests that the hydrostatic water level in the Early Dilmun period was between the two, a figure much lower than the 12 m hypothesized by Larsen (1983, 137 and Fig. 29). It also indicates a much more gradual depletion of the underlying aquifer between the Early Dilmun period and modern times.

[115] **A Housing block**
Houses 1–4 demonstrate the general similarity of Saar private houses, with some differences of detail. Houses 2–4 have the inner room positioned just inside the door on the left, whereas in House 1 it is opposite the entrance. Houses 2 and 4 each have a door at the back into a space shared with another building, but House 3 has a private courtyard of its own at the back, and House 1 has no extra space at all.

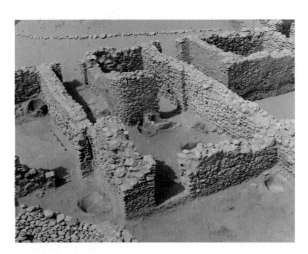

[116] **House 204**
In this 'typical' Saar house the entrance from the street gives into an L-shaped outer room, with a basin and pot-stand just inside the door. The door to the inner room is round the corner, and the cooking range built against the wall next to the door. From the back of the outer room another door leads through to an area shared with the next-door house, and probably unroofed.

[118] **Cooking arrangements in House 204**
On the right is a barrel-shaped *tannur*, or bread oven, of the kind still in general use in the Near East today. An open-ended, baked clay cylinder is heated by an open fire at the bottom, and disks of unleavened bread are cooked by being slapped onto the inside surface. At Saar, the clay cylinder is always supported by an outer skin of masonry. Built partly against it and partly against the wall is a low, semicircular open hearth, constructed of ashy plaster. At the back are the remains of three narrow supports which form a 'tripod'. These are made of small stones coated with ashy plaster. They are always found in conjunction with a semicircular hearth, while the *tannur* is often in a separate location.

[117] **Water installation in House 204**
Just inside the doorway of most private houses was a double installation apparently connected with the use of water. A stone platform with a shallow, carefully plastered depression on top forms a basin, and next to it is another, lower, stone support, this time with a smaller, deeper hollow. The latter sometimes contains the remnants of a medium-sized, round-bottomed pot.

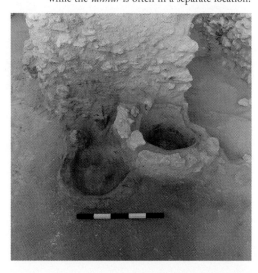

Type No.	Description	Characteristic Unit (Thin-section: unit no)
104	**packing/levelling material**	
104.1	packing, loamy sand with 20–30% carbonate rock fragments	84:19
104.2	packing, sandy loam, 5% carbonate rock fragments	86:1
104.3	packing, fine-very coarse sand	86:11
105	**fine plaster**	
105.1	grey silt loam, 20% voids from platy microstructure	13:6
105.2	silty clay loam, olive brown, micro-contrasted particles	85:2
105.3	silty clay-silt loam, pale greyish brown, no micro-contrasted particles	85:3
106	**medium plaster with 5–25% carbonate rock fragments**	
106.1	sandy silt loam, 20% rock fragments	4:7
106.2	sandy silt loam, 20–35% plant remains	4:8.2
106.3	sandy loam, heavily burnt, 5–10% carbonate rock fragments	84:3
106.4	sandy silt loam, heavily burnt, 10–20% carbonate rock fragments	84:9
106.5	sandy loam, brown calcitic inclusions	84:7
106.6	loamy sand, pale greyish brown, 20% carbonate rock fragments	84:11
106.7	sandy loam, greyish brown, <10% carbonate rock inclusions	79:25
106.8	sandy silt loam, aggregates of yellowish clay	3:8.2
106.9	sandy silt loam, aggregates of silty clay-silt loam	86:6
107	**gritty plaster with 30–40% carbonate rock fragments**	
107.1	sandy silt loam, 30–40% carbonate rock fragments	79:31
107.2	sandy silt loam, rubified, >30% carbonate rock fragments	84:13
107.3	sandy clay loam, 30% carbonate rock fragments	86:8
107.4	sandy silt loam, pale greyish brown, 30% rock fragments	13:4
108	**gypsum and other plasters**	
108.1	gypsum plaster	86:11
109	**matting**	
109.1	dark pigmented/charred date palm leaflets	4:9.5
110	**occupation deposits with less than 5% plant remains**	
110.1	sand	4:9.3
110.2	sand, <5% plant remains and trampled plaster aggregates	13:5
110.3	loamy sand, no plant remains	86:3
111	**occupation deposits with 5–40% plant remains**	
111.1	loamy sand-sand, 20% plant remains	4:9.6
111.2	sandy loam, >20% dark pigmented/charred date palm remains	13:10.1
111.3	sandy silt loam, organo-mineral fine material	14:12.6
111.4	sandy loam, <20% dark pigmented/charred remains	13:4
111.5	sandy silt loam, date palm leaflets	13:9
111.6	sandy loam-sandy silt loam, 20% pseudomorphic voids of plant remains	3:8.1
112	**occupation deposits with more than 40% plant remains**	
112.1	silt loam, 30% pale date palm leaflets, c. 10% melted c. 10% ashes	4:6.1
112.2	silt loam, 30–40% dark pigmented/charred date palm	4:9.8
112.3	silt loam, 50% well preserved pale yellow date palm leaflets	14:12.1
112.4	silt loam, inter-bedded lenses of dark, pale yellow, and grey ash	13:12
113	**occupation deposits with organic staining/rubified**	
113.1	sandy silt loam, 5–10% dark pigmented plant remains	84:2
113.2	sandy silt loam, >20% dark pigmented plant remains	84:6
113.3	sandy silt loam-silt loam, 2–5%, pale and dark date palm leaflets	84:14
113.4	silt loam, 30% well preserved date palm leaflets	79:20
113.5	silt loam-sandy silt loam, mottled brown and dark brown	79:28
118	**silt lens associated with use of mats**	
118.1	sandy silt loam, compacted	86:4
121	**naturally laid deposits: wind**	
121.1	medium sand, sterile	1:1
121.2	sandy loam, anthropogenic inclusions	2:2.1
122	**naturally laid deposits: other**	
122.1	bedrock, carbonate	11:0
126	**indeterminate**	
126.1	plaster floor/occupation deposit	4:6.2

[4] Deposit types in thin-sections, with brief reference to the key characteristics of the subdivisions within major deposit type groups

The deposit types have been identified by analysis and comparison of a wide range of depositional attributes and characteristics in thin-section. Although the basic sets of characteristics which are significant to interpretation of activity areas are discussed below, detailed micromorphological descriptions and attribute terminology have not been used in this report which is intended for a wide readership. The detailed micromorphological descriptions of the 118 depositional units are recorded as archival material in a computerized database at The McDonald Institute for Archaeological Research, University of Cambridge.

The detailed sequence of deposits from each field section from the altars is illustrated [202].

Micromorphological Characteristics of Floors and Deposits

Microstratigraphic evidence for activities within the temple is based on analysis of four principal sets of depositional characteristics, each of which will be examined in turn. These characteristics include the type of floors or surfaces, the impact of activities on those surfaces, the nature and deposition of residues from human activities, and the extent of post-depositional alterations.

Types of floors and surfaces

Three different types of packing or levelling material were laid as a foundation to the floors in the temple, Deposit Type 104. The first of these types is a pure medium-coarse sand, which was laid as a foundation to Phase 3 of the temple, and was between 60–100 cm thick. The second type of foundation material is a sandy loam packing with 30% calcitic rock fragments, which was laid on top of the pure sand in the temple at Saar in order to provide structural stability, in a layer approximately 20 cm thick. The third type of foundation material comprises a range of sandy to sandy loam sediments with 2–25% calcitic rock fragments. This material was principally laid in areas away from the altars, such as Area 200 and in both of the storerooms, in order to raise the floors up to the level of those around the altars, where burnt residues from offerings accumulated to considerable depths.

Four major types of plaster were used in the temple. The two most frequent types were made from sandy silt loam to loamy sand sediments, and were laid on the temple floors and on top of the southern altar. Of these two, Type 106 [178] has fewer carbonate rock fragments, 5–25%, than Type 107 [179] which has 30–40% carbonate rock fragments. A fine silt loam-silty clay loam mud plaster, Type 105 [180], was used to line the hollow depressions in the two storerooms. A hard gypsum plaster, Type 108 [181], was used to line the surfaces of benches in the NE of Area 200 and the basal floor at the side of the central altar. All of these types of plaster were also used in domestic houses.

Identification of the sources of raw materials used in the manufacture of these plaster floors requires future collaboration with geologists and geomorphologists. Analysis of the materials in thin-section, however, does enable us to suggest the probable general nature of the source areas. The sandy loam to sandy silt loam plasters, Types 106 and 107, were probably made from gravelly soils on top of carbonate bedrock. The fine silt loam to silty clay loam plasters, Type 105, were most probably made from calcareous muds deposited in the inter-tidal flats in the sheltered embayment to the NE of the site during the Holocene transgression (Doornkamp *et al.* 1980, 323). The fabric of these fine plasters includes <2–5% mollusc shell fragments up to 6.5 mm in length, which are likely to have been present in the calcareous muds (see Glover, this volume). These fine plasters, Type 105, also include 5–10% carbonate rock fragments less than 2 mm in length, and <2% micro contrasted organic inclusions, which are also present in the carbonate rich muds. Five to ten percent of the fabric of the fine plasters has thin curvilinear spaces from plant remains which have since decayed. These plants have been identified as small Gramineae (grass) fragments from the epidermal silica bodies which adhere to the sides of many of these empty voids. These grass fragments were probably added during manufacture of the plaster to serve as stabilizers, which would have provided tensile strength and cohesion in the plaster, and would have reduced cracking during drying and use (Norton 1986, 32). Generally, less than 2% spaces from decayed plants are present in the more sandy and gravelly plaster floors Types 106 and 107, rarely 5–10%.

The gypsum plasters, Type 108, were probably made by adding water to a pre-prepared 'plaster of Paris' to form a paste which tends to harden quickly. Plaster of Paris is prepared by heating gypsum to 100–200° C to form a hemihydrite of calcium sulphate. By the addition of water, this powder can be reconverted to its original chemical structure, calcium sulphate dihydrate (Moorey 1994, 330). The crystals of the gypsum plaster at Saar are generally small, less than 10–15 µm, but are larger around empty holes in the plaster fabric [181].

Impact of activities on floors and surfaces

Analysis of the boundaries between different floors and occupation deposits, both in the field and in thin-section, has enabled identification of the imprint and impact of human activities on floors and surfaces, and study of changes in depositional agents and processes (Gé et al. 1993; Matthews & Postgate 1994).

Footprints were uncovered during excavation near the central column, preserved in a moist plaster which had subsequently hardened. In thin-section the surfaces of some plasters are covered in a fine lens of dislodged aggregates, from trampling and surface abrasion.

Thin white or charred strips of fragile plant remains were visible during excavation, especially on the floors at the front and side of the southern altar. These have been identified in thin-section as the remains of well-preserved, overlapping, date-palm leaflets, which may have been matting, or a layer of loose leaflets. Impressions of probable matting have been identified on the upper surfaces of compacted lenses of fine sediments in loamy sand deposits in a thin-section sample from the NE of Area 200, close to the benches.

The impression of the base of an artefact, perhaps a standard, is preserved in the surface of sandy deposits at the side of the altar, below a layer of burnt date-palm leaflets [182], Units 11.1–11.2. One side of the impression has been disturbed by subsequent insect activity. The preserved impression is of an object which curves down towards a slightly raised and flattened base. The extant impression is 1.2 cm wide. If the original object was symmetrical, it would have been at least 2.4 cm wide. Unusual impressions have also been detected in a plastered surface on top of the altar [183], in Units 5–7. Here, the impressions are only 1.1–1.9 mm wide and resemble the tapering edges of a knife or cutting implement. These impressions were overlain and in-filled by fine silty sediments, and preserved below a thin layer of charred date-palm and subsequent layer of plaster.

The tops of the altars were regularly cleaned after ritual burning and before replastering. The deposits between each layer of plaster were truncated and disturbed, and only survive in layers less than 0.2–1.6 mm thick.

Nature and deposition of residues from human activities

The contribution of micromorphology is that we are able to analyse artefactual remains, organic residues, and sediments, in their depositional context within individual layers. We can study not only a wide range of properties for each individual component, but also the abundance of each component and its depositional relationship to other components.

Plant remains

One of the most surprising discoveries in thin-section has been the remarkable quantity and preservation of plant remains in occupation deposits at Saar. This is in contrast to the results from flotation at the site. Only 82 g of charred plant remains were recovered during initial flotation of 6,804 litres of soil from 82 different contexts (Nesbitt 1993). In thin-section it is evident charred plant remains represent less than 30% of the plant material around the temple altars at Saar.

Many fragile plant remains are well preserved in large thin-sections. It is evident that plant remains at Saar survive not only as charred material, but as desiccated, silicified, vitrified and ash remains, and as spaces within sediments which have been preserved in the shape of the original plants, since decayed. None of these traces were visible in the heavy residues from flotation at Saar where very few charcoal remains were sinking (Nesbitt 1993, 21), nor often during excavation, due to their fragile nature and often small size. For the first time, therefore, we are able to study not only the seeds, wood, and distinctive elements of plants which were charred in antiquity, but in addition, we are able to identify and quantify the plant remains which had not been charred, or which had been burnt at temperatures generally greater than 400° C. Boardman and Jones, in their study of charring on cereals, have established that the types of burnt residue from fires vary according to plant component and species, burning temperatures and duration, and oxidizing and reducing conditions (Boardman and Jones 1990).

The articulated plant remains in thin-section from Saar have been studied by plant anatomists at the Jodrell Laboratory, Royal Botanic Gardens, Kew, and identified by comparing the morphology and organization of the articulated plant cells to extensive modern reference collections of plants in thin-section.

What is surprising at Saar is that although plant

remains occur in great abundance in thin-section they derive almost entirely from the date-palm. This is not a product of the technique. Very sparse silicified fragments from the epidermis of a small grass have been identified as less than 2% of the components in two layers of occupation deposits in front of both altars, and in the fabric of some plasters at Saar [184]. These silicified fragments are sinuous-walled, epidermal long cells of a small grass (Gramineae), and are only 5–10 μm wide and less than 1.4 mm in length. Their sparse presence indicates that other plant remains do survive at the site, but only in small quantities. Indeed, a range of charred cereal grains, seeds, and other woods have been recovered by flotation, but, again, generally in low quantities. (Nesbitt 1993; de Moulins, this volume) These other types of plant remains are not present in the thin-section samples from the temple and other contexts yet studied, almost certainly because of sample size and the generally low density of the plant remains in question. By contrast to this lack of variety at Saar, a wide range of abundant plant remains from grasses, cereals, reeds, shrubs, trees and dung have been identified in thin-sections from other sites elsewhere in the Near East in Iraq, Syria and Turkey. Thin-section analysis has added further weight to the conclusions that the inhabitants of Saar depended heavily on the products of the date-palm in the early second millennium BC (Nesbitt 1993).

The use of date-palm remains in the temple can be identified by thin-section analysis of the date-palm part, fragment size, preservation, degree of burning and the context of deposition. We have been able to distinguish between the anatomical structure of date-palm leaflets and the more woody petiole, rachis and stem fragments (Tomlinson 1961; Winton *et al.* 1916). Isolated strands of vascular bundles may represent fragments of string, and have been identified in three units in front of the southern altar, Units 9.8, 11.1 and 11.2 [185].

Date-palm leaflets are well-preserved and abundant in thin-section. The leaflets range in thickness from 180–480 μm, and in length from 100 μm to more than 1 cm, and survive in a range of burnt and unburnt material forms. Many date-palm leaflets survive as desiccated remains which are pale yellow in thin-section, and in some instances may have been partially burnt [186]. Other date-palm leaflets are pigmented very dark brown to black. As yet it is not possible to determine whether these dark pigmented leaflets are partially decomposed or whether they have been charred at temperatures of less

than c. 400° C. Further experiment and analysis of the diagenesis, decay and combustion of date-palm and other plant remains is required. Some leaflets are translucent pale grey in thin-section and have been partly or entirely melted at temperatures probably close to or greater than 600° C, the melting point of silica. Lenses of calcitic ashes may originate either from leaflets or woody materials and could have been produced at a range of temperatures, depending upon conditions of combustion (Boardman and Jones 1990). The spherical silica bodies in date-palm are distinctive and readily identifiable. These silica bodies are small, with a diameter of usually 5–12 μm, or occasionally 24 μm, and occur close to the edge of the leaflet epidermis, and around the edges of vascular bundles. In deposits where the plant structure has been disrupted by physical agencies or combustion, they occur randomly distributed or in clusters, as in the thin lenses of burnt residues on top of the altars [187].

It is possible to distinguish between the charred woody fragments of date-palm branches (petiole/rachis) and those of the trunk (stem) in well-preserved fragments. The vascular bundles in date-palm stems tend to have wider, lignified bundle sheaths than those in the petiole/rachis (Fahn *et al.* 1985 pl. 82b). The vascular bundles in thin-section range in diameter from 250–720 μm. Stem fragments have been identified with some degree of certainty in one unit on top of, and two units in front of, the southern altar, and in two units at the side of the central altar. The largest fragment of stem in the thin-section samples from the temple is 8.5 mm in length.

Fragments of plant remains with less than approximately 10 cells are unidentifiable and indeterminate. These remains occur as both pale yellow and dark pigmented fragments, and do not suggest the presence of any plant other than date-palm in the thin-section samples.

The frequency and concentrations of all of these different types of plant materials are shown in the graphs [104–106]. The number of units in which each type of plant remains occurs is illustrated for the area on and around the altars, the NE corner of Area 200, and Test Pit 1, Phase 0.1 [104]. The frequency of occurrence is expressed as a percentage of the total number of occupation deposits in thin-section, which are 52, 7, and 5 respectively, for each area. Date-palm leaflets are the most widely occurring plant remains, being present in 80% of the occupational units around the altars. Dark woody date-palm remains only occur in 23% of units. Spherical silica bodies from the date-palm occur in at least 42% of the deposits and are embedded in the identifiable plant remains listed above. The least frequent types of plant remains are melted leaflets, 6%, spaces in the sediments from plants which have since decayed, 6%, and grasses, 4%. The sparseness of spaces from decayed plant remains in occupation deposits may be explained partly by the coarser sandy texture of many of the deposits at Saar, which will not readily form a fine mould or cast around fresh or decaying plant remains, as in the siltier deposits in Mesopotamia and Anatolia which have been analysed in thin-section.

The maximum and mean (average) concentrations of each type of plant remains in individual depositional units are shown as a percentage of the total area of deposits in thin-section [6 & 7]. Date-palm leaflets occur in the highest concentrations, constituting up to 70% of single depositional units. Pale yellow uncharred date-palm leaflets constitute a much higher average of occupation deposits around the altars than dark pigmented/charred leaflets, at 14% as opposed to only 3.5%. Dark/charred woody date-palm fragments constitute up to 40% of some units, for example at the side of the southern altar, but usually only constitute 2–5% of deposits, with an average of 2%. Spherical date-palm silica bodies are numerically abundant, but due to their small size, 5–24 µm, never represent more than 5% of deposits, and an average of less than one percent.

The series of bar charts illustrates the abundance of different types of plant remains for each of the contexts sampled [195–201]. Discussion of this information is incorporated into the contextual analysis of activities and the use of space.

Plant remains are the most abundant residue from human activity both within the temple at Saar, and on many ancient settlements in the Near East. As a consequence, the occupation deposits in the temple have been subdivided and analysed in three major groups, which are defined on the basis of plant remains content. Deposit Type 110 has less than 5% plant remains, and often comprises a layer of sand, which was probably brought in as an expedient floor surface. Deposit Type 111 has more than 5% but less than 40% plant remains, and often comprises trampled or mixed layers of sand and burnt plant remains. Deposit Type 112 has more than 40% plant remains and little sediment, and is associated with activities directly related to the use and deposition of plant remains. These major groups relate to significant

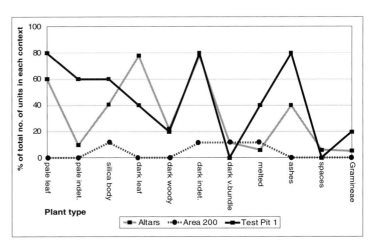

[5] Frequency of plant types in depositional units as a percentage of the total number of units in each context

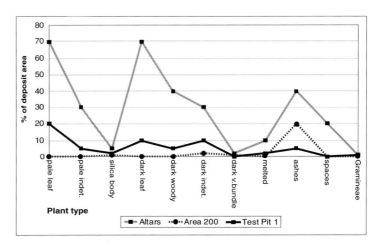

[6] Maximum concentrations of plant types in single depositional units

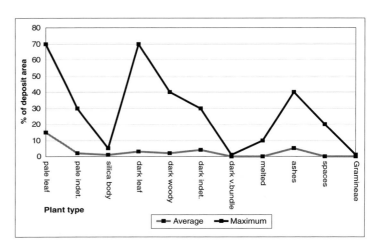

[7] Maximum and average concentrations of plant remains from the altars

differences both in the character of deposits, and in the nature of activities, both at Saar and at other sites in the Near East (Matthews & Postgate 1994, 192).

Bone fragments

Bone fragments occur in 16 of the 52 occupation deposits in thin-section samples from the temple altars. These fragments constitute no more than 2% of the components in all of these deposits, and range in size from 60 μm–1 mm. Bone was incorporated incidentally during manufacture into the fabric of two plasters of Type 106 on top of and in front of the southern altar. The remaining 16 occurrences of bone are in thin-sections of accumulated occupation deposits and can be summarized as follows:

	Southern Altar			Central Altar	
Deposit type	Top	Side	Front	Side	Front
111	0	3	0	2	2
112	0	2	0	1	0
113	5	1	0	0	0
Total	5	6	0	3	2

The presence of admittedly small fragments of bone in 31% of deposits, particularly on top of and at the sides of the altars, suggests that offerings of fish or meat may have been made at the altars. None of these bone fragments was identifiable due to their small size.

No bone fragments were identified in the depression sampled in the storeroom. In the NE of Area 200, near the benches, sparse fragments of bone, <2% in quantity and <4.5 mm in size, occur in the fabric of one packing and two plasters. The only fragment from accumulated deposits in this corner of the temple is a small fish-bone or scale (0.5 mm), in a compacted lens, Unit 9.1, perhaps below a mat.

Bone fragments are more abundant in Test Pit 1, Phase 0.1, in the wind-blown sand deposits and layers of intermittent occupation. Burnt and unburnt fragments of fish-bone and vertebra occur in Unit 2.1 at 2%, <1 mm, and at 2–5%, <4.5 mm, in Unit 2.2. Burnt bone fragments also occur at 2%, <1 mm, in a layer of *in situ* burning, and were particularly abundant in the field section. The wind-blown sands covering this layer are more sterile, with <2% bone.

Mollusc/shell fragments

Shell fragments occur in 7 of the 52 occupation deposits in thin-sections from the temple altars. These fragments constitute <2% of the components in all of these deposits, and range in size from <400 μm–2.5 mm. Shell fragments are also present in the fabric of two plasters, Type 105 and 107, and in plaster aggregates in three occupation deposits, one of which was on top of the altar. The shell fragments in plasters were probably present in the sediment from the original source area, as in the fine plaster, Type 105, lining the depressions in the storeroom (Area 220). The occurrence of shell in the seven occupation units can be summarized as follows:

	Southern Altar			Central Altar	
Deposit type	Top	Side	Front	Side	Front
111	0	0	0	2	2
112	0	1	0	1	0
113	0	1	0	0	0
Total	0	2	0	3	2

None of these shell fragments was identifiable in thin-section due to their small size, nor was any shell identified in residues in thin-section on top of the southern altar.

More than half of the shell fragments in thin-sections from Area 200 occur in the fabric of foundation materials and plasters. Shell fragments occur in three sandy deposits and in one compacted lens, perhaps below a mat. One of these shell fragments is large, at 1.7 cm, and is filled with a fine sediment from the original source area. Only one medium sand-size fragment of shell occurs in the thin-sections from Test Pit 1, where it was in wind-blown sand, Unit 2.1.

Pottery fragments

Pottery fragments were identified in 8 of the 52 occupation deposits in thin-section from the altars. The incidence of pottery can be summarized thus:

	Southern Altar			Central Altar	
Deposit type	Top	Side	Front	Side	Front
111	0	2	0	2	2
112	0	1	0	0	0
113	1?	3	0	0	0
Total	1?	6	0	2	2

These fragments range in size from less than 1.3 to 9.8 mm, and constitute less than 2–5% of deposits. One sherd at the side of the southern altar is bitumen coated. A fragment in Unit 22 on top of the altar is either from a pot, or from a clay object with a high mica content.

No pottery fragments occur in the sample from the NE of Area 200. One possible fragment of medium sand-size, <400 μm, occurs in Test Pit 1, Phase 0.1, in wind-blown sand deposits, Unit 2.1.

Bone, shell and pottery fragments only occur together in thin sections of 3 of the 52 occupation deposits, two of which are at the side of the central altar, and one of which is at the front of the southern altar.

Other artefactual residues from human activity

Few other artefactual residues from human activity occurred in thin-section samples around the temple altars. One of the questions relating to activities around the temple altars is whether or not incense was burnt during ritual ceremonies, as in other parts of the ancient Near East in the second millennium (Groom 1981; Nielsen 1986). Amorphous organic staining occurs in many of the deposits on top of the altar, and may in part originate from the burning of incense. This, however, cannot be established until chemical analysis for traces of incense has been conducted by Dr. R.P. Evershed at the University of Bristol as part of a forthcoming frankincense research project.

Small aggregates of bitumen, medium to coarse sand-size, 240–600 μm, occur in four occupation deposits, Type 111.5, around the central altar, and in the fabric of one plaster on top of the southern altar. Similarly, small sand-size fragments of possibly igneous grindstones occur in two units, one at the side and one on top of the southern altar. One fragment perhaps of copper, only 70 μm in size, is present in a plaster on top of the altar. The small sand-size, low concentrations at <2%, and infrequent occurrence of this group of artefactual residues in thin-section, make interpretation difficult. They may have been random inclusions in the sand or have been brought in incidentally adhering to the surface of date-palm leaflets.

Two medium sand-size aggregates of bitumen occur in a layer of packing, and a plaster in the NE corner of Area 200. None occur undisturbed in the samples from Test Pit 1, Phase 0.1. No other artefactual remains occurred in deposits sampled in thin-section.

It is possible to distinguish between primary residues from activity in thin-section, which are deposited in the location in which they were used or generated, and residues in secondary contexts, by the orientation, distribution, compaction and associations of components, and observations on size, surface abrasions, and burning for example. Residues in a secondary context may be present as incidental inclusions in plaster, displaced and trampled aggregates, or in dumped refuse deposits, for example (Matthews & Postgate 1994 and Matthews 1995).

Post-depositional alterations

The principal post-depositional alterations at Saar are physical disturbance by insects, small animals, plant roots, and recrystallization of salts, particularly gypsum. The areas of deposit affected by insect, animal and plant disturbances are clearly visible in thin-section as in-filled channels and chambers, and have been excluded from analyses of residues from human activities. These disturbances are present throughout the depositional sequences from Saar, including deposits immediately above bedrock in Test Pit 1, more than 5.40 metres below the current surface of the site. Soil fauna is sparse in comparison to that of temperate regions, but ants are abundant, and active in breaking down plant material, and have extensive subterranean channels and chambers (Doornkamp *et al.* 1980, 357). Root casts have been identified at the side of the central altar in Unit 13.2, for example. Deposits affected by the recrystallization of salts in solution may have been wetted either from the surface, or by evaporation of water in the soil profile. Recrystallized salts at Saar often occur as a combination of salts in-filling channels and chambers, or as salts which have impregnated the fabric and have disrupted the structure of the deposit in localized areas or horizons. There is some organic staining, particularly of deposits on top of the altar, which requires future chemical investigation. Occupation deposits with organic staining are classified separately as deposit Type 113.

Microstratigraphic Sequences and Uses of Space

We have studied the thickness, frequency and microstratigraphic sequence of floors and deposit types in each of the field sections and thin-sections, which are characterized in the microstratigraphic columns and tables [202 & 203]. Even at a general level there are clear differences.

Southern altar, top

The microstratigraphic sequence of plasters and burnt residues on top of the altar, Phase 3–5, was analysed in a vertical section which was excavated up to 10 cm into the western edge of the altar top. The surviving sequence was 19–22 cm thick.

The top of the altar was frequently cleaned and replastered. Ninety-four percent of the sequence comprises deliberately laid plasters and packing, while less than 6% comprises lenses of burnt residues [93, 115, 116]. A layer of packing 3 cm thick separated two series of plastering and use, Series 1 being the earliest. The number of microstratigraphic units in each series can be summarized as follows:

SERIES NO.	NUMBER OF UNIT			
	Packing Type 104	Plaster Type 106	Plaster Type 107	Residues Type 113
1	1	6	3	10
	1cm thick	0.5–1.7cm thick	1–1.5cm thick	180μm–1.44mm
2	1	4	3	8
	3cm thick	0.5–1.4cm thick	0.4–1.25cm thick	50μm–1.4mm

There is a total of 16 layers of surviving plaster and 18 layers of burnt residues on top of the altar. The base of the altar was built of stone. The first layer of plaster on top of the altar stood 50–60 cm above the first floor. The deposits around the base of the altar accumulated at a faster rate than those on top of the altar. The latest surviving plaster on top of the altar is only 28–34 cm above the latest surviving floor. The first series of plaster layers on top of the altar slopes down towards the back, perhaps to stop any burning residues or libations from spilling off the front. The second series of plaster floors is more disturbed in the centre and at the back of the microstratigraphic section, and it appears to have lipped up against a step, or an object such as a censer, in the centre of the altar. These plasters are only present in the front 14 cm of the altar. Beyond the lip in the plasters there is a layer of ash 4 cm thick, perhaps from the base of a censer.

The plasters in the centre of the altar in Series 1 were heavily reddened by burning, suggesting that the fires were burnt directly on top of the plaster surface. The microscopic boundaries are slightly irregular, following the undulations of exposed rock fragments and coarse sand grains in the surface of the plasters. One plaster surface, Unit 5, has two impressions, perhaps from the tapering edges of a knife, or the sharp base of a metal object [99].

The top of the altar was cleaned periodically, and before replastering. The surviving lenses of burnt residues are very thin, at less than 50 μm to 1.4 mm. These deposits often include unoriented, and randomly distributed, fragments of date-palm leaflets and clusters of silica bodies, which had been disturbed by repeated cleaning

[187]. All of the plant remains in the lenses in the centre of the altar are dark pigmented and charred [195], with the exception of Unit 14. This predominance of charred remains is characteristic of reducing conditions (Boardman and Jones 1990) and may have been induced by lack of oxygen at the base of the embers at the contact with the plastered surface, where combustion is likely to have occurred in a reducing condition, also noted by Groom (Groom 1981, 8). The dark coloration and reducing conditions may also have been induced by damp conditions, perhaps from the pouring on of libations. Further evidence for libations on top of the altar is perhaps suggested by the presence of a silty clay lens on top of plaster layer Unit 5, and the presence of secondary, post-depositional anhydrite in plaster layers Units 20, 23 and 30. Anhydrite, dehydrated gypsum, tends to form in hydrothermal conditions which are likely to have been generated if libations were poured on top of burning embers on the altars, as documented in later texts (Nielsen 1986; Groom 1981). This evidence, however, is not conclusive and requires confirmation by chemical analyses and experiment. The anhydrite is a post-depositional alteration, and may have been induced by either human or natural agencies.

Pale yellow date-palm leaflets which had only been desiccated or only partially burnt, occur in deposits at the front of the altar top, in Series 2 [195]. Here they are likely either to have been at the edge of any fire or to have fallen in front of a censer. One plaster in this series is slightly reddened, perhaps from burning embers. There are few lenses of calcitic ashes or melted leaflets on top of the altar, in contrast to the base of both altars, where ashes constitute up to 40% of deposits. Ashes and melted silica derive from more complete combustion than charred remains, and tend to occur away from the very base of a fire. They were probably brushed off the top of the altar, and redeposited around the base.

Fragments of bone occur in 6 of the 18 lenses of burnt deposits in thin-section, one in the centre of the altar in the first series of deposits, five at the front of the altar in the upper series [188]. These bone fragments, however, are small and sparse, less than 1 mm in length, and only constitute less than 2% of the deposits. The presence of bone fragments in thin-sections of 10 other units around the base of the altars may add further weight to the suggestion that bone was burnt on top of the altar.

Although deposits on top of the altar have some amorphous organic staining, there is no conclusive micromorphological evidence to suggest that incense was burnt. Modern incense bought in the *suq* in Manama, Bahrain, has been sampled in thin-section. In its fresh state it does not resemble any components in thin-section. One aggregate of pale yellow, isotropic material, with layering, is currently the only contender as a fragment of incense. Future research is needed in combustion and diagenesis of incense and date-palm leaflets and wood, and analysis of burnt residues in conjunction with chemical analyses. Isolated sand-size grains of bitumen and igneous rock also occur in the burnt lenses, but may have been brought in incidentally on the surface of the date-palm leaflets for example.

Southern altar, eastern side

The microstratigraphic section studied is parallel to the eastern side of the altar, 30 cm from the side of the stone base, and is one metre in length. This surviving sequence was 42 cm in height when studied. After later excavation it could be established that the sequence survived to a total height of at least 52–60 cm above the layers of foundation materials.

Accumulated layers of occupation debris constitute as much as 82% of the sequence studied, by contrast to the top of the altar where lenses of debris only represent 6% of deposits [202 & 203]. The microstratigraphic sequence can be summarized as follows:

Deposit	Plaster	Occupation				Layered
Type	106	110	111	112	113	111/112
No. of layers	7	4	4	9	1	5
% of sequence	18	8	10	37	1	26

More than half of the deposits at the side of the altar have more than 40% plant remains, Type 112 [186]. These deposits principally comprise date-palm remains which had been burnt at a range of temperatures, and in some instances were unburnt [196]. Some of the plant remains are well-preserved and had either been shovelled from the top of the altar with little disturbance, or in some instances may have been burnt at the side of the altar where there were irregular stone settings. At the bottom of the sequence studied, layers of plant remains accumulated to a depth of more than 12.5 cm before another plaster floor was re-laid. Later in the sequence layers of plaster, Type 106, or sand Type 110, were periodically laid on top of layers of plant remains less than 5 cm thick. There does appear to be some periodic alternation

between deposits rich in plant remains and those with less [196], perhaps reflecting increases and decreases in ceremonial activity.

Two particularly well-preserved cyclical series are represented by Units 9.3–9.7, and Units 9.8–11.2. In the first microstratigraphic sequence a layer of sand was deliberately laid down in order to cover an underlying layer of trampled debris, and to provide a thin foundation layer for a well-prepared, orange plaster floor. This floor was covered by date-palm matting or loose leaflets [189]. Accumulated deposits on this floor comprised firstly a layer of amorphous organic stained deposits similar to those on top of the altar, and secondly a layer of burnt plant remains, principally ashes, which included trampled plaster aggregates, a pottery sherd and 2% bone fragments. This first sequence is then followed by two layers of trampled sand and plant remains, Units 9.8 and 11.1. The last of these trampled layers has a possible standard impression on its upper surface, which is preserved under an immediately succeeding layer of burnt date-palm leaflets and ashes, Unit 11.2, presumably from burning on the altar [182]. The nature of this impression is discussed above.

Bone occurs in five units, 9.1, 9.6, 9.7, 11.1 and 11.2, all fragments are less than 1 mm in thin-section, and constitute 2% or less of deposits. Possible charred string fragments represented by isolated clusters of vascular bundles occur in Unit 11.1 [185].

Southern altar, front

The microstratigraphic section at the front of the altar is 30 cm from the stone base of the altar, and 1.3m in length. The microstratigraphic sequence [93, 115] can be summarized as follows:

Deposit	Plaster	Occupation					
Type	106	110	111	112	111/112	110/112	113
No. of layers	8	3	4	8	4	1	1
% of sequence	21	5	12	27	27	7	1

The proportions of deposit types in front of the altar are similar to those at the side [203]. There are, however, more discontinuous lenses and compound layers of burnt plant remains and sand in front of the altar, and fewer thick layers with more than 40% plant remains [197]. This difference suggests that the front of the altar was an active area where only thin lenses of burnt residues accumulated between thin layers of perhaps deliberately strewn sand and plaster floors [204], whilst the eastern side of the altar was generally used as a dumping area for burnt residues from the top of the altar.

Microstratigraphic Units 6–10 were analysed in thin-section. The top and bottom layers were very disturbed. Unit 7 is a sandy loam plaster, Type 106.1, which was burnt up to 3.5 mm below the surface, preserving date-palm leaflet structural stabilizers in the fabric of 10% of the plaster. A layer with almost 40% burnt and unburnt plant remains accumulated on this surface to a depth of 2.6 cm. This layer, Unit 8.1, is unusual, for it includes 20% relic voids of plant remains which have since decayed, leaving spaces in the surrounding sandy silt loam sediments. The edges of these spaces are lined with a thin layer of hypo coatings of fine sediments, <60 μm thick, which, together with the presence of salts, suggests the deposits were damp, perhaps from libations. Half of these relic plant voids have date-palm silica bodies from leaflet fragments, and one fifth have Gramineae (grass) epidermal long cell fragments. The remaining plant remains comprise pale yellow date-palm leaflets, and sparse, dark-pigmented, date-palm vascular bundles, ashes, and melted silica.

Units 8.2, 9.1, 9.2 and 9.3 comprise alternating layers of plaster and accumulated deposits. There is periodic variation between high and low concentrations of burnt plant remains in these accumulated deposits, which may represent increases and decreases in ceremonial activity associated with burning, also attested at the side of the altar. Unit 9.1 has more than 60% pale yellow date-palm leaflets and sparse ash, whilst Unit 9.3 has only 5% dark pigmented date-palm and indeterminate fragments. Unit 9.8 is rich in charred date-palm woody fragments and pale yellow leaflets.

The only other residues from human activity in the thin-section samples are <2% bitumen and bone fragments in Unit 9.8 in thin-section.

Central Altar, west side

The microstratigraphic section at the western side of the central altar is 15 cm out from the base. It is 1.10 cm long, but only 53 cm is well preserved. The height remaining for study was 28.5 cm. The microstratigraphic sequence [202 & 203] can be summarized as follows :

Deposit	Plaster			Occupation			
Type	105	106	107	110	111	112	111/112
No. of layers	1	1	3	1	6	4	2
% of sequence	2	4	5	4	51	14	18

Eighty-nine percent of the sequence comprises layers of accumulated deposits from human activity and mixed sandy layers. Only 11% of the sequence comprises deliberately laid plaster floors.

Although deposits with more than 40% plant remains, Type 112, only represent 14% of the sequence, nearly half of the trampled sandy layers, Type 111, have almost 40% plant remains [198]. Sandy deposits at the side of the central altar may have been subject to more disturbance as they lay adjacent to routes to and from the storerooms at the back of the temple.

Most of the plant remains survive as pale yellow date-palm leaflets, which may constitute up to 70% of deposits, with calcitic ashes at 10–20%. Pottery fragments are only present in Unit 9, at <2%, <1.8 mm. Bone is only present in Units 9, 12.1 and 13.4, at <2%, <1 mm.

Central Altar, front

The microstratigraphic section at the front of the central altar is 1.05 cm in length and, although stepped, is currently 33 cm high above foundation levels. The microstratigraphic sequence [93, 115] can be summarized thus:

Deposit	Plaster		Occupation+sand		Occupation with more than 40% plant remains	
Type	106	107	110	111	112	111/112
No. of layers	10	4	1	6	4	7
% of sequence	15	5	3	38	12	28

Almost twice as many plaster floors were laid in front of the central altar as at the side. This calculation excludes the five layers of orange plaster which occur at 1.0–1.5 cm intervals at the top of the sequence, but which are eroded at the side. Compound layers of sand and plant remains are more frequent in front of the altar than at the side, as is the case at the southern altar.

The plant remains in front of the altar are more varied but less abundant than at the side, and include slightly more dark pigmented or charred date-palm fragments [190 & 199]. Pottery fragments are more common and occur in Units 9, 10.3, and 11, but still only as 2% of deposits or less, and <5 mm in length. They often occur with plaster aggregates as in Units 10.3 and 11. Bone fragments occur in Units 9 and 10.1 as <2% of the components, and <1 mm in length.

Area 200, NE corner

The NE corner of Area 200 has benches built against both the northern and eastern wall faces. The surface of one bench, the high bench, has a rectilinear impression which may have been from the base of ritual statue or votive figure. The western face of a test excavation in this corner provided a section through the extant floors in Phases 3–5. As in other areas of the temple, the floors of Phases 3–5 were founded on a thick layer of pure sand, which was stabilized by a capping of silt loam 5 cm thick, with calcitic rock fragments.

Only an 11 cm high sequence remained for study during the sampling period at Saar. All of these surviving layers were remarkably clean and virtually devoid of even microscopic plant remains and residues from human activity [191], in contrast to the sequences around the altars. The sequence of deposits above foundation layers can be summarized as follows:

Deposit	Packing	Plaster	Plaster	Matting	Sandy deposits
Type	104	106	107	109	110
No. of layers	1	3	2	3	5
% of sequence	19	17	17	3	35

The types of plaster floor in this area differ slightly from those around the altars. Firstly, plaster Type 106.9, rather unusually, includes 10–20% aggregates of calcareous silty clay. These aggregates are from the same source materials as the sediments used to manufacture the fine plasters Type 105, which lined the depressions in the two storerooms. Secondly, plaster Type 106.6 has rather high concentrations of calcitic rock fragments for this group, at 20%. Thirdly, plaster Type 107.3, Unit 8, has a finer, denser and more orange, sandy clay loam matrix than other plasters in this group. One aggregate within this plaster has unreworked layers of water-laid orange clay silt, suggesting the fine sediments were of water-laid origin. These fine sediments appear to have been subsequently mixed with sandy deposits and carbonate rock fragments, which together formed a durable plaster floor.

At least three depositional layers attest the use of mats. Three lenses of compacted fine deposits have upper surfaces which bear undulating impressions suggestive of matting or woven floor coverings. These lenses are only 0.1–3.5 mm thick. Two occur within accumulations of sandy deposits [191]. One occurs on top of fine plaster aggregates and sparse fish-bone fragments, on top of the durable plaster, Unit 8.

Plant remains only occur in three units at very low concentrations [200]. Less than 2% date-palm silica bodies, which were perhaps abraded from a mat, occur

above a thin compacted layer, Unit 4. Two-percent, pale yellow, date-palm leaflets and indeterminate plant remains occur in sandy deposits, Unit 9.2, and 3% dark pigmented/charred indeterminate and possible string fragments occur in Unit 9.3.

The only other inclusions in occupation deposits are 10% trampled plaster aggregates above plaster floor Unit 3, 2% shell fragments in sandy deposits Units 9.2 and 9.4, and a large fragment of gypsum plaster 5.7 cm long in a layer of sandy packing, Unit 11, and a smaller fragment in packing Unit 1. These plaster fragments are the same as the plaster used to coat the benches in this area, and were probably dislodged during general modifications of the area. The manufacture of gypsum plaster is discussed above. Both the layer of packing, Unit 11, and probably the sandy deposits Type 110, were probably laid in order to raise the floor surface in this area up to those around the altars, which were accumulating at a faster rate, due to the accumulation of residues from burning on top of the altars.

Area 220, NW storeroom

The plastered depressions in the two storerooms of the temple were lined with layers of fine plaster, Type 105, [96] which ranged in thickness from 3.5 mm to 8 cm. Each depression was usually replastered two to five times before disuse. Two rather similar types of plaster were used, a pale brown silty clay loam with small organic particles, and a pale greyish brown silt loam with no organic inclusions. The source materials and manufacture of these plasters are discussed above.

Microscopic residues only occurred on top of one of the five layers of plaster in the depression sampled for thin-section analysis. These only comprised isolated date-palm leaflet fragments, less than 0.5 mm in length, and a thin discontinuous lens of organic staining, and are insufficient indicators of the use of the depressions. Chemical analysis of the organic staining may shed further light on the use of the depressions. The boundaries between the other layers of plaster are either smooth [180] or slightly serrated. There was extensive post-depositional recrystallization of gypsum salt crystals at the base of the first plaster in the depression sampled. This restricted occurrence suggests that the fine plaster lining may have acted as an impermeable layer which stopped salts rising from the ground onto the base of items such as large storage jars or sacks supported by the depression.

Test Pit 1

Three thin-section samples have been analysed from Test Pit 1, Phase 0.1. The first sample was prised from the bedrock surface at the bottom of the sounding in order to study the characteristics of the Eocene carbonate which forms the back-slope on which the site is located. The remaining two samples were cut out of the east section of the Test Pit in order to determine the nature and origin of the sandy deposits immediately overlying the bedrock, and the lenses of burnt material from the earliest, perhaps intermittent, occupation at the site [125].

The bedrock sample was 3.4 cm thick, and had partially weathered from the rock surface. It was impossible to hammer out a fragment from the solid rock due to the instability of the sandy sides of the Test Pit. The rock fragment was pale grey in thin-section and was formed from irregular zones of silt size calcitic crystals, 6–60 μm in size. The edges of the rock fragment and irregular internal voids, 5–10%, were partially lined with larger calcitic crystals up to 1 mm in length. Some edges of the rock had post-depositional iron staining, micro-contrasted organic particles, and gypsum salt crystals.

This carbonate rock fragment is very similar to the rock fragments in the mortars, foundation materials, and plasters Types 106 and 107, at the site, illustrating that all of these architectural materials were manufactured from locally-available building materials. The bedrock is currently exposed to the south-east of the site, and is very close to the surface to the west of the site where many Dilmun tombs were built. Six samples of plaster on top of and around the altars include rock fragments which are more weathered than the bedrock sample analysed. These more weathered fragments originate from the same carbonate rock. The crystals, however, are more isolated, and are surrounded by a matrix of pale yellowish brown clay, which has a distinctive reticulate birefringent structure in cross-polarized light under the microscope.

The sand immediately on top of the bedrock, Context 1729, is 7–42 cm thick. In thin-section it comprises a moderately sorted medium sand with no microscopic inclusions from human activity, suggesting its origin predates any occupation at the site [192]. This is in contrast to subsequent layers of sand in Phase 0.1, all of which include reworked and wind-blown residues from adjacent but probably intermittent occupation.

The sterile layer of sand on top of bedrock comprises 30% quartz, <720 μm, 20% carbonate sands, <840 μm, 2–5% carbonate bedrock fragments <1 cm, and 5–10%

assorted minerals, all of which are wind-blown and sub-rounded [192]. Because there is very little fine mineral material, <2%, the sand grains tend to touch one another, leaving extensive complex packing voids between the sediments, and up to 30% of the fabric is spaces. The sand grains are unoriented and randomly distributed. The site of Saar lies right on the boundary of quartz-rich sands to the west, and carbonate sands to the east (Doornkamp *et al.* 1980, Figure 10.1). These sands were blown onto Bahrain by a north wind during the late Pleistocene phase of low sea-level when Bahrain was not an island, but part of the Arabian mainland. It has been suggested that the quartz-rich sands originate from the Arabian mainland, and the carbonate sands originate from the carbonate-rich deposits of the Arabian Gulf (Doornkamp *et al.* 1980, 201–3).

There has been some post-depositional disturbance of the layer of sterile sand in Test Pit 1. Sparse fragments of bitumen and dark pigmented date-palm fragments have been introduced into this layer, down well-defined insect and small animal burrows, and along root channels. The location and extent of these channels and chambers are clearly visible in the field and in thin-section. There has been some post-depositional reprecipitation of gypsum crystals at the base of the sand, at the contact with the bedrock.

The sterile sand is overlain by a layer of wind-blown sandy loam, which has the first traces of human activity, microstratigraphic unit numbers 2.1–2.3, Context 1728. This activity is represented by the presence of 10% fragments of date-palm leaflets, wood, and ash <1 mm; 2% burnt and unburnt bone, including a fish-bone and vertebra, <2% pottery/baked clay aggregates <400 μm, <2% shell <360 μm, and a denser organo-mineral fine material which constitutes 25% of the fabric. The co-occurrence of these burnt and unburnt remains suggest they originate from preparation and cooking of food. All of these fragments have been reworked and blown about by wind, suggesting they may originate from a hearth either in an open or unroofed context, or from a tent or light structure, which may have been only intermittently used. This layer is 11–25 cm thick. It does include one lens, Unit 2.2, of relatively undisturbed layers of burnt and unburnt date-palm leaflets at 25% [201], bone 2–5% less than 4.2 mm, and 2% highly calcitic rock fragments less than 1.4 mm, perhaps from a grindstone. The moderately good preservation of the date-palm leaflets and their strong parallel orientation and distribution, suggest they were discarded very close to the original hearth.

Unit 3, Context 1727, is a silt loam with well-preserved burnt remains. This layer is only 2 to 7 cm thick. The plant remains are entirely from date-palm and are well-preserved in thin-section [193], they can be summarized thus [201]:

Pale yellow leaflets	Dark leaflets	Woody	Melted	Ashes	Dark indeterminate
10%	10%	5%	2-5%	5%	10%
3.5 mm	4.9 mm	<8.5 mm	2.1 mm	3.5 mm	<500 µm

The presence of highly-melted date-palm leaflets and vesicular melted silica suggests the fire was well ventilated and may have been fanned by wind in an open unroofed context. Patches of the underlying sand in the field section were reddened, indicating that this area is the actual location of several fires. Fish-bone was identified in thin-section, but only as 2%, <1 mm. In the field section and during excavation, larger fragments of fish-bone and charred date fruits were recovered. No associated architectural structures were encountered during the excavation.

This layer of burning was later covered by wind-blown medium-coarse sand with few inclusions from human activity, Unit 4, Context 1725, suggesting another hiatus in activity or occupation.

All of these layers had been subject to burrowing and root disturbance, which could be isolated and separated in thin-section analysis. The ratio of quartz to carbonate sands in deposits with residues from human activity was similar to that of the sterile sand immediately above bedrock, at 4:3.

Conclusions

Analysis of the microstratigraphy of floors and occupation deposits has provided evidence on the nature and cycle of activities in different rooms and areas of the temple.

The NE corner of the temple, to the right-hand side of the entrance, was kept remarkably clean. Two thirds of the sequence comprised structural packing and floors, with some evidence to suggest the use of mats. The remaining third comprised sandy deposits, only a few of which had very sparse plant remains, <3%. There is no evidence for burning in this area of the temple. The packing and sandy deposits may have been laid to raise

the level of the floor in this area up to that around the altars, where floors were accumulating more rapidly due to the accumulation of burnt debris.

The central and southern altars were both used for ritual burning. There is some alternation in the accumulation of deposits with high and low concentrations of plant remains, which may have been associated with increases and decreases in ceremonial activity. The periodic distribution of sandy deposits would also have affected the apparent concentrations of burnt residues, diluting them, where plants were trampled or mixed into the sandy deposits.

A surprising number of plant remains were observed for the first time in deposits in thin-section. Two thirds of these plant remains are not charred, and many are so fragile they are usually lost during standard flotation procedures. All of the plant remains both on top of and around the altars are from date-palm leaflets and woody fronds or stems, in the thin-section samples, with the exception of rare Gramineae fragments. This demonstrates further the great reliance on date-palm products by the inhabitants at Saar (Nesbitt 1993), although in flotation samples other plant remains have been identified (de Moulins, this volume).

Although the burnt layers on top of the southern altar are very thin, less than 0.2–1.4 mm, we have been able to detect diagnostic date-palm fragments in all of the layers. Tiny fragments of bone, less than 1 mm, occur in one third of these deposits. They occur at such low concentrations, both here and at the base of the altars, that it is difficult to confirm whether or not meat or fish was burnt as offerings. Although no recognizable fragments of incense have yet been identified, assessment of its presence requires future chemical analyses.

Burning on temple altars is closely tied to many ritual activities and intercessions with the gods (Groom 1981; Nielsen 1986). There are no significant differences in the microstratigraphic sequences or nature of deposits which could suggest differences in the role of the two altars in the temple at Saar. The only noticeable difference is that the deposits around the central altar are generally slightly more trampled than those around the southern altar. This increase in activity can probably be related to its more central position with routes to the storerooms either side of the altar. At both altars more floors were laid in front of the altars than at the side. Layers of burnt plant remains brushed from the altar tops tended to accumulate particularly at the sides of the altars.

The second series of plasters on top of the southern altar appears to have lipped up against a step, or object such as a censer, located in the centre of the altar top.

An impression of the base of an object, perhaps a standard or a tall incense stand, has been identified in the surface of a layer of sand at the side of the southern altar, covered immediately by a layer rich in burnt date-palm leaflets and ash. Thin tapering impressions, perhaps from the blade of a knife or object, have been identified in the surface of one plaster on top of the altar. These impressions are in-filled with a fine silty clay, which with other occasional characteristics may suggest the practice of libations at the southern altar.

The depression sampled in the back room Area 220, was lined with a fine, silty clay or silt loam, calcareous plaster with vegetal stabilizers. There are no microscopic residues on the surfaces of the plasters in the depression to suggest function. It is likely that the depressions were completely covered by an object such as the base of a pot, which would have prevented the build up of even microscopic dust. Sacking is likely to have left some residues, and therefore may perhaps be ruled out. The base of the first plaster in the depression sampled has been extensively disrupted by recrystallization of gypsum salts, suggesting the fine plaster may have been laid as an impermeable barrier to prevent salts damaging the base of an object such as a storage pot, or perhaps even penetrating through the fabric of the pot into its contents and thus spoiling it.

The lowest layer of sand in Test Pit 1, Phase 0.1, is sterile and wind-blown. Overlying layers of wind-blown sand have low but consistent densities of burnt and unburnt date-palm and bone, from adjacent and intermittent human activities. One layer in the east section of Test Pit 1, Context 1727, has *in situ* burning, and large fragments of fish-bone. This layer is only 2–7 cm thick, and is overlain by another thick layer of almost sterile wind-blown sand, suggesting intermittent occupation or activities, probably in an open area.

Chapter 4. Seals and Sealings: Fragments of Art and Administration

The most frequent and interesting of the finds from the temple are fragments of clay, some with designs stamped on them, apparently originally used to seal jars and packages which were stored or used in the temple. These pieces of clay functioned just like sealing wax. Forty-eight batches of these sealings or fragments of sealings were registered. In some cases groups of fragments found together were recorded under a single registration number. Most are made of a fine unbaked, yellow clay, although grey clay is occasionally used instead. All the designs identified on the clay fragments were originally made by circular Dilmun seals and the fingerprints of the person who affixed the seal are visible on almost a third of the examples recovered. Only one Dilmun seal was found in the building, but the design on it does not match any of those on the sealings.

The temple sealing corpus from Saar is the first large assemblage of stamp-impressed clay sealings ever to be recovered from a Dilmun-period site in Bahrain, or indeed anywhere in the Dilmun world. A great many of the Saar sealings have been recovered by use of systematic sieving procedures. The dearth of sealings from other Dilmun period sites is probably to be explained by the lack of such systematic procedures. However, sieving carried out at Failaka between 1958 and 1963 recovered only four sealings, and 363 stamp seals were found during these seasons (Kjaerum 1980 & 1983). It is suggested that seals were being manufactured at this site and as many came from badly disturbed, redeposited material the more fragile sealings from the same contexts might not have survived. More recent work at Failaka has continued this trend of finding large numbers of seals but few or no sealings (Beyer 1986 & 1989; Pic 1990). More locally on Bahrain, from the Barbar temple a total of nine seals and six sealings was recovered (Mortensen 1971), while from City II at Qala'at al-Bahrain came twenty-four seals and three impressions, one on a lump of bitumen (Højlund & Anderson 1994, 319–350).

Elsewhere, in Mesopotamia and south-western Iran, finds of Dilmun glyptic appear to be restricted to seals, with little or no representation of sealings with seal impressions (Amiet 1986; Kjaerum 1986; Mitchell 1986; Porada 1971). Further afield still, at Açemhöyük, far to the north in Anatolia, a few sealings of related type were found (Crawford 1991, 257). These sparse finds of Dilmun-period sealings emphasize the importance of the Saar temple corpus as a unique collection of administrative artefacts from secure contexts within a discrete and functionally distinct building at the centre of the settlement. The 80 pieces of sealings from the temple at Saar represent the largest single assemblage of clay sealings from any architectural context at the site, although smaller numbers occur in several of the houses.

Seals, and the sealings made from them, have traditionally been regarded as works of art in miniature. They are judged to have varying degrees of artistic merit and, incidentally, through the scenes they depicted, to throw light on the beliefs and mythologies of their creators. They also provide the archaeologist with a relative chronology based on stylistic change which is independent of both historical documentation and scientific techniques. More recent studies have tended to concentrate on other attributes. Seals, and the impressions from them, are now also recognized as recording systems which represent the fossilised, though incomplete, remains of the economic and administrative systems of the people who used them. Each sealing is seen as evidence for a transaction of some sort and clues to the type of transaction can sometimes be found in the nature of the item to which the sealing was originally attached and the place where it was found. For example, it has been shown that at Arslan Tepe in south-east Turkey the sealings removed from goods as they entered a temple store were retained for a period of time as a means of accounting for the goods which had been received (Ferioli & Fiandra 1983). At the end of the accounting period they were thrown away. The only possible remains of some kind of accounting system at Saar are represented by circular pin-holes pushed through four of the sealings from the temple, in some cases obliterating part of the design [9 & 19]. A rectangular hole, obviously made by a different shaped implement, can be seen on a fifth sealing which shows a seated insectivorous creature [17]. A circular hole is also to be seen on what may be a tag or label (1581:04). These labels are of different types and the best preserved is broken in two. The surviving piece is hemispherical and the impression of the string which originally ran through the centre of the little clay ball is clearly visible (1597:10). All these holes must have been made soon after the sealing was applied or the clay would have become too dry for the hole to have been made, and all are pierced from the front. The holes are plainly not random, but had a definite purpose and we can guess that they may represent some checking of a consignment of goods before despatch.

The design on the seal is another source of information and will occasionally give some indication of who owned it. In some cases the name and position of the owner may even be inscribed on the seal and will form part of the design, as for example on many seals of late third millennium date in Mesopotamia (Collon 1987). However, none of the Saar seals carries such an inscription. It is also possible that the picture itself may sometimes relate to the office or the profession of the user as Nissen and Dittman have suggested (Nissen 1977; Dittman 1986). They discuss one class of fine, well-cut seals of late fourth millennium date from Mesopotamia which shows a figure usually identified as a priest/king, engaged in ritual or warlike activities [205] while a second, much less well made, shows groups of people engaged in mundane tasks like weaving or potting [206]. The first class seems to have been used by high officials, the second by the temple workshops. The seals with the priest/king on them are sometimes found apparently counter-signing seals of the second type, again implying a difference in status between the users of the two. More recently it has further been suggested that closely related people may have used seals with closely related designs, so-called 'Look-a-like seals' (Weingarten 1990, 76). This suggestion has also been made about one class of seals from Saar showing a rotating wheel-like design of animal heads, which it was proposed may have been used by a group related, not by blood, but by their profession (Crawford 1991, 257).

Studies of the way seals were used suggests that they were more than just signatures. They could also be badges of office used to validate formal transactions of many sorts such as land transfers or bills of sale (Gelb 1991). It is possible that they were also used as trademarks by manufacturers so that a population which was probably largely non-literate could distinguish between different signatures and makes of goods. It is likely that the designs on seals represent individuals, products, or great offices of state; each is specific to the user. Many were no doubt instantly identifiable within their own community.

The Sealings

The sealings from the temple form a homogenous stylistic group. Nearly all of the Phase 1 and 2 floors remained unexcavated, and the sealings are therefore mostly from the later phases. Only seven came from Phase 2, and the rest from Phases 3 and 4. Of the 80 fragments recovered, 39 have legible impressions on them and they are all in the classic early Dilmun style. None of the Phase 2 fragments had a legible design.

The designs on the sealings are very varied, though as most of them are incomplete, we may have several motifs which came originally from the same seal. The designs are comparable to those found in the settlement at Saar, at the Barbar temple, in City II at Qala'at al-Bahrain (Højlund & Andersen 1994) and on the period Ia/b seals published by Kjaerum from the island of Failaka. The last forms the most extensive collection so far available for comparison (Kjaerum 1983). Two thirds of the designs from the temple include a human figure engaged in a variety of pursuits. One of the very few complete impressions found shows two crouched or seated human figures on either side of a hatched rectangle which seems to be stretched on a frame resembling a horizontal loom [13]. A second, incomplete impression apparently shows a similar scene [9]. Another broken example depicts a scene of sexual intercourse [20]. There are also five broken pieces, probably from the same seal, which show a line of figures in tiered skirts who seem to be dancing [14 & 15]. The reverse of the pieces suggest that they may all have come off a big jar which was sealed several times with the same seal. The same design may be present on sealings from House 224, but as the pieces are broken it is difficult to be sure of this. Duplicate sealings are rare, but two sealings both show a seated figure facing a curious symbol

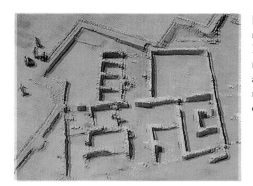

[119] House 53 and its neighbours, looking south-west
House 53 had no less than 11 rooms or open areas, including a large square courtyard and a row of 4 small storerooms opening off a kitchen area.

[120] The temple from the air
In the foreground is the junction of Main Street with Temple Road (seen from the NE). The shape of the temple is in contrast to the surrounding rectangular houses.

[121] The temple terrace
Buildings to the south and north of the temple showed signs of being terraced into the settlement mound. This can be demonstrated by plotting the highest floor levels in each building on a north–south axis. Note that the vertical scale has been exaggerated. The slope is steeper NE of the temple, down Temple Road.

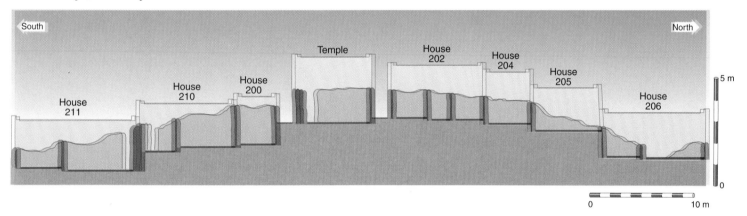

[123] Location of Test Pits
The investigation of the pre-temple history of this area began with the excavation of Test Pit 1 against the NW wall. This was the only area where virgin soil was reached.

[122] Temple dimensions in Phase 5

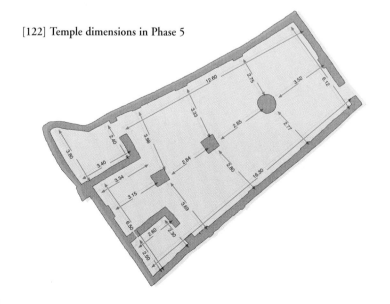

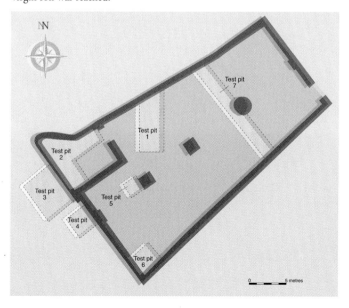

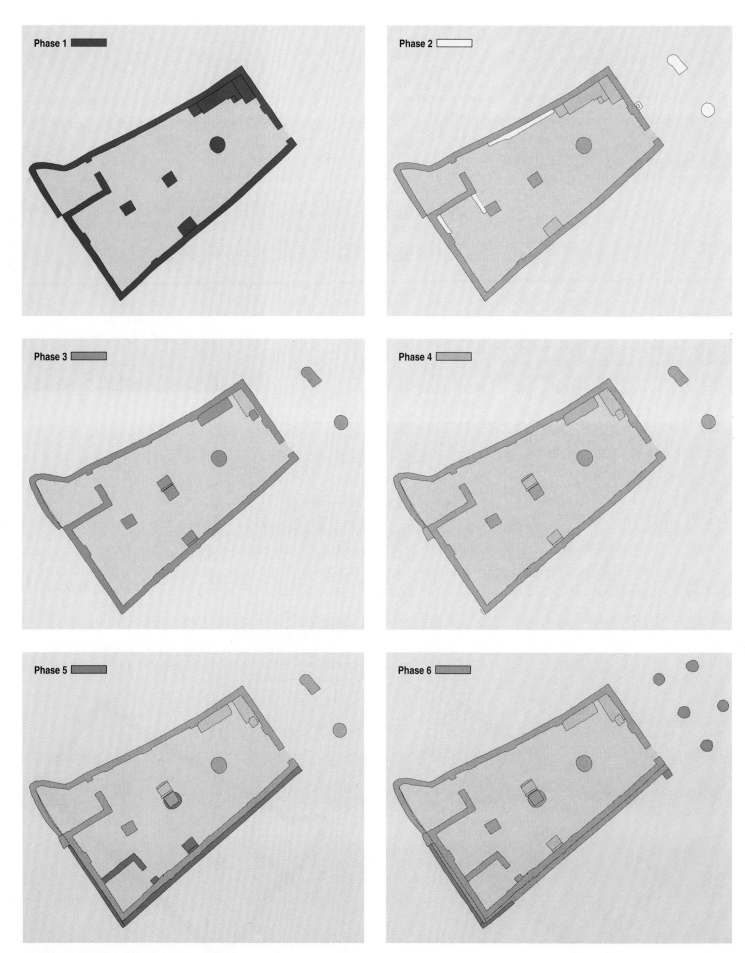

Phase 1

Phase 2

Phase 3

Phase 4

Phase 5

Phase 6

[124] Phase-by-phase schematic plan

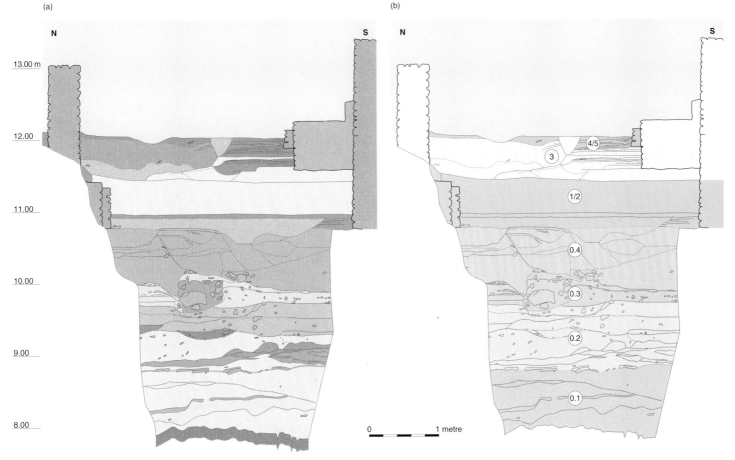

(a)   (b)

N   S   N   S

13.00 m

12.00

11.00

10.00

9.00

8.00

0   1 metre

[125] The north-east section of Test Pit 1 against the central column

The surprising depth of pre-temple Phase 0 deposit is clearly illustrated in this section. The Phase 0.3 wall can be seen in the middle of the section, between a depth of 9.60 m and 10 m, sealed by a layer of sand which it is assumed indicates levelling activity before the temple was built.

PHASE	OBJECT NO.	MATERIAL	LABORATORY REFERENCE	RESULT BP	POSSIBLE CALIBRATED DATE RANGES (BC)	
					68% PROBABILITY	95% PROBABILITY
0.1	1533:06	DATE STONES	BM-2673	4000 +/- 50	2565-2465	2865-2815
						or 2695-2680
						or 2665-2450
						or 2425-2395
						or 2375-2370
0.2	1516:02	DATE STONES	BM-2672	3740 +/- 40	2275-2250	2290-2035
					or 2205-2130	
					or 2075-2045	
0.2	1521:02	DATE STONES	BM-2670	3700 +/- 80	2275-2250	2455-2445
					or 2205-1975	or 2355-1885
1	1923:01	ASH	OxA-5913	3320 +/- 130	1760-1440	2000-1300

☐ Pre-temple   ▨ Temple

[126] Carbon 14 dates from Test Pit 1 and the temple

Three samples of charred date-stones from a sequence of layers below the temple were sent for C14 dating at the British Museum. They fit reasonably well into current chronological orthodoxy and show that the origins of the settlement at Saar recede back into the third millennium BC. The result of accelerator-dating one further sample, ash from a Phase 1 floor, suggests that the foundation of the temple should be put in the second millennium BC, though not, perhaps, as late as the 95% probability range suggests.

[127] Phase 0.3: Pre-temple buildings in Test Pit 1

Running through the middle of Test Pit 1 (SW to NE) was a substantial wall which predated the temple. Behind it, in the side of the excavation, is the NW wall of Phase 1. The foundation and base of the subsequent Phase 3 wall can be seen above it.

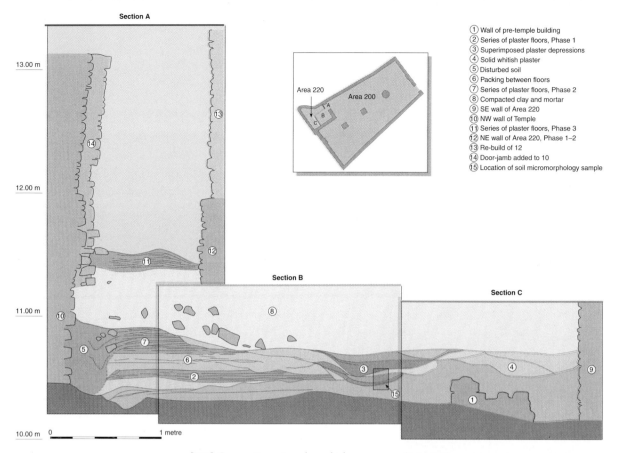

Section A

13.00 m

12.00 m

11.00 m

10.00 m

0   1 metre

Section B

Section C

Area 220

Area 200

① Wall of pre-temple building
② Series of plaster floors, Phase 1
③ Superimposed plaster depressions
④ Solid whitish plaster
⑤ Disturbed soil
⑥ Packing between floors
⑦ Series of plaster floors, Phase 2
⑧ Compacted clay and mortar
⑨ SE wall of Area 220
⑩ NW wall of Temple
⑪ Series of plaster floors, Phase 3
⑫ NE wall of Area 220, Phase 1–2
⑬ Re-build of 12
⑭ Door-jamb added to 10
⑮ Location of soil micromorphology sample

[128] Composite section through the storeroom (Area 220)
The Phase 0.3 wall is at the bottom right (1), sealed by hard packed material which separates it from the construction of the temple. The in-filling that separated Phase 1/2 from Phase 3 of the temple is also shown (8), with a disturbed area (5) indicating perhaps where the Phase 1/2 door-jamb had been removed.

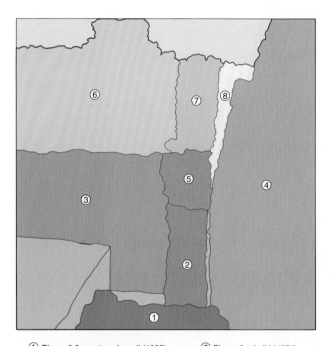

① Phase 0.3, pre-temple wall (1935)
② Phase 0.3, pre-temple wall (1934)
③ Phase 1 temple wall (1935)
④ Phase 1 temple wall (1934)
⑤ Packing for Phase 3 rebuild
⑥ Phase 3 rebuild (1674)
⑦ Phase 3 rebuild (1668)
⑧ Phase 4 door-jamb insertion (1932)

[129] The south-west corner of the storeroom (Area 220)
A section of walling (2) from the underlying building was reused for the temple. But where the earlier wall was not in a convenient position to be included in the new building it was simply cut down, and the stumps subsequently covered by the storeroom floors, as can be seen in the foreground (1). The wall on the right (4) is part of the looping wall at the back of the temple. It can be seen that it almost misses rejoining the back wall of the temple. Indeed, by the time of the Phase 4 insertion of a door-jamb for House 206 (8) it had slumped away from the back wall, by then rebuilt (7).

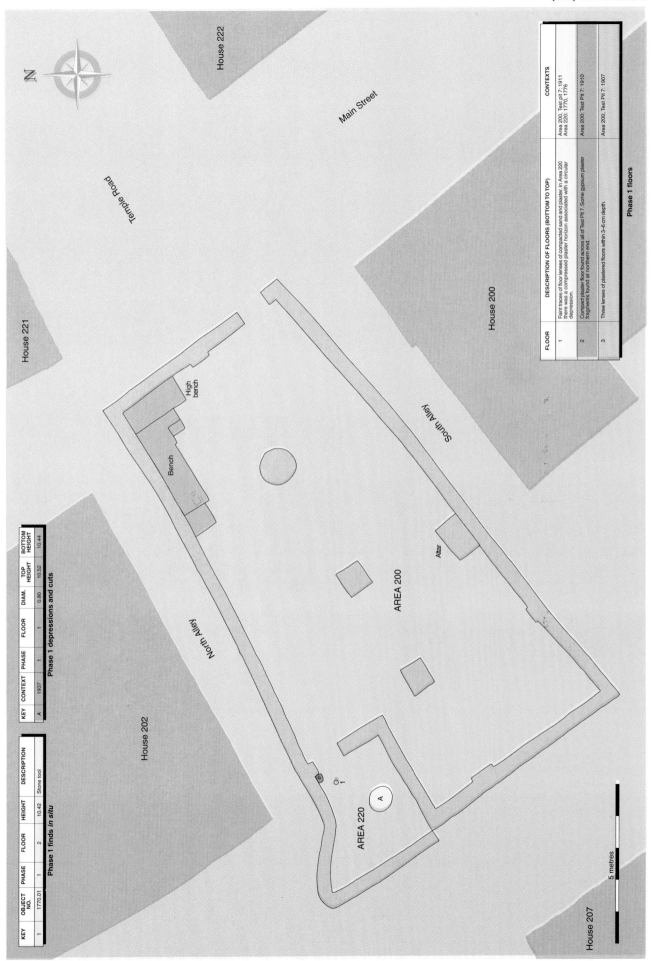

N

House 222

House 221

House 202

Main Street

Temple Road

North Alley

South Alley

House 200

House 207

AREA 200

AREA 220

High bench

Bench

Altar

A

Phase 1 finds *in situ*

KEY	OBJECT NO.	PHASE	FLOOR	HEIGHT	DESCRIPTION
1	1770.01	1	2	10.42	Stone tool

Phase 1 depressions and cuts

KEY	CONTEXT	PHASE	FLOOR	DIAM.	TOP HEIGHT	BOTTOM HEIGHT
A	1937	1	1	0.80	10.52	10.44

Phase 1 floors

FLOOR	DESCRIPTION OF FLOORS (BOTTOM TO TOP)	CONTEXTS
1	Faint traces of floor lenses of compacted sand and plaster. In Area 220 there was a compressed plaster horizon associated with a circular depression.	Area 200, Test pit 7: 1911 Area 220: 1770, 1776
2	Compact plaster floor found across all of Test Pit 7. Some gypsum plaster fragments found at northern end.	Area 200, Test Pit 7: 1910
3	Three lenses of plastered floors within 3–6 cm depth.	Area 200, Test Pit 7: 1907

5 metres

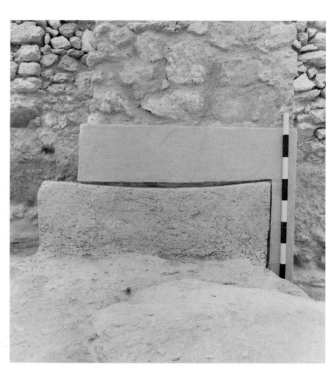

[132] The Phase 1/2 altar
The altar was partially preserved beneath the southern altar of Phase 3 as a rectangular block, 80x112 cm and at least 66 cm high. The smooth-plastered area in the middle is a modern support put in to prevent the collapse of the Phase 3 altar, the stonework of which can be seen above it.

[131] Phase 1 features in Test Pit 7
Beneath the circular column at the NE end of the temple was a plastered depression with a raised edge, forming a shallow basin, 103x35x11 cm. It was lined with a well-rendered layer of plaster and was perhaps used for mixing materials required in the construction of the building, such as mortar or wall-plaster.

[134] Rectangular impressions in the long bench
Faint multiple impressions were visible in the plaster of the long bench (1824). The indentations suggest that a rectangular box or stand, approx. 16x14 cm, was repeatedly moved around on top of the bench before the plaster was properly set.

[133] The suite of installations in the north-east corner of the temple
The NE corner of the temple was a focal point for religious activities in the building. On the left, two low benches (1824, 1825) seemed to have served as tables. The high bench in the corner of the temple may have been a permanent support for other objects connected with the temple rituals.
Dimensions:
High Bench (1653): 62–77x186 cm; original height 139 cm.
Long bench (1824): 85–95x294 cm; excavated height: 34 cm.
Bench (1825): 68x75 cm; original height: 60 cm.
Top step: 17x46x64 cm; lower step: 12x46x64 cm.

[135] Detail of plastered top of long bench
The plasterwork of the suite of installations survived in pristine condition. Even the swirls created by the plasterer's fingers were still preserved in places.

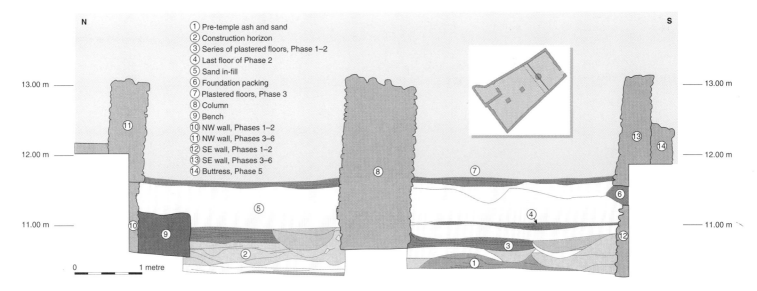

① Pre-temple ash and sand
② Construction horizon
③ Series of plastered floors, Phase 1–2
④ Last floor of Phase 2
⑤ Sand in-fill
⑥ Foundation packing
⑦ Plastered floors, Phase 3
⑧ Column
⑨ Bench
⑩ NW wall, Phases 1–2
⑪ NW wall, Phases 3–6
⑫ SE wall, Phases 1–2
⑬ SE wall, Phases 3–6
⑭ Buttress, Phase 5

N

S

13.00 m — — 13.00 m

12.00 m — — 12.00 m

11.00 m — — 11.00 m

0   1 metre

[136] **The north-east section of Test Pit 7**
Two separate sequences of finely plastered floors of Phases 1–2 are visible south of the column, but these appear to be conflated to the north. Shallow depressions similar to those found at the western end of the temple were also noted here in section where they show up as ellipses of smooth plaster.

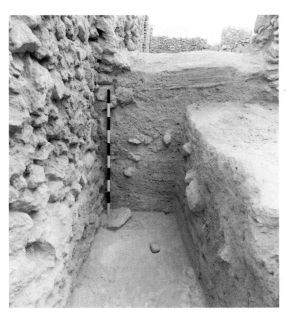

[137] **Flooring sequence, looking out through the storeroom**
The floors of Phases 1–2 can be seen at the bottom of the section. There is some 50 cm of accumulated flooring, with Phase 3 levelling material and floors above. The Phase 1 door-socket can be seen under the scale.

[138] **Inside the temple, looking north-east**
The floor level is excavated down to Phase 2. Seventy centimetres higher, on the left (NW) side of the central square column, is the base of the Phase 3 altar underpinned by our modern plasterwork. Higher still, on the right-hand side, and again underpinned, is the Phase 5 skirt added to the column.

[139] **Burnt material next to the altar**
Accumulated on the floor next to the altar was a deposit of burnt ashy material, perhaps representing a localized fire, or debris from whatever was burnt on top of the altar.

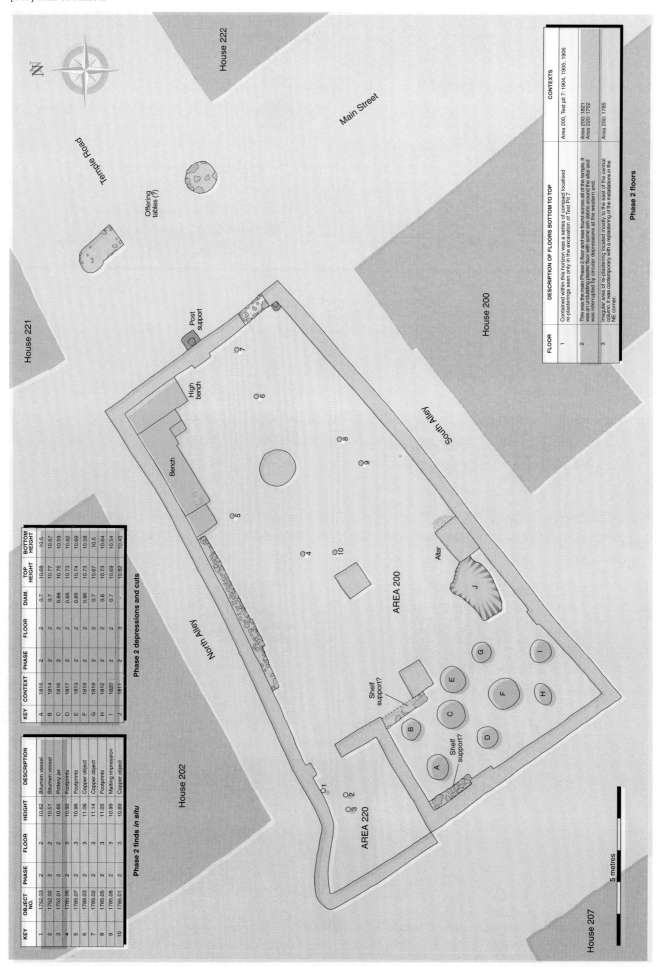

Phase 2 finds *in situ*

KEY	OBJECT NO.	PHASE	FLOOR	HEIGHT	DESCRIPTION
1	1752.03	2	2	10.62	Bitumen vessel
2	1752.02	2	2	10.51	Bitumen vessel
3	1752.01	2	2	10.65	Pottery jar
4	1785.06	2	3	10.92	Footprints
5	1785.07	2	3	10.96	Footprints
6	1785.03	2	3	11.06	Copper object
7	1785.02	2	3	11.14	Copper object
8	1785.05	2	3	11.05	Footprints
9	1785.08	2	3	10.99	Matting impression
10	1785.01	2	3	10.89	Copper object

Phase 2 depressions and cuts

KEY	CONTEXT	PHASE	FLOOR	DIAM.	TOP HEIGHT	BOTTOM HEIGHT
A	1815	2	2	0.7	10.68	10.5
B	1814	2	2	0.7	10.77	10.67
C	1816	2	2	0.88	10.75	10.59
D	1817	2	2	0.66	10.73	10.62
E	1813	2	2	0.85	10.74	10.69
F	1818	2	2	0.96	10.73	10.58
G	1819	2	2	0.7	10.67	10.5
H	1812	2	2	0.6	10.73	10.64
I	1820	2	2	0.7	10.69	10.54
J	1811	2	3		10.82	10.43

Phase 2 floors

FLOOR	DESCRIPTION OF FLOORS BOTTOM TO TOP	CONTEXTS
1	Contained within this horizon was a series of compact localised re-plasterings seen only in the excavation of Test Pit 7	Area 200, Test pit 7: 1904, 1905, 1906
2	This was the main Phase 2 floor and was found across all of the temple. It was an undulating plaster floor with some ash debris around the altar and was interrupted by circular depressions at the western end.	Area 200: 1821 / Area 220: 1752
3	Irregular area of re-plastering located mostly to the east of the central column. It was contemporary with a replastering of the installations in the NE corner.	Area 200: 1785

like a figure of eight on the far side of which is a horned animal looking back at the seated man [18 & 25]. Even if duplicate sealings from the same seal are rare, certain themes, such as the standing man touching the head of a horned animal, are repeated with minor variations [21, 24 & 28]. Another of the temple fragments [12], which shows the hindquarters of a standing animal, can be matched by a piece from a nearby House 203 (1622:02) indicating, perhaps, that both were receiving goods from the same supplier.

About ten percent of the sealings show one or more graceful horned animals which often resemble gazelle or oryx, sometimes with humans, when a hunting scene may be represented, as we suggested above, sometimes with other animals. Many of the scenes are impossible to interpret. There is, for example, the curious row of human heads in profile which protrude from a hatched strip running horizontally across the sealing [23]. The lower part of the design is missing.

Only one seal was found in the temple during the current excavations [21]. It is a classic Early Dilmun circular stamp seal, perforated for suspension, and made of what is usually called chlorite/steatite, although no tests have been carried out to determine the exact chemical composition of the stone. It has a diameter of 1.9 cm and a low humped back 1.2 cm high which is decorated with three incised lines at right angles to the perforation, flanked by four dot-and-circle motifs, two on each side of the lines. The profile of the seal is slightly concave. Kjaerum, who has studied these seals most extensively, divides them into different groups on the basis of the profile which can also be straight, convex, angular or grooved. His study would place this seal in the Variant II Group (Kjaerum 1983, 14).

Kjaerum has also classified these seals on stylistic grounds and on his criteria our seal shows characteristics of his Groups Ia and b (Kjaerum 1980, 46). Group Ib is characterized by human figures shown in profile in a more linear style than in Group Ia where the torso is often shown front view. The temple seal is finely cut in a linear style, but the shoulders of the man are shown as if from the front. The two groups overlap in time and the difference may reflect the traditions of different workshops or craftsmen. The design on the seal shows a naked male figure, his bearded face and lower body in profile, but his shoulders front view, while to the right he holds with one hand the horns of a long-horned caprid, which looks back over its shoulder towards him. To the left he

holds a shield-like object and beyond that there is an oblong motif. Although the details and the execution are very different the theme is similar to that found on an impression from near the central altar and on another fragment from Area 220. A similar theme is also found at Failaka (for example, Kjaerum 1983, nos. 202/203).

Information on the types of goods to which the sealings were applied comes from their backs, which often retain the negative impression of the object, providing evidence for containers and wrappings, even though these may have been perishable.

Sealing Functions

As the Saar temple sealings are small and fragmented, the necessary evidence for sealing function, as attested by impressions on the reverse faces, is generally of a restricted nature. Even when complete, and only five of the 80 pieces appear to be so [9, 13, 16, 17 & 28], the Saar sealings do not readily yield information on their original functions. Nevertheless, some important information has been recovered.

Sealing clay composition is not here explored, beyond a brief colour description in each catalogue entry. Most sealings are of a yellow-grey-green or light grey-whitish clay, usually not burnt or baked. One sealing, 1785:04, is of a distinctive dark grey clay with sizeable mineral inclusions. This fact, taken with the unusual string impressions on its reverse face, suggests the sealing may have arrived at Saar attached to imported goods. Chemical analysis of clay composition by X-ray fluorescence, particularly if integrated with analyses of clays used in pottery production, could shed much light on the original provenance of clay sealings found at Saar. In general terms, the Saar clay sealings can be divided into four groups. Firstly, there is a large group of sealings for which it is impossible to identify any sealing function. Secondly, on some sealings it is possible to identify string impressions but no further diagnostic markings. Thirdly, there is a group of sealings which have impressions of a curved object and string on their reverse faces. Fourthly, some sealings take the form of circular or oval disks with string impressions on the reverse. We can look at each of these groups in turn.

Group 1: sealings of uncertain function
In all, 31 sealings, or 40% of the temple corpus, have unknown functions, largely due to their small and frag-

mented nature. These pieces are extremely hard to interpret and in some cases are unlikely to have functioned as sealings at all. Ten of these functionally indeterminate sealings, or 32% of the 31, have detectable seal impressions on their obverse face, substantially less than the 51% of the temple corpus (39 out of 77) with detectable seal impressions. This fact is likely to reflect, on the one hand, the fragmented nature of the Group 1 sealings and, on the other, the possibility that some of these pieces are not true sealings, but shaped pieces of clay for other purposes.

Group 2: sealings with string impressions only

Twenty sealings, or 26% of the temple assemblage, have impressions of string on their reverse surfaces. In no case are there additional markings to assist in a functional interpretation, so that all we can say is that these pieces of clay were at some stage affixed to lengths of string which must originally have enveloped or secured some object. The sorts of objects bound by string and sealed by these clay pieces cannot with confidence be ascertained, but we may reasonably speculate that Group 2 sealings are mainly fragmentary versions of sealings in Groups 3 or 4.

Seven of the Group 2 sealings, or 35%, have visible seal impressions on their obverse face, a slightly higher proportion than in Group 1. The comparatively low proportion of pieces with detectable seal impressions in Groups 1 and 2 indicates that the obverse faces of these sealings are as fragmentary as the reverse faces.

While we are unable to identify the precise function of these sealings we can at least retrieve some information concerning string technology [8]. On 15 of the Group 2 sealings the string impressions are too faint, smudged or distorted for any precise measurements to be taken. The remaining five pieces, 1539:05 (1), 1550:06 (5), 1596:02 (2), 1763:05 (2) and 1763:09, yield consistent results as here summarized, with all measurements in centimetres:

Strand diameter average	range	String diameter average	range	Twist period average	range	String spin direction Z	S
0.27	0.2–0.3	0.32	0.25–0.35	0.67	0.65–0.7	-	5

There is considerable uniformity in these measurements of string details, with a narrow range of values for each category. The exclusive use of S-spun string is especially striking. There is also consistency in the type of fibres used in the string attested on the Saar temple sealings, across all functional groups, with a medium-coarse fibre always employed, its coarseness giving a slightly stiff and

unfinished appearance to the string, as impressed on the sealing reverses. There can be little doubt that the string employed at Saar was manufactured from date-palm fibre, a versatile substance well known for string production (Popenoe 1973, 118).

Many examples of modern date-palm fibre string are on display in the ethnography section of the Bahrain National Museum. Some were measured and tallied extremely well with the Saar sealing evidence, with strand diameters of 0.25–0.3 cm, string diameters of 0.35–0.4 cm and twist periods of 0.7–0.9 cm. In every single case the string spin direction was S-spun, with no instances of Z-spun.

In any case it is not surprising that the inhabitants of Saar made every use of the natural products of a tree which must have dominated their environment. It is worth commenting that at the Early Dynastic cities of Fara and Abu Salabikh in southern Mesopotamia (around 2,500 BC), reverse impressions on clay sealings show a marked preference for Z-spun string, almost certainly made from goat hair, with only a few instances of probable date-palm fibre string (Matthews 1991, 5; Martin and Matthews 1993, 37).

Group 3: sealings with curved reverse faces and string impressions

Seventeen sealings, or 22% of the temple assemblage, have reverse faces with some degree of curvature and generally with associated string impressions. Estimated diameters of the curved objects covered by the sealing vary substantially, so that it is unlikely that all Group 3 sealings were used on the same type of object.

In all, 13 of the Group 3 sealings, or 76%, have detectable seal impressions on their obverse surface, a much higher proportion than the 32% of Group 1 and the 35% of Group 2 sealings with seal impressions. This high proportion almost certainly reflects the generally better state of preservation of the Group 3 sealings, with both obverse and reverse faces being more readily intelligible.

There is some variety in the nature of the curved object to which the Group 3 sealings were affixed. Three of the sealings, 1581:04.2, 1599:01 and 1763:08, have gradual curves with diameters of 9.0 cm or more, in each case with string impressions, probably reflecting adhesion to a pot neck secured with string [207].

Five other pieces, 1542:04, 1543:06, 1550:06 (1), 1587:05 and 1750:05, have short stretches of smooth curved impression with diameters ranging from 1.2 to 2.8 cm, averaging 1.7 cm. All but 1542:04 have string impressions. These pieces appear to have been applied to smooth pegs secured with string [208]. In one case, 1750:05, at right angles to the peg impression can be seen a tiny surviving flat area of the sealing with clear wood grain impressions, suggesting that the peg had been originally affixed to a wooden object, such as a door or chest [208c]. Two other sealings, 1550:06 (9) and 1612:10, have traces of a smooth level surface which might have been a plastered wall or container.

Four sealings, 1597:01(3), 1612:09(1), 1763:05(1) and H13:12:01, have clear impressions of a peg with parallel striations running the length of the peg impression, diameters ranging from 1.3 to 3.8 cm, averaging 2.5 cm. These sealings were affixed to lengths of peg manufactured from reed, as indicated by the distinctive striated marks. Each of these four sealings also has string impressions around the peg [209]. Finally, several pieces have indeterminately curving reverses with string impressions.

Only two of the Group 3 sealings, 1542:04 and 1598:01 (1), lack any string impressions. Of the remaining fifteen Group 3 sealings, six have string impressions which are too faint for any detailed measurement, while nine pieces yield some form of quantified information. The string impressions on the Group 3 sealings are here summarized:

Strand diameter		String diameter		Twist period		String spin direction	
average	range	average	range	average	range	Z	S
0.28	0.25–0.3	0.34	0.3–0.5	0.76	0.5–0.9	-	8

In every case the string fibre is of medium-coarse texture. These string details bear close comparison with those already presented for Group 2 sealings, and reinforce the idea that the Saar string was manufactured from date-palm fibre. The mode of use of the string on the Group 3 sealings is for the string to be wrapped around the curved object, often in several parallel rows. In no case has the sealing been applied onto a knot in the string.

Our overall interpretation of Group 3 sealings is that they were affixed to curved objects which had been bound with date-palm fibre string. It is likely that at least pots and pegs are represented by the curved reverse faces of the Group 3 sealings, in some cases the pegs being made of reed. In one instance, there is evidence that the sealed peg protruded from a level wooden surface such as a door or chest but in most other cases it is not possible to

determine what the sealed peg had originally been stuck into. Evidence from Early Dynastic south Mesopotamia suggests a strong connection between peg sealing and security of storeroom doors (Matthews 1991; Martin and Matthews 1993), but it is perfectly feasible that some of the Saar temple sealings of Group 3 were used to seal pegs, with string, which in some manner acted as security for containers such as boxes. It is highly likely, however, that many of the Group 3 sealings were affixed to pegs connected to door sealing.

We can summarize the functional make-up of the Group 3 sealings as follows:

Category	No.
Pot	3
Smooth peg & string	5
Reed peg & string	4
Smooth surface on curved object	2
Unknown	3

Group 4: disk-shaped sealings with string impressions

Nine of the Saar temple sealings take the form of a circular or oval disk with string impressions on the reverse. All nine, or 100%, have clear seal impressions on their obverse face. The only two complete, unfragmented sealings in the temple corpus are of this group (1539:01, 1596:01). These sealings take the distinctive form of little cakes of clay, some 3.0 cm in diameter across the obverse face, with a single clear seal impression stamped in the middle of the obverse. They are a little over 1.0 cm in thickness and frequently have clear fingerprints around the edges of the obverse, where the clay has been pressed onto the sealed object.

All nine Group 4 sealings have string impressions across their reverse faces. In three cases the impressions are not clear enough for detailed measurement, while the remaining six sealings yield the following results:

Strand diameter		String diameter		Twist period		String spin direction	
average	range	average	range	average	range	Z	S
0.28	0.25–0.3	0.34	0.3–0.4	0.8	0.7–0.9	2	4

As with the other sealing groups all string fibres are of a medium-coarse texture, again almost certainly date-palm fibre. In the categories of strand diameter, string diameter and twist period, we see results very similar to those from Group 2 and 3 sealings. With string spin direction, however, there is for the first time a slight change, with a 33% representation of Z-spun string against 66% of S-spun. The two sealings with Z-spun string, 1539:01 and 1785:04, are the only ones with this characteristic in the entire temple assemblage. As already noted, 1785:04 is made of a distinctive clay, dark grey in colour and with large mineral inclusions, suggesting that the sealing may have been imported into Saar from outside attached to unknown goods. Sealing 1539:01, however, is made of a yellow-green clay common amongst the temple sealings. On the reverse of sealing 1596:01 there is the impression of a loose knot in the string.

Group 4 sealings were clearly placed over lengths of string, but it is difficult to say more about their functions. In the case of 1539:01 [9], there are suggestions on the reverse faces of leather impressions, probably from a pot covering secured with string. The diameter of the reverse face curve, at ca. 10 cm, supports an interpretation of this piece as being originally affixed to the neck of a closed vessel as shown [210]. Other Group 4 sealings may also have sealed a range of vessels.

Summary of sealing functions

We can here summarize the information about sealing function which has been presented so far.

Group	Function	Qt.	% of total
Group 1:	uncertain function	31	40
Group 2:	string	20	26
	pots	3	4
	pegs	9	12
Group 3:	curved/smooth object	5	6
Group 4:	disk & string	9	12
Total:		**77**	**100**

It is worth pointing out that collections of sealings from south Mesopotamian urban contexts of the rather earlier Early Dynastic period (2,900–2,350 BC) bear some similarities to the Saar temple assemblage. Large groups of sealings have been recovered from burnt dumps, often interpreted as the rubbish regularly cleared out from urban temples. Such sealing collections are known from Fara and Ur in the Early Dynastic I period (Martin 1988; Matthews 1991 & 1993) and from Abu Salabikh in the Early Dynastic III period (Martin and Matthews 1993). In functional terms these temple sealing groups are dominated by the practice of door sealing, and as with the Saar assemblage the sealing obverses display large quantities of different seal impressions.

Secondly, in considering the evidence for sealing function, it is possible that many of the Saar temple sealings were used to seal containers, some perhaps secured by means of pegs employed in the manner of toggles or fasteners with encircling string. If so, it would be of great value to establish whether the sealed containers were portable or non-portable, for portable containers may attest trade over some distances, while non-portable containers are more likely to reflect mainly intra-site activity (Duistermaat 1994, 65).

It is still possible, however, that a sizeable proportion of the Saar sealings were in fact used to seal doors between the storage rooms and the main body of the temple. A series of door sockets were found in the small storeroom in the NW corner of the temple (Area 220) so a door existed to be sealed. In this case we can envisage a substantial peg, such as the reed pegs attested on several sealings, protruding from a wooden door which could be secured by wrapping date-palm fibre string around the peg and attaching the string to a fitting in the adjacent wall. A clay sealing could then be affixed to the peg and string and stamped with a seal, acting as a form of guarantee against illicit entry into the storerooms. Control over room access, through the use of door sealing, may have been in the hands of specific officials empowered to oversee the access of other seal-bearing individuals to their stored goods within the rooms. Such a two-tiered sealing system, with a small corps of door-sealing officials in control of rooms storing commodities sealed by a wider group of seal-bearing individuals, is also attested by sealings from level IV of the temple of Inanna at Nippur, dating to the Third Dynasty of Ur (Zettler 1987, 227) and therefore approximately contemporary with the Saar temple. However, if such a system had indeed been in use at Saar, we might expect a higher number of duplicate sealings than in fact occur.

Thirdly, if we allow that the temple sealings were employed in many cases to secure containers, then we may rightly consider the question of what commodities were inside these sealed containers. In this matter we receive little help from the sealings. The large storage vessels may have held a wide range of commodities, from liquids such as beer or milk products to solids such as dates or grain. Sealed boxes may have held more precious items, such as stones, metal ingots or textiles. All these commodities may have participated within a system of offerings or tithes and redistribution within the temple.

Finally, it is hoped that future analyses will assist interpretations of the functioning of clay sealings within administrative and social conditions. In particular, chemical composition of sealing clays and residue analyses of sealed storage vessels are techniques likely to provide important new information.

Distribution

More than two-thirds of the sealings come from the western end of the temple building, from the storeroom in the NW corner (Area 220) and from the adjacent area at the back of the main room. In Phases 1–4, evidence for depressions, interpreted as settings for storage jars, were concentrated in these areas. In Phase 5, an additional room was constructed in the SW corner of the temple. In Phases 3–5, 66% of all sealings (53 out of 80) were found at the western end of the temple (including the storerooms). Two of the pieces in the main room of the temple were found close to the altars. One of these, an almost complete sealing about 2.5 cm in diameter [28], shows a standing male figure with a tiered skirt holding a shield-like object in one hand and touching the forehead of a horned gazelle-like animal with the other. The animal looks back over its shoulder towards him and, as on the seal, there is an oblong object in the far field beyond the shield. The reverse of the sealing shows the impressions of three parallel cords and a peg. It is one of the possible door sealings, although it could also have come off a container closed with a peg.

The second impression came from a pit full of ash close to the north-east corner of the southern altar, but the design is broken [12]. It shows part of a standing male animal, and it is interesting that a sealing apparently from the same seal (1622:02) was found in House 203 to the north of the temple. It is tempting to suggest that both the sealings found in close association with altars came originally from goods which were offered on them to the god.

Interpretation

If we look at the evidence provided by the distribution of the finds and by the designs on the sealing we can make certain tentative deductions about the way the people who owned the seals behaved. More than two thirds of the sealings came from the western end of the temple

building and in some cases they were associated with shallow plastered depressions in the floor which are thought to have supported large storage jars. Some of them probably came from these jars. Others came from parcels and packets whose nature cannot be determined, while a few may have come from a door between Areas 220 and 200. It has been suggested before that the presence of sealings in a building indicates that goods were being received there (Woodburn & Crawford 1994). Sealings are probably not removed from goods which are about to be sent out of a building. It seems likely, then, that incoming goods for use by the temple were stored in these areas, though they could, of course, have been repackaged for distribution later on.

There are, perhaps, as many as thirty different designs on these sealings, but we must remember that the temple was in use for a considerable period of time and the sealings are not all contemporary. Three possible interpretations can be suggested for the presence of such a diversity of sealings: they may have come off goods which entered the temple stores over a considerable period of time from a number of different individuals who sealed them at source; there were thirty or so officials working in the temple who sealed the goods on receipt; or there were one or two temple officials guarding and sealing the stores while the rest of the seals belonged to different individuals who were sending goods into the temple. The considerable number of seals and sealings found in the houses throughout the settlement at Saar, and the relatively small size of the temple itself makes the first possibility an attractive one, but it has been shown that some door sealings may be present in our collection in which case we can suggest that the third option is also plausible. The one or two temple officials would have used their seals on the door to the room in which goods sent in by a number of different individuals were stored. The problem with this interpretation is, as mentioned above, the lack of duplicate impressions which one would expect if the same officials were opening and closing the door on a regular basis. The second option seems the least likely as the Saar temple is surely too small an institution to have supported thirty or so officials.

Which ever model we accept to explain the wide range of designs the checking represented by the holes in the faces of a small number of the sealings was carried out when the goods were originally sealed and the clay was still wet. The designs, all in the early Dilmun style, indicate that the goods involved originated within Dilmun itself, or at least that if goods from Mesopotamia or the Indus valley were involved, they had been repackaged by someone owning a Dilmun seal.

It can then be suggested that the goods came into the temple from a variety of different individuals, but we do not know whether these were temple servants, sending goods from temple lands, or members of the community contributing offerings or even taxes. In Mesopotamia the temples owned large estates, but in Dilmun there is no evidence of any sort on this point. In Mesopotamia offerings were made to the god by royalty and commoners of a huge range of goods which included furniture, jewellery and food, while the temple of Nannar at Ur also seems to have levied a tithe on successful trading expeditions to Dilmun (Leemans 1960, 23). In Dilmun we can only speculate that some of the sealings may have come from

similar offerings brought in by the local inhabitants, while others may represent goods which arrived as taxes, or produce from the temple's own lands.

Only one seal was found in the temple, apparently dropped by accident rather than deliberately deposited. Although it is a very fine one, there is nothing to suggest that it may have belonged to an official of the temple, or that it was part of the temple's administrative machinery. It is interesting that no other administration tools, such as weights, or pots in standardized sizes have been found in this building, although weights have been found elsewhere on the site. Their absence may indicate that the temple at Saar was primarily a religious building at the heart of its community, but without an elaborate bureaucracy. There is no conclusive evidence for wider economic or administration functions.

CATALOGUE OF SEALS AND SEALINGS

All string measurements refer to the real string, rather than to the mirror image attested on the clay surface. Thus Z-spun string will give an S-spun impression on the clay sealing, but will be identified as Z-spun in this catalogue and report. The spin direction refers to that of the string rather than that of the strands making up the string, which are assumed to have a spin direction opposite to that of the string. For further discussion on string description see Hurley 1979 and Martin & Matthews 1993.

[8] The terminology and measurements used in the description of string

Abbreviations
di.   diameter
sd. di.   strand diameter
sg. di.   string diameter
TP   twist period
SSD   string spin direction
All measurements are in centimetres.
All objects are clay sealings unless otherwise stated.

1505:08 Bitumen sealing. Irregular, flattish piece of bitumen. One side smooth with a flat surface, the other irregular. On one edge of this side are parallel concave impressions. Dimensions 8.4x4.3x1.1. Phase 4.5.

1508:03 Two small fragments of yellow/green unbaked clay.
1) Small fragment, irregular, unclear string impression on reverse. Dimensions 1.5x0.9x0.6.

2) Obverse: figure in net pattern skirt. To the left he holds a long straw which leads into a pot at his feet. Reverse lost. Segment of edge remains. Dimensions 1.7x1.4x0.6. Phase 4.5.

1539:01 Complete sealing.
Roughly circular lump of yellow/green unbaked clay, with complete impression of stamp seal with an estimated di. of 2.2. Smoothed edges with fingerprints visible. Obverse: hatched rectangle down the centre with a seated bearded figure to the right, hands outstretched towards it. On the left of the rectangle, an unidentified motif, possibly an animal head. Small circular hole, di. 0.2, in the centre of the rectangle punched from the front. Reverse: disk-shaped piece with slight curve to reverse face, di. ca. 10.0, generally smooth surface crossed by three rows of string impressions. Sd. di. 0.25, sg. di. 0.3, TP 0.8, SSD Z-spun, medium/coarse fibres. Traces of possible fold impressions from a covering, perhaps leather. Disk on string. Dimensions 3.0x3.2x1.1. Phase 4.4.

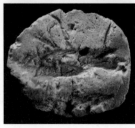

[9]

1539:05 Four fragments of unbaked yellow/green clay, string marks on one, remains of design on a second.

1) Reverse: string impressions. Sd. di. 0.3, sg. di. 0.35, TP 0.65, SSD S-spun, medium/coarse fibre. Dimensions 2.2x1.7x0.6

2) Obverse: Edge of seal impression showing human arms, torso, legs. Fingerprints also visible. Dimensions 1.3x0.9x0.7.

3) Dimensions 1.4x0.9x0.6.

4) Dimensions 2.0x1.2x0.8.

Phase 4.4.

1542:01 Fragment of yellow/green unbaked clay.

Obverse: a horned animal, couchant, looking back over its shoulder to the left. Behind it are three vertical motifs, the middle one appears to be a leg or snake. A horizontal line runs under the scene. Reverse broken away. Dimensions 2.4x1.8x0.7. Phase 4.3.

[10]

1542:03 Originally five small pieces of yellow/grey clay of which two remain. Four had fingerprint impressions on them.

1) Fragment of yellow clay. Obverse: part of a impression showing two lines at right angles, with hatched squares in the angles. Irregular in shape. Dimensions 1.6x1.2x0.4.

2) Obverse: clear fingerprints, but no trace of impression.

3–5) Fingerprints, but otherwise featureless.

Phase 4.3.

1542:04 Fragment of soft grey clay. Smooth edge. Obverse illegible. Reverse: smooth curved surface. Di. 2.8. Possible peg impression. Dimensions 2.5x1.5x1.7. Phase 4.3.

1543:03 Dark grey clay. Fragment of clay with fingerprint impressions. Very flaky damaged sealing. Dimensions 2.5x1.5x2.1. Phase 4.3.

1543:06 Hard white clay.

Obverse: a standing figure in a net skirt, one hand outstretched to the left towards perhaps a tree. Unidentified motif to the right. Reverse: smooth curved peg impression, di. 1.6, crossed by 2 rows of string impressions. Sd. di. 0.3, sg. di. 0.35, TP 0.7, SSD S-spun, medium/coarse fibres. Peg and string. Dimensions 2.5x1.4x0.7. Phase 4.3.

[11]

1550:06

Nine pieces of yellow/green unbaked clay and one grey/white clay.

1) Obverse: a hatched square, perhaps a fish, and a palm tree/standard. Reverse: smooth impression of circular peg, di. 1.2, length >1.4. Peg bound by 3 rows of string impressions. Sd. di. 0.3, sg. di. 0.35, TP 0.9, SSD S-spun, medium/coarse fibres. Peg and string. Dimensions 2.6x1.8x1.0.

2) Pale green clay, fingerprints on two surfaces. Obverse: Faint remains of seal impression. Reverse: no clear markings. Dimensions 2.4x2.0x1.5.

3) Pale yellow/green clay. Obverse: no clear markings. Reverse: unclear string impressions. Dimensions 1.9x1.8x1.1.

4) Pale yellow/green clay. Reverse: unclear string impressions. Dimensions 1.7x1.4x0.6.

5) Pale yellow/green clay. Reverse: string impressions. Sd. di. 0.3, sg. di. 0.35, TP 0.7, medium/coarse fibres.

6) Pale yellow/green clay. Reverse: very unclear string impressions, medium/coarse fibres. Dimensions 1.7x0.8x0.6.

7) Yellow/grey clay. Reverse: very unclear string impressions. Dimensions 1.3x0.9x0.6.

8) Yellow/grey clay, no clear markings on either face. Dimensions 1.2x0.8x0.7.

9) Grey/white clay. Obverse: traces of possible seal impression. Reverse: one surface flat and smooth, second surface at right angles to it has unclear string impressions. Dimensions 1.7x1.2x0.9. Phase 4.4.

1581:04 Three pieces of yellow/green, unbaked clay.

1) Obverse: no seal impression, but clear fingerprints. Hole, di. 0.15, pierced through sealing from obverse to reverse. Reverse: two smooth flat surfaces, rest broken. Possibly a tag/label. Dimensions 2.1x1.4x1.4.

2) Obverse: no seal impression, smooth surface. Reverse: slight curve to reverse face, three rows of string impressions. Sd. di. 0.3, sg. di. 0.3, SSD S-spun, medium/coarse fibres. Perhaps a pot and string. Dimensions 1.8x1.2x0.6.

3) Obverse: no seal impression. Single incised line. Reverse: no clear details. Dimensions 2.1x1.3x0.5. Phase 4.2.

1587:02 Three fragments of hard gritty greenish clay.

1) Reverse: small area of flat surface, perhaps from peg. Scattered string impressions, medium/coarse fibre. Dimensions 2.0x1.7x0.8.

2) No markings on either side. Dimensions 1.8x1.6x0.6.

3) Obverse: perhaps an impression of an animal head. Fingerprints on both sides. Dimensions 1.7x0.9x0.6. Phase 4.1.

1587:05 Fragment of hard yellow/green clay. Obverse: left edge of impression. Design shows the net skirt of a standing figure facing right and holding perhaps a spear in one hand. Reverse: 2 faces at right angles. One shows unclear string impression, the other an impression of a smooth curved peg with di. 1.6, length >0.8. Peg and string. Dimensions 1.3x1.2x0.7. Phase 4.1.

1593:01 Soft grey clay, originally disk shaped but now broken in half. Obverse: standing male animal, body, hind legs and tail extant, the rest broken with a rosette or plant below its belly. Another illegible motif behind it. Probably from the same seal as 1622:02 (from House 203). Reverse: faint string impressions. Disk on string. Dimensions 1.7x1.6x0.7. Phase 4.1.

[12]

1596:01 Yellow/green hardened clay with complete circular seal impression. Diameter of seal 2.14. Obverse: a hatched rectangle down the centre, with a schematic human figure seated either side, arms outstretched to hatched rectangle, which is outlined by a post on either side. Perhaps a weaving or netting scene. Reverse: disk-shaped piece with tangled mass of string impressions on reverse. Sd. di. 0.3, sg. di. 0.35, TP 0.8, SSD S-spun, medium/coarse fibres. String is probably in form of loose knot. May originally have been disk on string. Fingerprints round the edge of the disk. Dimensions 3.0x2.6x1.2. Phase 4.1.

[13]

1596:02 Four fragments of yellow/green hardened clay, all with fragmentary seal impressions. Three fragments join and are from the same, almost complete sealing.
1–3) Obverse: three standing human figures, wearing flounced dresses, and facing left. The seal is the same as that used on 1596:03. Reverse: scattered string impressions. Disk on string. Fingerprints round edge. Overall di. (reconstructed) 2.7. Actual dimensions 2.9x2.7x0.6. Drawing is composite.
4) Obverse: feet of a human and the rest is lost. Reverse: string impressions. Sd. di. 0.25, sg. di. 0.3, TP 0.7, SSD S-spun, medium/coarse fibres. Dimensions 1.7x1.3x0.6. Phase 4.1.

[14]

1596:03 Yellow/green hardened clay with most of an impression preserved. Estimated di. of seal 2.3. Obverse: two standing human figures and the faint outline of a third, with flounced skirts standing in a row facing left, the central figure holds a jar to the left. From the same seal as 1596:02. Reverse: string impressions. Sd. di. 0.25, sg. di. 0.3, TP 0.8, SSD S-spun, medium/coarse fibres. Angle of reverse suggests a jar sealing. Dimensions 2.5x2.2x1.5. Phase 4.1.

[15]

1597:01 Three fragments of yellow/green clay.
1) Obverse: no impression. Fingerprint. Reverse: unclear string impression. Dimensions 1.6x1.5x1.3.
2) Obverse: smooth. Reverse: parallel impressions of fibrous vegetal matter. Dimensions 1.6x1.0x0.7.
3) Small edge piece of an impression. Reverse: two faces at right angles, one has clear string impressions. Sd. di. 0.25, sg. di. 0.3, TP 0.5, SSD S-spun, medium/coarse fibres. Other face has clear impression of peg shaft, with di. 1.3, length >1.1, and with parallel striated impressions. Clearly a length of reed used as a peg and bound with string. Dimensions 1.4x0.9x0.8. Phase 3.1.

1597:02 Yellow/green unbaked clay. Obverse: traces of hatched triangle. Reverse: no clear markings. Dimensions 2.2x2.1x1.2. Phase 3.1.

[16]

1597:05 Two fragments of grey unbaked clay.
1) Obverse: edge of an impression showing a man on the right, with arms raised, in front of a crescent-topped(?) standard. Rosette within arms of the standard. Reverse: no clear impressions. Dimensions 1.2x1.2x0.5.
2) Edge of a sealing, with fingerprints. Reverse: 3 or 4 rows of unclear string impressions, medium/coarse fibres. Dimensions 1.6x1.2x0.8. Phase 3.1.

1597:10 Yellow/green unbaked clay. Hemispherical, broken in half, originally with string through centre. Obverse: smoothed with traces of triangle enclosing hatched lines. All other surfaces lost. Di. 2.4, height 1.0. Phase 3.1.

1598:01 Five pieces of light grey unbaked clay.
1) Obverse: triangular hatched design, next to a standing figure(?) Reverse: impressions of two surfaces at right angles, one smooth, perhaps from peg. Details unclear. Dimensions 1.7x1.1x1.3.
2) No seal impression, but reverse has very faint string impression. Dimensions 1.3x1.3x0.9.
3) No impression. Dimensions 1.3x0.8x0.6.
4) No impression. Dimensions 0.9x0.8x0.6.
5) No impression. Dimensions 1.2x0.8x0.5. Phase 3.2.

1599:01 Complete sealing. Yellow/orange clay.

[17]

Diameter of seal: 2.2. Obverse: the design is obscured by a rectangular hole in the centre of the scene punched from the front. There is a seated(?) insect or monkey-like figure on the left, with a hatched rectangle on the far right-hand side. Reverse: gently curving surface with two rows of string impressions. Sd. di. 0.3, sg. di. 0.35, TP 0.8, SSD S-spun, medium/coarse fibres. Jar sealing(?). Dimensions 3.9x3.2x1.1. Phase 3.2.

1599:07 Grey/green unbaked clay. Obverse: the upper torso of a male figure, holding a long shield(?). Now irregular in shape. Reverse: no clear details. Dimensions 1.3x1.0x0.4. Phase 3.2.

1599:09 Grey unbaked clay. Obverse: circular impression with the head of an animal facing left towards two curved lines, possibly the horns of a second animal. Reverse: unclear string impression. Fingerprints on the edge. Dimensions 1.9x0.9x0.5. Phase 3.2.

1599:10 Grey clay lump with fingerprint impressions. Edge of seal visible on one surface, possible string marks on reverse. Dimensions 3.0x1.9x1.2. Phase 3.2.

1599:11 Grey clay fragment, probably from sealing. Reverse: smooth and concave. Irregular in shape. Dimensions 2.1x1.5x0.4. Phase 3.2.

1599:12 Dark grey clay fragment. No design, fingerprints are visible along one edge. Hole made by a stick(?) jabbed into obverse. Hole: 0.35 in di., 0.4 deep. Dimensions 2.8x2.2x0.8. Phase 3.2.

1599:13 Light grey lump of hardened clay. No design visible. Reverse: unclear string impression. Dimensions 2.7x2.1x1.0. Phase 3.2.

1600:01 Dark grey unbaked clay, about half of impression extant comprising right and lower left of design. Obverse: seated, bearded, nude figure, with arms held up to either side. To the right he touches caduceus-like symbol, perhaps twisted palm leaves, with an animal leg hanging from the top. To the left of the symbol are the hind quarters of an animal. Above the back of the animal is a fish(?). From the same seal as 1763:09 and 1853:95. Reverse: sub-circular piece with impression of smooth curving surface, di. 4.1, surrounded by 3 or 4 rows of string impressions. Sd. di. 0.3, sg. di. 0.35, TP 0.8, SSD S-spun, medium/coarse fibres. Disk on string. On the edges of the clay are fingerprints. Overall di. 2.8. Phase 3.1.

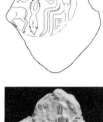

[18]

1600:02 Light pinkish unbaked clay. About half of disk-shaped piece extant. Obverse: a central 'standard' topped with a crescent, with a horned animal on either side of it. Both animals are looking back over their shoulders at each other. In the left field, above the animal's head, is a branch(?). There is a pinhole, di. 0.1, through the rump of the right-hand animal. Reverse: part of disk-shaped piece, with 3 or 4 rows of string impressions. Sd. di. 0.3, sg. di. 0.35, TP 0.7, SSD S-spun, medium/coarse fibres. Disk on string. Fingerprints on edge. Dimensions 2.3x2.2x0.9. Phase 3.1.

[19]

1600:05 Yellowish unbaked clay. Obverse: on the left a standing animal facing right, but looking back over its shoulder. On the right, a standing figure in a net skirt, probably facing left. A vertical line appears between the figures, perhaps a spear. Very worn. Reverse: faint string impressions, SSD S-spun, medium/coarse fibres. Dimensions 2.2x1.6x0.7. Phase 3.1.

1610:03 Yellow/green unbaked clay fragment. Obverse: an erotic scene, the frontal view of a figure with widely splayed legs, a crescent below one arm, and part of a male figure, perhaps engaged in sexual intercourse. Various illegible motifs in the field. Reverse: unclear string impression, medium/coarse fibres. Dimensions 2.4x1.7x1.4. Phase 3.1.

[20]

1612:01 Seal. Creamy soft stone. Obverse: a standing, nude male figure, looking to the right. In his right hand he holds a shield, in his left the horns of a long-horned animal which looks back over its shoulder at him. An oblong symbol appears in the left field and a crescent in the right, behind the head of the animal. Reverse: standard Dilmun type, with three incised parallel lines across the boss at right angles to the perforation and four incised circles with central dots equally spaced around the edge. Edge: Failaka Variant 2 (Kjaerum 1983). Di. 1.9, height 1.2, weight 5.7 gm. Phase 3.2.

[21]

1612:09 Two pieces of dark grey, burnt clay.
1) Obverse: the head of a horned animal on the right, looking towards a 'ladder' motif. To the left of the ladder a human figure crouches, one arm outstretched towards the 'ladder'. Behind him is an illegible motif. Reverse: smooth curved surface, di. 1.5, with vegetal striations from reed peg and one row of unclear string impressions, medium/coarse fibres. Reed peg and string. Dimensions 1.9x1.6x1.0.
2) Piece of clay with one flattened and smoothed surface, but no impression. Reverse: faint string impressions, medium/coarse fibre. Dimensions 1.1x1.0x0.4. Phase 3.2.

[22]

1612:10 Fine pale grey clay. Obverse: a hatched rectangle, probably originally horizontally across the centre of the design. On one side is a row of bearded human heads facing left, the necks touching it at right angles. Three are preserved, with traces of a fourth. On the opposite side of the rectangle is part of a different, unidentifiable motif. Reverse: two faces at right angles, on one there is a string impression. Sd. di. 0.3, sg. di. 0.5, TP 0.9, SSD S-spun, medium/coarse

[23]

fibres. The second face is smooth and flat. String and wall or container. Dimensions 2.8x2.0x1.3. Phase 3.2.

1612:11 Dark grey unbaked clay. Fingerprints on one side. Irregular in shape. Dimensions 2.0x1.3x0.9. Phase 3.2.

1750:05 Fine light grey unbaked clay with salt crystals visible. Obverse: lower half of a seal impression. Standing nude male figure, head missing, facing left, holding a male horned animal by its head. Animal looks back over its shoulder towards him. Possibly from the same seal as H13:12:01. Reverse: impressions on two

[24]

faces at right angles. On one face is the impression of a smooth curved peg, di. 1.2, length >1.2. On the second face are string impressions. Sd. di. 0.25, sg. di. 0.3, TP 0.7, SSD unclear, medium/coarse fibres. Also on a small part of this face is an impression of a flat surface with clear striated grain, probably from wood. This suggests the peg was inserted into a wooden door or container. Dimensions 1.6x2.4x1.35. Phase 3.

1750:10 Light grey clay lump, uneven. Surfaces smoothed. One surface shows impression of wood/leaf(?). Dimensions 2.6x1.8x1.5. Phase 3.

1752:06 Three possible sealing fragments of light grey clay.
1) Burnt. No clear markings apart from finger prints. Dimensions 1.9x1.9x1.3.
2) No visible markings. Dimensions 1.7x1.6x1.1.
3) No visible markings. Dimensions 1.6x1.4x0.8.
Phase 2.2.

1763:05 Twelve fragments of light green sandy clay. Two with definite impressions.
1) Obverse: no impression. Reverse: stretch of curved peg, di. 3.8, with unclear string impressions of medium/coarse fibres. Reed(?) peg and string.
2) Obverse: no impression. Reverse: two rows of string impressions. Sd. di. 0.2, sg. di. 0.25, TP 0.6, SSD S-spun.
The remaining fragments have no markings.
Phase 3.1.

1763:08 Fine light grey clay. Obverse: upper central part of a seal impression preserved but the design is illegible with the exception of a possible animal head. Reverse: four rows of string impressions. Sd. di. 0.3, sg. di. 0.35, TP 0.9, SSD S-spun. Jar sealing(?). Dimensions 2.5x1.9x0.5.
Phase 3.1.

1763:09 Fine grey unbaked clay with salt crystals visible. Obverse: badly damaged human head and arm facing left and touching broken 'caduceus' with animal leg hanging from the top. Two small holes pierced from obverse over impression. Same seal as 1600:01 and

[25]

1853:95. Reverse: two parallel rows of string impressions. Sd. di. 0.3, sg. di. 0.35, TP 0.7, SSD S-spun. Dimensions 1.0x1.2x0.6. Phase 3.1.

1763:10 Fine unbaked grey clay. Obverse: part of standing figure in long skirt with one arm raised to the right, perhaps holding a long shield. Reverse: part of smooth surface with faint string impressions. Dimensions 1.9x1.2x0.6. Phase 3.1.

1763:11 Fine grey clay. Two pieces joined together. One quarter of the seal impression is preserved, intact to the edge. Obverse: bottom left quadrant of a seal impression showing leaping(?) naked figure above a long, notched, curved object, like a long animal horn. Below this at an angle of 90 degrees is the head and ruffed neck of a short-horned animal. For similar design see seal 2070:05. Reverse: part of disk with unclear string impression. Dimensions 2.3x1.5x0.7. Phase 3.1.

[26]

1785:04 Dark grey clay with mineral inclusions. About three quarters of sealing preserved. Obverse: all but the top left of design preserved, showing stylized palm tree in the centre, seated figure with head missing to left, holding trunk of tree with both hands. Badly damaged motif to right of tree, possibly an animal. Reverse: almost complete disk with

[27]

three overlapping rows of string impressions. Sd. di. 0.3, sg. di. 0.4, TP 0.9, SSD Z-spun. Unusual string and clay suggest origin outside Saar. Dimensions 2.2x2.3x1.1. Estimated di. of seal 1.8. Phase 2.3.

1785:09 Five fragments light grey sandy clay with inclusions. One fragment has illegible design on obverse. No clear impressions on reverse. Dimensions 1) 2.0x1.1x0.9. 2) 1.6x0.9x0.4. 3–5) <1.0. Phase 2.3.

H13:12:01 Complete sealing. Pink clay.
Obverse: oblong impression, the lowest part broken off, fingerprints on edge. Standing figure wearing a flounced skirt, arms up to either side. To the right he holds a shield(?), and on the right of that there is a hatched vertical oblong. To the left of the figure there is a horned animal facing left with head turned to look back over its shoulder. Compare Kjaerum 1983, 201 and 202. Reverse: stretch of peg impression, di. 3.4, length >1.0 with parallel

[28]

striations, clearly from a reed peg. Three rows of string impressions round peg. Sd. di. 0.25, sg. di. 0.3, TP 0.7, SSD S-spun medium/coarse fibres. Reed peg and string. Dimensions 2.5x2.2x1.0. Phase 3.2.

Chapter 5. Temple Paraphernalia: Tools, Containers and Other Items

Copper Items

Forty-three items of copper were recovered from the temple, as well as 4 small pieces of copper slag and one of indeterminate metal slag. Of the copper items, 9 were recognized as objects or partial objects, the rest being small corroded fragments or groups of fragments. No metal from Saar has been analysed, and the term 'copper' is used here to denote all metal which appears to the excavators to be copper or copper alloy. It is usually found thickly corroded to a green oxide. Metallic fragments not corroded to green have been termed 'metal'. Their exact composition is similarly unproven.

The recognizable pieces included: a possible vessel [29]; a ring [30]; an object resembling the shape of a shoehorn [31]; a nail [32]; and a complex wire link [33]. After cleaning it was possible to identify 8 more fragments as being something other than irregular blobs of corrosion: a strip with notched end [34]; a split tube [35]; a broken fish-hook and tiny strip,1611:2; two shaped but unidentifiable pieces [36 & 37]; part of a haft, 1763:7; and a loop or link [38].

It is, of course, unlikely that copper was being smelted or cast in the temple, and there is certainly no evidence that it was. The presence of numerous copper fragments and a few of slag is not in itself remarkable, as they are common throughout the excavated deposits at Saar. It is interesting to note, however, that they were virtually absent from the pre-temple levels sampled in Test Pit 1. Excavations there produced only one fragment of copper slag, 6 unidentifiable copper fragments or groups of fragments, 2 fragments of indeterminate metal ore and one of metal slag. Whatever other activities took place on the temple site before it was built, metalworking was not apparently one of them, nor was any going on in the immediate vicinity.

It is possible that the small fragments simply came into the temple with the material used for the floors, or

they may represent disintegrated items or furnishings actually belonging to its use. Of the items for which a shape, if not a use, can be ascertained, two in particular are peculiar to the temple, and contrast with the usual fish-hook and haft fragments found in domestic contexts at Saar. These are the clasp-like item of thick copper wire [33], and the thoroughly enigmatic piece reminiscent of a shoehorn, or the disembodied spout of an Arabian coffee-pot [31]. Knowing as little as we do about Dilmun cult practices, the imagination can be allowed free-rein with these objects. Perhaps the 'horn' was a scoop to transfer small quantities of a substance such as incense; perhaps the link was part of an ornate fastening for some vestment.

Also likely to belong to the temple are the remains of a vessel or other object of sheet-copper [29], which was found in such an advanced state of disintegration that little could be done to conserve it. Bitumen adhered to the inside, and when first excavated it was possible to discern the impression of woven or knitted textile in the copper corrosion of the inside surface. It is conceivable that it was a copper-covered object with bitumen core, but there is really too little left to do more than speculate, and its find-spot in the storeroom, Area 221, supports more its interpretation as a vessel.

Apart from the 'vessel', all the objects and the vast majority of the fragments came from the main room of the temple. With such a small quantity of data, no spatial or chronological analysis would have much meaning. There were fewest occurrences in Phase 5, which was in any case partly removed before our excavations, and otherwise a greater concentration in Phases 3 and 4 than in Phases 1 and 2.

Outside the temple, in the sand which accumulated in the street by the main entrance, was found a large and well-preserved copper nail [32]. Also from this sand deposit came a group of fragments of mixed iron and copper, including a piece of copper sheeting with iron

[29] **Fragments of a copper bowl**
1502:01. Traces of possible woven impressions can be seen on the fragment at the top right, and bitumen adhering to that on the bottom right. Width of largest piece 5.0 cm.

[30] **Copper ring,**
H13:14:04. (Scale 2:1)

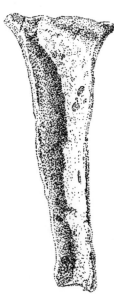

[31] **Copper object**
Of unknown function, shaped like a shoehorn or an Arabian coffee-pot spout, 1610:01. (Scale 1:1)

[32] **Copper nail,** 1874:02.

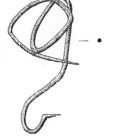

[33] **Link or clasp of copper wire,**
H13:09:01. (Scale 1:1)

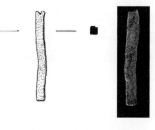

[34] **Copper strip**
With notched end, perhaps a graving tool, 1505:03. (Scale 1:1)

adhering to it (1874:01). Nearby, against the front wall of the temple, was the Phase 2 rectangular feature, perhaps a setting for a post or standard. If that interpretation is correct, then the copper nail and sheeting may have been connected with it.

Objects of Shell and Ivory

A single object of worked shell was recovered from the temple, a pierced cockle-shell [39] from the main room in Phase 3.1. Several such pieces have been found in the settlement, and although it is not always possible to be sure they are deliberately worked, some of them certainly are. They would have worked as weights for the kind of fishing net designed to float just below the surface of the water to trap surface-feeding fish (Brian Irving, personal communication). They could presumably also have been strung or stitched to clothing as ornaments.

From Test Pit 1 (Phase 0.2) came a minute pearl [40] with an even smaller protuberance on one side. About a dozen pearls have been found at Saar to date, most of them larger.

More unexpected was a fragmentary length of ivory [41], found on the Phase 2.2 floor. Although it is badly cracked and split, it is clear that it has been deliberately shaped and polished. Preliminary examination shows that the structure of the ivory is consistent with that of elephant or dugong, with the latter presumably more likely (identified by James Rackham). Similar pieces of dugong tusk were found in the 'warehouse' at Umm an-Nar (Frifelt 1995, 223).

Artefacts of Bitumen

Pieces of bitumen, in the form of small objects or fragments, are found in most occupation deposits at Saar. The waterproofing quality of bitumen, combined with its light weight, must have made it a most desirable commodity around the village. It was presumably particularly useful for activities connected with exploitation of the sea, such as boating and fishing, though we have as yet little direct evidence of such applications from the excavation.

While bitumen was clearly far from scarce, it was apparently not locally obtained. Three samples from the temple (1597:09, 1843:02, and 1928:04) have been subjected to molecular analysis (by Jacques Connan, Senior Scientific Adviser, Elf Aquitaine), and preliminary results suggest that their best source match is Khuzistan, in western Iran. The local source which allegedly existed in the Jebel Dokhan region of Bahrain until earlier this century was either unknown to the inhabitants of Saar, or perhaps just too far to walk to. It may actually have been simpler to buy bitumen coming by boat from a great distance than to organize supply from a waterless, land-locked place 16 km away.

Bitumen-coated woven vessels

Of the seventy bitumen objects registered in the excavation of the temple, fifty-one were remains of vessels woven from palm-leaf, then given a bitumen coating. Most survive only as groups of fragments and flakes of bitumen, which retain the impressions of the woven leaves. In at least some cases, the containers were coated both inside and out, and fragments which are smooth on both sides tend to split, after excavation, to reveal the basket-weave impressions inside. Four groups of fragments were found in the Phase 5 storeroom (Area 221), nine in the main storeroom (Area 220) [41 & 43], three in Test Pit 1, and the rest came from the main room (Area 200).

Preserving these bitumen vessels defied most attempts at conservation. Even when a substantial part of the vessel was visible in excavation, it was very hard to lift it intact. The fabric was always extremely brittle, and became more so as soon as removed from the ground. The very impermeability which made bitumen so useful to ancient peoples renders it virtually impervious to consolidants. Some success in this field has recently been achieved (by Kirsty Norman) by using Primal, but the general policy for bitumen objects recovered from the temple was to photograph as soon as possible, if necessary without cleaning.

Three containers were sufficiently well preserved for their original shape to be still recognizable, and all of these came from Area 220 [44–46]. All had square, or sub-rectangular, bases. Pieces of another, very fragmentary vessel [43] suggest, however, that there were round-based ones used here as well. One container [46], was altogether elliptical, both at rim and base. It may have been manufactured as a pouch-shaped vessel, or perhaps just became flattened from the weight of the earth above it.

Woven containers waterproofed with bitumen seem to be fairly common in Dilmun-period graves from Bahrain

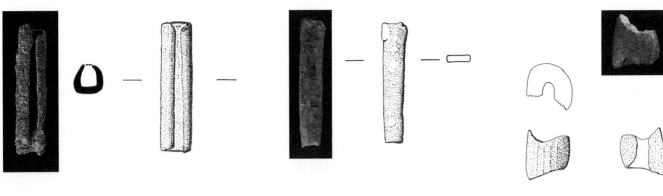

[35] Split copper tube
Perhaps the haft for a small
tool, 1529:02. (Scale 1:1).

[36] Flat copper strip,
1612:08 (1). (Scale 1:1)

[37] Copper fragment
Part of a robust tubular object of
unknown function, 1612:08 (3).
(Scale 1:1)

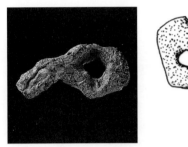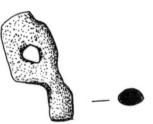

[38] Copper loop or link,
1896:03 (2). (Scale 2:1)

[39] Pierced cockle-shell
Glycymeris pectunculus, (1610:02). The
edges have been smoothed and a deliberate
hole cut out. Diameter 3.8 cm.

[40] Tiny pearl
1516:09. Diameter
0.18–0.25 cm.

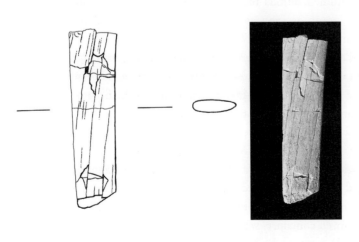

[41] Object of ivory
1821:01. From a tusk shaft.
The surfaces have been
polished. Ends broken.
(Scale 1:2)

[42] Fragments of a bitumen-coated woven vessel
1750:02. The palm-leaves which formed the container
have, of course, disappeared, but the impression of the
weave is very clear. Largest piece 4.7 cm wide.

(Højlund 1995), but few are published as yet. Something of the variety of possible shapes can be ascertained from a group from the Saar mound-field (Ibrahim 1982, Pl. 52). The temple containers with round rim and square base are not apparently made by the same technique as that used for the ones from the graves, i.e. the bottom formed by making each of the four sides end in a point, and the points then folded inwards and sewn together, so the base has diagonal stitched seams from all four corners into the middle. Baskets like this are still manufactured in Bahrain. Those from the temple, however, seem to be the result of a different technique, the details of which cannot be ascertained from what is left.

The concentration of fragments of bitumen-coated vessels in Area 220 is entirely in keeping with our interpretation of this space as a storeroom for the temple. These vessels must have been easy and cheap to manufacture, and presumably useful for storing something which needed a light, waterproof container. Dates would be an obvious possibility, if the vessels were not so small. There again, the many shapeless fragments recovered may well have come from larger baskets, the shapes of which are not recoverable. Against this might be argued that dates are still packed in palm-leaf baskets in Bahrain and elsewhere, and they are not waterproofed, but just allowed to become very sticky.

Lids and bungs

Five lids, stoppers or bungs, in various states of preservation, were found in the temple: a rather large one from Area 220 [47], one from Area 221 [49], one from the SE wall of the main room [48], and one each, in very fragmentary state, from the floors of the main room and from Test Pit 1. The one from Area 220 was unusually large, consisting of a thin flat circle of bitumen, with a cylindrical projection at the centre. The end of this projection carried the impression of woven palm-leaf. Bitumen objects of this kind are common throughout the excavations at Saar. The types which were obviously made as lids, perhaps transferable from one vessel to another, are sometimes hard to distinguish from roughly-shaped pieces intended to stop up permanently a hole or break in a vessel. The latter were made by pushing a thin piece of bitumen into the hole, then smoothing whatever was left flush with the container wall. The bitumen piece, when parted from the container again, is mushroom-shaped if still intact, and very similar to a disk-shaped lid with a knob on top, especially if abraded.

Beads

A single large bitumen bead [51] of a type fairly common elsewhere in the Saar settlement, was recovered from Area 200. No satisfactory explanation has yet been put forward as to what these were for. They would have made most unattractive and clumsy jewellery, as they are crudely fashioned and often contain pieces of grit or organic matter. Bitumen beads covered with gold foil as a substitute for solid gold are known from other sites in the Near East, such as Ur (Plenderleith 1934, 295) and Abu Salabikh (Postgate and Moon 1982, Pl. Vc), but none of those from Saar bears the slightest trace of any covering. Occasionally, as with this example, they bear the impression of a palm-leaf mat. Perhaps they were laid out on mats to harden after manufacture. Could they have been components for an abacus? Perhaps a use as net or line floats is more probable, in which case the bead which occurred in the temple should be seen as an incidental find.

Miscellaneous impressions in bitumen

Some of the bitumen fragments from Test Pit 1 bore various impressions, including a possible wood-impression (1527:01), a possible cloth impression (1513:02), and some reed or stalk impressions (1536:06). A possible sealing, with parallel impressions of grass or leaf 'string' (1505:08), came from the main room.

Stone Artefacts, including Ground-Stone Tools

Of the thirteen stone artefacts recovered from the temple excavations, all but five were tools of one kind or another, which are described below. A tubular bead of banded agate [52] was found in the main room just south of the storeroom.

More likely to represent part of the temple furnishings is a segment of a dark grey softstone vessel with a finely-made flange around the edge [53a], found on the floor of Phase 4.4 in the main room. There is no decoration on it, and we cannot be sure if it came from a flat plate or from a lid. By one of archaeology's occasional extraordinary coincidences, a second fragment of the same vessel [53b] was found in a different context some four years after the first, lying just a few metres away from the temple entrance in an open area at the back of House 222. It actually fits the first piece, the break between the two

[43] **Pieces from the base (above) and rim of a bitumen-coated woven vessel**
1597:09. This vessel was comparatively robust, the base and rim being especially thickly waterproofed. The technique of finishing the rim with a plain horizontal strip of leaf was common. Lower piece 7.0 cm wide.

[44] **Woven vessel, coated with bitumen inside and out**
1599:02. Only half of the vessel has survived, and much of the inner lining has come away, revealing the basket-weave impression of the original palm-leaf structure. The rim is circular, but the base is sub-rectangular. Diameter 7.7 cm.

[45] **Bitumen-coated woven vessel with sub-rectangular base**
1752:03. Photographed shortly after excavation. Height 6.0 cm.

[46] **Bitumen-coated woven vessel**
1752:02. Enough is preserved to show that the rim was round and the base sub-rectangular, although the whole thing is now elliptical. Height 6.5 cm.

[48] **Small bitumen stopper**
(1662:01) Height 3.9 cm.

[47] **Lid or stopper of bitumen**
1597:03. The sides of the object are quite smooth, but the smaller circular end has obviously been in contact with something made of woven palm-leaf. Width 11.4 cm.

[49] **Small bitumen bung**
1772:01. Presumably intended to stop up a leak in a pot or other vessel. (Scale 1:1)

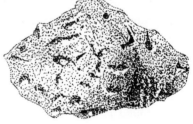

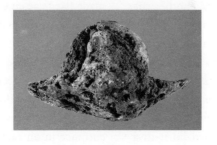

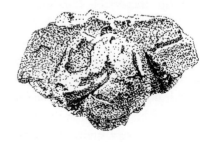

being perfect and unworn, but definitely not new. In fact, the two fragments have weathered to slightly differing over-all colours as a result of their long deposition in different surroundings.

A piece of limestone hollowed out to serve as the socket for the storeroom door from Phase 1 (1775:01) is the only other definite stone artefact, apart from tools, found in the excavations of the temple. There were in addition a fragment of a fossilized shell (1512:07) found in Test Pit 1 (Phase 0.2), and a piece of calcite (1598:05) from the Phase 3.2 floor in the main room, but these were not definitely worked.

Stone tools from the temple

Simple stone tools for grinding and pounding, smoothing and rubbing, are found distributed throughout the settlement at Saar. While it is not known exactly what they were used on, the very probable domestic nature of their function makes it no surprise that the temple is distinguished by having fewer of them than other buildings. Only two were found in the temple itself, and one of these came from the storeroom, Area 220. There the Phase 1 floor produced a typical well-used compound tool of brown sandstone [54], and from the make-up for a later floor (Phase 3.1) came a smooth, water-worn grey pebble with one slightly polished face (1750:09). In the main room, a small triangular piece broken from a larger worked stone (1529:04) was found in the same context as the vessel fragment described above [53].

Stone tools from Phase 0.2

Three tools and two probable fragments of tools were found in pre-temple levels. Two were typical compound tools, their ends scarred by repeated pounding, and the sides worn to varying degrees by smoothing [55 & 56], while the third (1512:10) had certainly been used for smoothing, with one edge scarred from possible pounding too. All would appear to be fashioned from the limestone or quartzite which can be found on Bahrain today, except for one [56], which is of a dark grey metamorphic rock not local to the island. Tools of this hard, fine material are not as abundant at Saar as those made from local stone, but are nevertheless fairly common. Exact identifications or provenances for the imported stone types have yet to be made, but similar rock-types are found on the Arabian Peninsula. The three tools and one of the fragments (1516:06) all came from Phase 0.2, while the other fragment (H13:27:04) came from Phase 0.4.

Chipped Stone Tools

The chipped stone assemblage was made from varieties of flint and chert, and comprised a total of 60 artefacts: 16 from the temple, and 44 from the pre-temple phases of Test Pit 1. As no general differences between the two assemblages can be affirmed from the available sample, they will be considered as a whole in discussing the tools types and their manufacture.

There are hardly any chipped stone artefacts from Phases 1–2, but a small increase occurs in Phases 3–4 [50]. Phase 1 deposits were virtually devoid of stone tools altogether, containing only one ground-stone fragment. This dearth must be due in part to these layers being only partly removed in excavation. The tools from Phases 2–4 come mainly from floors, indicating that they were probably used in the building, rather than accidentally included in the deposits. With the exception of the blade and large borer, the repertoire of tools and the knapping techniques were no different from pre-temple Phases 0.1–0.4. However, there were several interesting carefully made types, such as the micro awl [57c] and double awl/scraper [57h] from Phase 2, the triangular scraper or component tool from Phase 3 [57j], and the backed awl and scraper/burin from Phase 4 [57g, m]. The lack of cores and the minimal amount of debitage suggests that flint knapping was not taking place inside the temple. In a religious structure it would presumably not have been appropriate to actually make tools. Those found must have been used by people who repaired and worked in the building, or to deal with the votive offerings brought in.

PHASE	Cores	Pounders	Awls	Borers	Scrapers	Blades	Scraper/Component	Retouched flakes	Flakes	Fragments	Total
0.1			1	1	2				1	1	6
0.2	2	1	3		1	1			13	5	26
0.3								1			1
0.4			1						9	1	11
Total	2	1	5	1	3	1	0	1	23	7	44
%	5	2	11	2	7	2	0	2	52	16	
1											0
2			2						1		3
3			3				1	2	2		8
4			1		1				1		3
5					1				1		2
Total	0	0	6	0	2	0	1	2	5	0	16
%	0	0	38	0	13	0	6	13	31	0	

Pre-temple ☐   Temple ☐

[50] Distribution of chipped stone by phase

[51] Bitumen bead
(1780:02) (Scale 1:1)

[53] Fragments from the rim of a softstone vessel
a A fragment from Phase 4 of the temple (1529:03). (Scale 1:1)
b A fragment found elsewhere in the settlement (6025:16) which fits the above. Diameter c. 14 cm. (Scale 1:1)

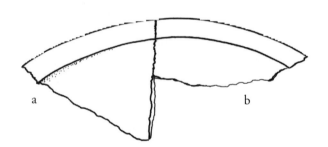

a   b

a

[52] Agate bead
1773:01. Length 3.3 cm.

[54] Compound stone tool
The long edges worn smooth from rubbing, the ends pitted from pounding. 1770:02. Length 8.1 cm.

[55] Stone tool
1512:04. Pink quartzite. One end is pitted from pounding. (Scale 1:2)

[56] Compound stone tool
1512:05. Compound tool made from hard, close-grained imported stone. The long edges are worn smooth and the ends pitted. Length 7.0 cm.

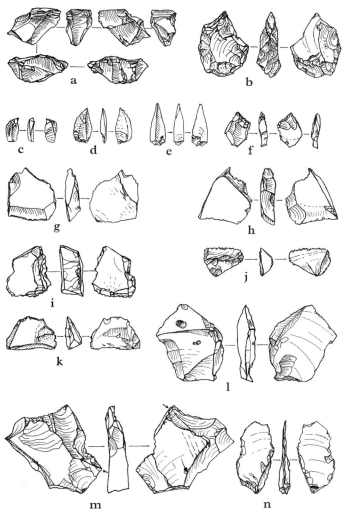

[57a–n]
Chipped stone (Scale: 1:2)
a Core. 1527:04 (1).
b Awl. 1527:04 (3).
c Micro awl. 1752:07.
d Awl. 1536:04 (1).
e Awl/point. H13:33:04 (1).
f Bifacial awl. 1527:10.
g Backed awl. 1587:01.
h Awl/scraper. 1905:04.
i Scraper. 1527:04 (2).
j Scraper/component tool. H13:20:05.
k Possible scraper. 1750:04 (6).
l Possible scraper. 1527:04 (6).
m Scraper/burin. 1596:09
n Re-touched blade. 1523:04 (1).

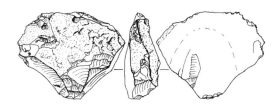

[58] Scraper 1536:04 (2). (Scale: 1:2)

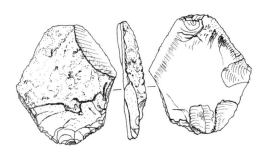

[59] Scraper 1536:04 (4). (Scale 1:2)

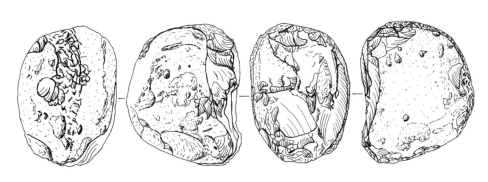

[60] Pounder 1512:06.
(Scale 1:2)

The proportion of chipped stone recovered from pre-temple layers also varies according to phase. Some of the deposits contained a range of types, such as context 1536 from Phase 0.1 with 3 tools and debitage, and 1527 from Phase 0.2 with a core, 2 tools and debitage. The presence of cores and the high proportion of flakes and debitage from the pre-temple phases indicates that prior to the temple's construction, the area was used for flint knapping. Several of the artefacts have been affected by heat, perhaps by being accidentally too close to a fire, or due to deliberate heat treatment of the stone to improve its flaking quality.

The stone favoured in the manufacture of the artefacts was predominantly brown flint, often mottled or with whitish blotches. For the pre-temple artefacts, grey, pinkish brown and chert-banded flint were used as well. The types of chert ranged from light to dark grey-brown. Some of the better quality light brown chert had been made into carefully retouched tools.

The limited range of stone and its similarity to flint found on the islands today probably indicates that most was extracted in Bahrain. The occurrence of the pounder and the larger cortical flakes in Phases 0.1–0.4 suggest that the larger flint-chert nodules were available at this relatively early phase, perhaps also locally. Most of the natural flint intrusions which can be observed eroding out of several of the local limestone strata are coarse and of a relatively small size. Some of the finer translucent flint and perhaps the shiny, grey-banded chert used in Phase 0.2 may have been brought from elsewhere, perhaps Qatar or Saudi Arabia. It is, however, possible that a local source or sources available previously are now exhausted or lie hidden. These views must be tentative until more work is done on the sources of flint as well as on the ground-stone tools.

The core and probable core fragment from Phase 0.2 exhibit different knapping techniques to produce both flakes and blades. The intact core has a single, slightly sloping, well-prepared striking platform [57a] whereas the core fragment (1513:03) was bipolar. The latter was rested on a hard surface (anvil) when flakes were being struck from it causing opposing concoidal fractures. Alternatively, due to the small size of the fragment it is possible that it was used in a similar way as a punch during indirect percussion. One Phase 0.2 flint nodule, however, was probably used as a pounder because of the large areas of percussion marks, or abrading, and the disordered flake scars on its surface [60].

Awls made up the commonest tool-type, most likely used to prise open shells or bore holes during processing of leather, bone, shell etc. [57b–h]. The fine point of each tool was usually formed by a double side strike, done equally either from both surfaces or only from the ventral surface. On occasion the point and adjacent edges were refined by unifacial retouch. Two wide double-struck awls, one being finely backed, were possibly also used as small scrapers [57g]. Another curious tool could have been used as a double awl, as well as a notched scraper [57h]. Some of the simple awls from Phases 0.1–0.4, with only one side strike having formed the tip, may have been used as projectile points [57d & e]. Many of the awls were very small and may fall into a microlith category, including one made of translucent brown flint that was carefully bifacially retouched [57f].

All the awl tips had some wear probably due to use. The only large awl or borer, found in Phase 0.1, was made using the same technique as the smaller versions but was very irregular in shape, due to the flaws within the flint. In addition five flakes were possibly also utilized as awls.

Scrapers were the second most common tool type [57i–m]. Three end scrapers have a working edge largely defined by minimal retouching and use wear [57l, 58, 59]. One heat-affected notched scraper on a thick flake has been carefully retouched [57i], but the most unusual came from Phase 0.1–2. This was a bifacially retouched large double concave scraper, which had two blunt tips, showing that it may have also been used as a burin [57m].

A retouched blade [57n] was found in Phase 0.2, and a small scraper or possible component tool [57j], made on a triangular flake, came from Phase 3.1 of the temple. The blade was bifacially retouched on both long edges and may have been used for cutting. The distal end was very thin and was broken either naturally or through use. The triangular tool may have been hafted as a barb or sickle blade, although there is no visible sheen near the retouched edge.

Three retouched flakes (two of which are broken) and four unretouched flakes may also have been utilized as scrapers. About half of the flakes have wear on one or more edges, but whether this was due to use is not certain. Lastly, there are 7 fragments of flint and chert that may have broken off flakes and tools, or chipped off pounders.

Despite the small size of the sample some general comments can be made. However, the following discussion will probably be modified once the entire Saar assemblage has been analysed, especially where it concerns Test Pit 1. The formal tools in the assemblage were only 32% of the total, with the flakes and fragments making up 56%. The actual proportion of utilized flakes is unknown, but future use-wear analysis may give additional information.

The tools, especially the awls, scrapers and blades, are best compared to those found in the vicinity of Saar by the Danish Expedition (Glob 1954, Site 24, Fig. 2a–c,f–l: this may actually be the site of Saar). Unfortunately, specific comparisons cannot be done until the chipped stone from other second millennium sites excavated in the Gulf, such as Qala'at al-Bahrain, other sites on Bahrain, and Failaka, are fully published (Bibby 1970; Mortensen 1986; Calvet & Salles 1986; Calvet & Gachet 1990; Kjaerum 1983; Højlund 1987). For the Emirates, the ground-stone tools from Tell Abraq are comparable to those from Saar, but only in the preliminary report of Shimal has mention been made of several flint concentrations (Potts 1990b; Vogt & Franke-Vogt 1987, 81, 83, 90 & 91).

The types of chipped stone tools discussed here appear to have been made over a long period of time, with comparative examples seen from sites in the region dating from the 6/5th–3rd millennia BC. There may be others from the mainly 4th millennium BC site of al-Markh in western Bahrain, but the lithics have not been published in detail (McNicoll n.d.; McNicoll & Roaf 1975; Roaf 1974 & 1976a & b). Similar awl-dominated tool kits have been found at coastal sites on the eastern province of Saudi Arabia dating to the 'Ubaid to Early Dynastic periods, such as Abu Khamis and Umm ar-Ramadh (Masry 1974, Figs. 81.2–8, 84.2–4; Piesinger 1983, 1028).

Awls, especially double-struck awls, have been recovered from an earlier site immediately north of the 2nd millennium settlement at Saar (Bellefroid, forthcoming). Others have been found on the west coast of Qatar (Kapel 1967, Figs. 9, 31–33 & 40), and the early fourth millennium settlement of Ras Abaruk 4 produced a very comparable wide double-struck awl (Smith 1978, Fig. 10.7). Similar awls and scrapers were also recorded during surveys in Saudi Arabia, in particular from the Northern Province (e.g. Jabal Umm Wu'al D & Rajajil. See McAdams et al. 1977, pls. 13–15; Parr et al. 1978, 40), and even west of the Rub' al Khali sands (Edens 1988, Fig. 9.6).

In conclusion, a very limited range of chipped stone tools was found in the pre-temple levels of Test Pit 1, and even fewer in the temple. Noticeably absent are projectile points, agricultural tools, and in the temple itself, blades and large borers. The copper arrowheads, spearheads, blades, larger tools and agricultural equipment found at Saar and at several other Gulf sites dating to the second millennium would indicate strongly that metal was now the material used for making these types of tools. Other reasons for the lack of variety may include the small size of the sample, multiple use of the tools, and the removal in antiquity of the more prized and carefully-made tools.

Pottery

The potential of the ceramic evidence

In this section, the ceramic inventory of the temple is described and comparisons drawn with the pottery from other sites in Bahrain, in the Gulf region, and in Mesopotamia. By comparing, too, the shape repertoire of the temple with that from the other households of Saar, we can examine the question of whether pottery was specially manufactured for the temple or not.

Furthermore, an attempt is made to gain some insight into the functions, activities and status of the institution in which the pottery was found. The various activities which took place in the temple, be they of a purely ritual or of an economic nature, should be reflected in the material remains of its contents, and clues to the position and status of the temple organization within the settlement ought also to be found in its archaeological inventory, including the pottery.

Chemical analysis of sherds from selected houses in the settlement has determined the composition of the clays, and also demonstrated what manufacturing techniques had been developed to ensure optimum suitability of the vessels for their intended function. The results of this analysis have elucidated the state of development of pottery technology at Saar, and particularly of firing methods. They should also make it possible to discover whether there is any variation in clay preparation or mode of manufacture which would comment on the status or special role of the temple, and whether the activities which took place there were exclusive to it or not. Examination of the shape repertoires from the three different rooms might show functional specialization of different areas. Comparison of the over-all temple repertoire with that of domestic dwellings in the settlement may shed light on the function and role of the temple.

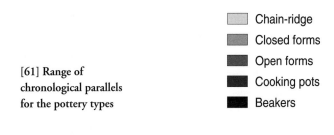

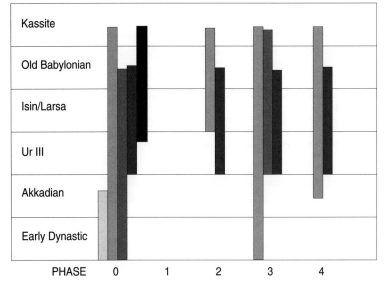

[61] Range of
chronological parallels
for the pottery types

Comparison with similar groups from neighbouring regions is offered with two objects in mind: to confirm the dating, and to provide pointers towards evidence of trade-linked activities in the temple.

General description and chronology of the ceramic types

The ceramic shape repertoire of the temple can be divided into four general vessel classes: closed forms (such as jars), open forms (plates and bowls), 'cooking pots', and 'storage jars'. In all areas there were of course body sherds which could not be ascribed to any vessel type. Different ceramic inventories are apparent for the two different rooms (Areas 200 and 220) into which the temple was divided during most of its life.

The date of the temple pottery is of course fundamentally determined by that of the much more extensive ceramic corpus from the rest of the settlement (Heinz 1994), the spectrum of shapes from the temple (and Test Pit 1) alone being necessarily more restricted. The general dating of the Saar pottery, at least of the undecorated forms, rests ultimately on comparisons with Qala'at al-Bahrain and the Barbar Temple on Bahrain itself; with Failaka (off Kuwait); the Dahran

mound fields (Saudi Arabia); the settlements of Abraq (U.A.E.); Hili (Oman), and with Mesopotamia. The last-mentioned are here specifically demonstrated by reference to two contrasting sites, the great urban centre of Uruk, in the south, and the small Diyala village of Uch Tepe.

These comparisons provide an apparent possible date range for the temple's duration from the Early Dynastic through the Kassite period [61]. Closed form comparisons range from Early Dynastic to Old Babylonian (Heinz 1994, 144–152). Parallels for the open forms can be found as far back as the Ur III period, with the latest similar types occurring up to Kassite times (*ibid.* 152–164). Comparanda for cooking pots begin around the Akkadian/Ur III transition and go on to the Old Babylonian period (*ibid.* 164–166). Storage vessels of the kind found in Area 220 can be found in Akkadian through to Kassite contexts elsewhere (*ibid.* 167). More precise comparison of specific forms, however, taking into account the pottery from the rest of the settlement, confirms the temple's date as belonging to the time of the Ur III/Old Babylonian period (Heinz 1994, 193ff).

Geographical distribution of comparanda

Parallels for closed forms and storage vessels from Saar are more widely spread than those for open forms and cooking pots (note that the illustrations of pottery represent types rather than actual sherds). The former range over the entire area from which comparisons have been drawn, including Mesopotamia. Certain closed forms [62a, g, l, n, o; 66m–o] are found at Uruk and Uch Tepe, on Failaka, at Tell Abraq, as well as on Bahrain itself. But parallels for the other closed forms concentrate in the Gulf region, mainly Tell Abraq and Bahrain. Comparable storage vessels [66b, t] have been found at Uruk, Tell Abraq, Failaka, and again on Bahrain. For the open forms and cooking pots, on the other hand, comparanda are almost exclusively confined to the Gulf, concentrating on Failaka and Bahrain (Heinz 1994). Cooking pots are also attested at Tell Abraq, though few to date.

Comparison of our pottery with similar forms found elsewhere would suggest therefore that Saar had connections with two different economic areas, one regional, connecting Bahrain with Oman and the rest of the Gulf, and the other supra-regional, reaching at least as far as Mesopotamia in the NW.

The temple assemblage compared with other pottery from Saar

Comparison of the ceramic assemblage of the temple with that of other households in the settlement shows that in general, the range of pottery shapes found in the temple is the same as that from elsewhere: no evidence can be discerned at Saar for any ceramic type made exclusively for the temple or specially connected with the cult, with the possible exception of the clay 'pedestal' found in the NW corner of Area 200 [74]. Nothing was found that could be identified as any form of offering, and nothing which could be interpreted as a luxury or prestige ware from its mode of manufacture. In fact, there was less decorated pottery in the temple than from anywhere else in the settlement: a mere two painted fragments were found, both from the main chamber [63j, k]. Elsewhere occurrences of paint, incision, decorated applied ridges, combing, reserved slip and smeared wash are all part of the normal household inventory at Saar (Heinz 1994).

This lack of any special features for the temple pottery is paralleled by the evidence of the chemical analyses. Analysis of pottery samples from selected areas of the settlement showed that two distinctive forms of raw material were employed (Heinz 1994). One group was made up of open and closed forms, bases and storage jars in a colour range of beige-brown, leather-coloured, yellowish (closed forms, bases and storage jars) to yellow-green (open forms), all made of similar clay. Cooking vessels formed the second group, distinguished not only by their shape but by the exclusive use of a red ware.

The colour of pottery is basically dependent on two factors: the composition of the clay, and the firing-temperature, atmosphere and length of time in the kiln. Brown, leather-yellowish and also red fabrics mean a firing temperature of 700 to 900° C. Yellowish-green colours on the other hand can only be achieved when the temperature reaches around 1,000° C, when a high content of fine, reactive lime produces the greeny yellow colour. The results of the chemical analysis showed clearly that the cooking pots differed from the other shape groups not only in their colour but also in the actual raw material of which their fabric was composed. Further conclusions may then be drawn about the methods of manufacture and the technical knowledge of the potters. Temperatures of up to 900° C can be obtained with an open fire, so a kiln was not essential for making closed forms and storage jars. Maintaining a constant tempera-

ture of 900–1,000° C, however, cannot be done with an open fire, and a kiln would have been essential for making the yellow-green open forms, so we may conclude that the Saar potters were masters of the requisite techniques for kiln-firing.

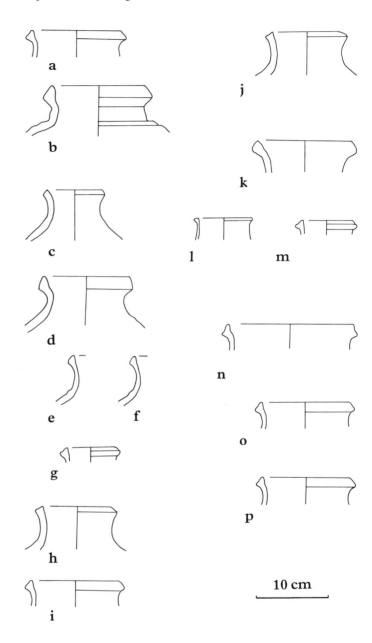

10 cm

[62]	Closed forms from Area 200				
	Context	Phase		Context	Phase
a	1526	5.1	i	1596	4.1
b	1526	5.1	j	1612	3.2
c	1528	4.5	k	1612	3.2
d	1505	4.5	l	1612	3.2
e	1538	4.5	m	1612	3.2
f	1538	4.5	n	1763	3.1
g	1529	4.4	o	1763	3.1
h	1596	4.1	p	1763	3.1

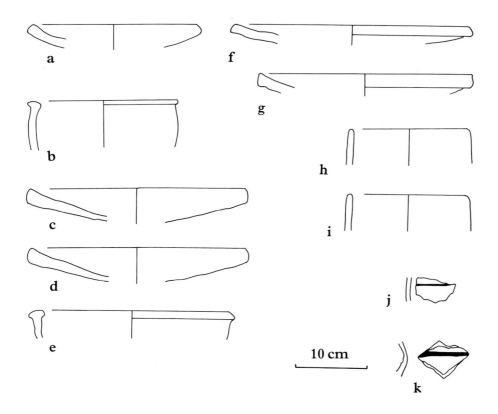

[63] **Open forms and decorated sherds from Area 200**

	Context	Phase		Context	Phase		Context	Phase
a	1508	4.5	e	1596	4.1	i	1763	3.1
b	1538	4.5	f	1612	3.2	j	1763	3.1
c	1587	4.1	g	1612	3.2	k	1763	3.1
d	1587	4.1	h	1763	3.1			

The cooking-pots show a deliberate relationship between shape, raw material and function. The designation 'cooking-pot' is taken from the round-bodied, round-based hole-mouthed shape and the frequency with which this type is heavily blackened on the outside. No other pottery types exhibit this characteristic at Saar. The type of clay chosen must have been ideal for its intended use, namely repeated heating over an open fire to a temperature of 300–500° C. The tempering material must not expand at a greater rate than the clay of the vessel when heated. The analysis showed that pottery from the temple and the rest of the settlement were made of the same raw material, so that no special selection was made either by manufacturer or procurer of temple pottery. The choice of raw material and its treatment in firing was determined solely by the form of vessel to be produced, not by its intended destination. There is no evidence at Saar for special temple pottery.

The question of whether Saar pottery was locally produced cannot be answered just from the chemical analyses. No correlation has yet been established between clay types from the excavations and from other locations on Bahrain: in other words, those tested do not represent the ancient source for the Saar pottery. A local origin is not of course out of the question: there may well be different types of clay on Bahrain. But our data and knowledge of the types and the local sources is just too incomplete to say more at present. Further clay analyses are necessary before local production or import can be determined with any certainty.

The ceramic evidence for activities inside the temple building

The pottery shape groups display very little variation from one phase to another, and thus no chronological change in the activities represented is to be concluded. As

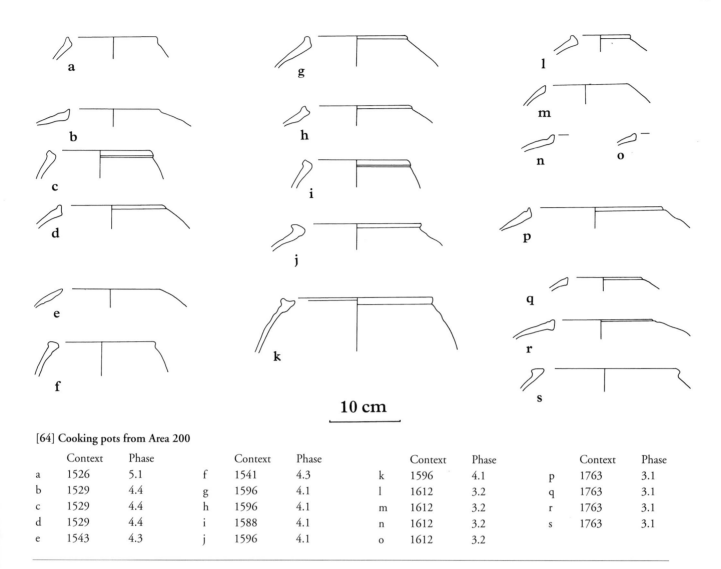

10 cm

[64] Cooking pots from Area 200

	Context	Phase		Context	Phase		Context	Phase		Context	Phase
a	1526	5.1	f	1541	4.3	k	1596	4.1	p	1763	3.1
b	1529	4.4	g	1596	4.1	l	1612	3.2	q	1763	3.1
c	1529	4.4	h	1596	4.1	m	1612	3.2	r	1763	3.1
d	1529	4.4	i	1588	4.1	n	1612	3.2	s	1763	3.1
e	1543	4.3	j	1596	4.1	o	1612	3.2			

to distribution, most of the pottery came from the main chamber, Area 200, but there was also some from the storeroom Area 220. The late addition, Area 221, produced nothing recognizable from the few deposits excavated. The main chamber produced a range of closed forms, or jars [62]; open forms, or plates and bowls, [63a–i]; cooking pots [64]; bases [65]; and two fragments with painted stripes [63j & k]. There was also a curious elongated object of baked clay [74, 161], probably a broken stemmed dish of the kind found in Barbar Temple IIb and at other Dilmun sites (Højlund and Andersen 1994, 86).

The ceramic repertoire of Area 220 differs from that of the main chamber on a number of counts. The usual jar-rims, bases and cooking pots are present [66]. There are, however, no open forms, and for the first time in the temple we find fragments of large storage vessels, decorated with a raised band with finger-impressions [66b, t].

Here also were found the only reasonably complete vessels to survive in the building. One was a small, wide-mouthed jar, found intact on the Phase 2 floor [70b, 73]. The other two were in the make-up for the succeeding Phase 3 floor. One is a large jar, ribbed all over its exterior, thickly coated with bitumen inside and out [70a, 71]. The upper part of the vessel is missing, but it had clearly been used in this broken state, as the bitumen ran over the broken edge. Furthermore, it had actually been used to contain bitumen, as opposed to being accidentally exposed to a spill, as there was a thick deposit in the base. With it was a smaller, rounder jar with ribs on the upper body [70c, 72]. This too had suffered damage, though only slight, and bitumen had been used to repair a hole in the lower body. It is possible that these pots had been used in the major refurbishment of the building which had just taken place, and, not being worth removing, were simply covered over by the new floor.

[65] Bases from Area 200

10cm

	Context	Phase		Context	Phase		Context	Phase		Context	Phase
a	1526	5.1	g	1543	4.3	m	1763	3.1	s	1763	3.1
b	1538	4.5	h	1596	4.1	n	1763	3.1	t	1763	3.1
c	1505	4.5	i	1596	4.1	o	1763	3.1	u	1763	3.1
d	1538	4.5	j	1588	4.1	p	1763	3.1	v	1764	3
e	1538	4.5	k	1596	4.1	q	1763	3.1	w	1764	3
f	1529	4.4	l	1587	4.1	r	1763	3.1			

The catalogue of temple pottery does not point to a specialized repertoire, with the partial exception of Area 220. The depressions in the floor of this room, presumed to be for the bases of large storage vessels, confirm the probability that this area was used as a storeroom. The small number of storage jar fragments, however, and the absence of large-scale storage facilities, suggest that the temple only stored materials for its own needs, as opposed to serving as a significant redistribution centre. In general, the range of types found in the temple is consistent with the provision and possibly the preparation and consumption of foodstuffs, and does not differ from that of other households in the settlement.

The possible function of the temple in controlling the economic activities of the settlement was mentioned above. Two aspects of the economy can be distinguished: the local economy, with agriculture, fishing and crafts serving the direct subsistence, and foreign trade as a supplementary branch. No control or organization of economic activities, however, can be surmised from the ceramic evidence. Texts from contemporary Mesopotamia show that the inhabitants of a settlement were bound to give produce as offerings to the temple, both to provide for the temple personnel and as sacrifices for the gods. A parallel tradition, with its connected assumption that members of the priesthood ensured their supplies by exercising definite control over local economic conditions (van de Mieroop 1992) cannot be demonstrated for Saar, but the possibility cannot be ruled out either.

Bahrain in the early second millennium functioned as a trading entrepôt for economic exchange between Oman and the Indus to the south and east, and mainly Mesopotamia to the north. The involvement of the temple in long-distance trade is shown by comparison of the pottery shapes found in it with pottery from the Gulf

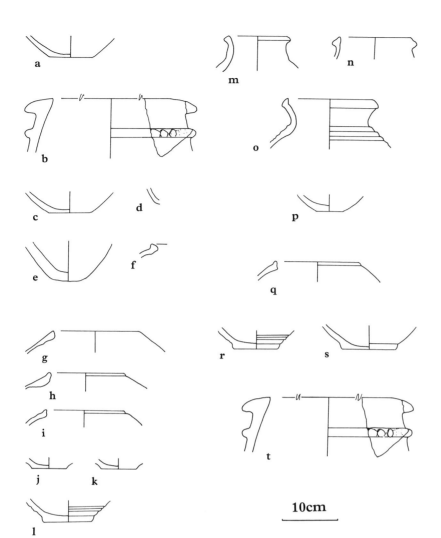

[66] Pottery from Area 220

	Context	Phase
a	1503	4.5
b	1617	3.1
c	1597	3.1
d	1597	3.1
e	1597	3.1
f	1750	3
g	1750	3
h	1750	3
i	1750	3
j	1750	3
k	1750	3
l	1750	3
m	1750	3
n	1750	3
o	1750	3
p	1752	2.2
q	1770	1.1
r	1770	1.1
s	1770	1.1
t	1770	1.1

10cm

and Mesopotamia, the similarities being especially marked in the case of the closed forms and storage vessels.

The vessels found in the temple cannot, therefore, be definitely taken as imports or local imitations of foreign style, nor can their local origin be proven. On the one hand, closed forms make up a fixed proportion of every Saar household's inventory, so their general abundance could be taken as an indicator of local production. On the other hand, the possibility of trade activities being the basis for parallels for other types should not be ruled out. Closed forms and storage jars, the two types which provide the most parallels with other regions, are ideal for transport, being easy to fasten up, move about, and stack in quantity on board ship.

Objects found in the houses and graves of the settlement show that the other households in Saar were also involved in long-distance trade, being either imported or made of imported raw material such as metal or semi-

precious stone (Crawford 1991, Heinz 1994). The distribution of imported goods makes it clear that trading was not restricted, and there were concentrations of imported goods in Houses 51 and 53 (Crawford 1993, Heinz 1994). Indeed a discrepancy is to be observed between the concentration of imports in the settlement and their scarcity in the temple. Further light on the respective roles of the temple and private individuals in trade must await more detailed analysis of the private houses and their contents, and of the spatial dynamics of the settlement. Saar is, of course, lacking the information on its trading activities which might be provided by written material. In southern Mesopotamia, on the other hand, texts show how at the beginning of the second millennium the organization and operation of foreign trade was becoming more and more the province of private merchants, while the temple was being reduced to the role of indirect receiver. This might

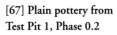

[67] Plain pottery from
Test Pit 1, Phase 0.2

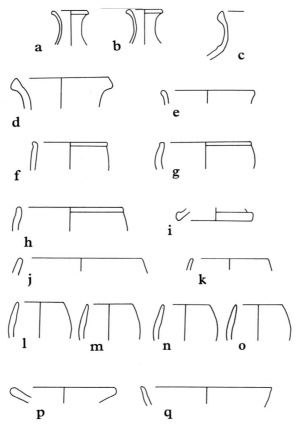
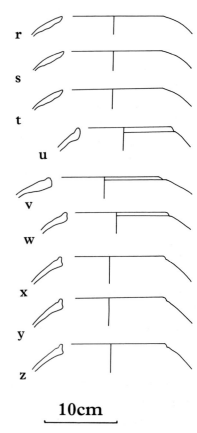

	Context
a	1527
b	1516
c	1527
d	1527
e	1516
f	1527
g	1527
h	1527
i	1512
j	1527
k	1527
l	1523
m	1527
n	1513
o	1516
p	1512
q	1527
r	1527
s	1513
t	1516
u	1527
v	1513
w	1516
x	1512
y	1513
z	1527

10cm

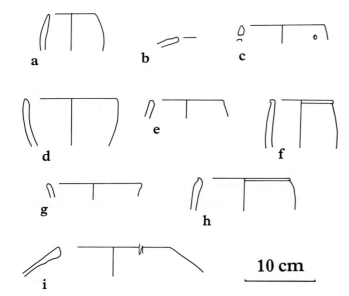

[68] Pottery from Test Pit 1, Phase 0.1.

a–h   context 1533
i   context 1536

10 cm

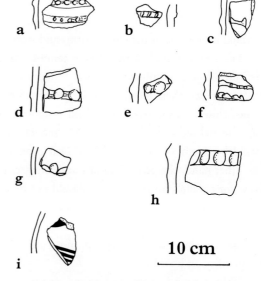

[69] Decorated pottery from Test Pit 1, Phase 0.2

a–c   context 1512
d–g   context 1516
h–i   context 1527

10 cm

well serve as a model for the organization of trade in Bahrain (van de Mieroop 1992).

Pottery from Test Pit 1

The area sampled as Test Pit 1 was too small to produce coherent building remains, and the pottery found in it cannot therefore be tied to building levels as such. It is, however, interesting for the glimpse it affords of ceramic styles at Saar in the period prior to the temple's construction. The pre-temple strata of Test Pit 1 are all referred to as Phase 0, and the pottery presented here was all found in the lowest levels, Phases 0.1 and 0.2.

The pottery from Test Pit 1 shows certain similarities with that of the temple itself, but also variations in the repertoire. Four classes of shape can be distinguished: open forms, cooking pots, closed forms, and 'beakers' [67–69]. Cooking pots and closed forms are in general comparable with examples of the corresponding shape types in the temple. A particularly slender and simple form of cooking-pot rim occurs three times in level 0.2 [67r–t]. Isolated occurrences of this type have been noted in later levels at Saar [64e], and at Qala'at al-Bahrain they persist into City II levels, but concentrate, however, in City I (Højlund and Andersen 1994, 142, Figs. 401–406; 136, Fig. 388).

The beaker forms have not so far been encountered in later levels. Five types of open form are also exclusive to Test Pit 1: shallow, round-bodied, and with short, everted rims [67f–h, 68f & h].

Parallels for the decorated sherds can only be found among the 'chain-ridge' ware. Chain-ridge fragments were found at Qala'at al-Bahrain in City I and City II levels, where it was noted that a larger type of chain-ridge is characteristic of City Ia and Ib levels, while a smaller version is found in City Ib and IIa (Højlund and Andersen 1994, 92; 136–137, Fig. 388). In the temple excavations at Saar chain ridge was only found in Phase 0.2, where both types were present [69a–h]. There are also examples from Tell Abraq from Early Dynastic and Akkadian-period contexts (Potts 1990b, 35, Figs. 7 and 28; 1991, 29, Figs. 16 and 17), and from Uch Tepe came an example of a decorated vessel with Early Dynastic affinities (Gibson 1981, 117; Fig. 67:5b and 8; Fig. 76).

If the same sites are used here for parallels as for the pottery from the temple building and the settlement, then cooking pots and closed forms fit into a date range of terminal Akkadian to the end of the Old Babylonian or start of the Kassite period. Shapes such as the beakers [67l–o, 68a] occur at Shimal, Hili and Tell Abraq (Heinz 1994:161) from the end of the third millennium BC to the middle of the second. The beakers, however, would appear to be limited to the Gulf region. For the open, sometimes round-bodied examples of open forms [67f–h] of Test Pit 1 there are parallels at Hili and Uruk. The Hili examples are from Phase 8E, F and H at the site, and date from the end of the Akkadian period to the beginning of the Old Babylonian. A similar piece from Uruk dates there to the end of Jemdet Nasr to Early Dynastic I (Pongratz-Leisten 1988, 178ff.)

The distribution of comparable material demonstrates

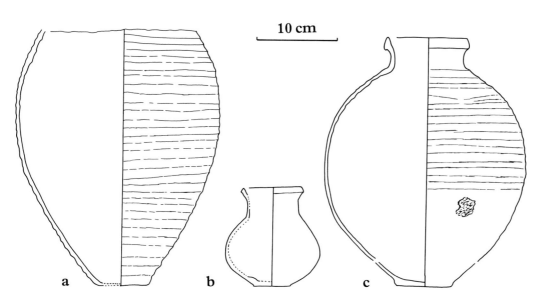

10 cm

a   b   c

[70] **Pottery vessels from Area 220.**

a   1750:07
b   1752:01
c   1750:08

[71] Broken vessel used to hold bitumen, 1750:07

[72] Pottery jar, 1750:08

[73] Small pottery vessel, 1752:01

[74] Pottery object, possibly a stand, 1541:01

connections between Bahrain and Mesopotamia going back as far as the middle of the third millennium BC. In other words, even before the construction of the temple, Saar had a wide range of trade contacts. In conclusion, comparanda for the plain and decorated pottery from Test Pit 1 suggest two separate dating blocks [61]. Chain-ridge ware is restricted to terminal Early Dynastic/Akkadian to Ur III. The plain forms, however, have a longer life-span, beginning in the Akkadian period and lasting up to the Kassite. In summary, our evidence suggests that the earliest occupation at Saar can be attributed to the end of the Early Dynastic period and that the settlement came to an end during the Old Babylonian period.

Chapter 6. **Food Remains**

A good deal of information about the plants and animals which influenced the lives of the people of Saar has already been assembled. Plant remains are overwhelmingly of the date palm (Nesbitt 1993), with only very sparse evidence for wheat and barley. Shellfish were exploited a great deal (Glover 1995), especially small clams. Preliminary results of the study of animal bone (Dobney and Jaques 1994) have confirmed that fish was a very important component of the diet, accounting for around 83% by weight of the bones recovered. Sheep and goat were the most popular domestic animals, and there was also evidence for the presence of cattle, equid, camel, and gazelle, and rare fragments of dugong, fox, mongoose, cat and cormorant. The temple, not surprisingly, generally contained less in the way of plant and animal remains than the domestic contexts which have been the subject of environmental studies at Saar so far, and only the fish bones give the impression of being in primary context. The pre-temple levels of Test Pit 1 provide small samples of environmental material earlier in date than any other which has been examined from Saar so far. Any special characteristics which distinguish either the temple assemblage or the earlier levels below it will probably not become fully apparent until the ongoing study of further domestic contexts is complete.

Plant Material

One botanical sample from within the temple was analysed as part of the existing study of plant remains from Saar (Nesbitt 1993, 23, Table 2 (H13:10:01)), and this contained the usual date remains. No more plant material has been found in samples taken subsequently from the temple building itself. Two samples from Test Pit 1, from Phase 0.1, again containing date material, were included in the same study (*ibid.*, H13:27:01, H13:28:01), and further material from Phases 0.1, and some from 0.2, is reported on here [196].

Methodology

Six soil samples were taken from contexts dating to Phases 0.1–0.2. One of these samples appears to have been from a burnt area, perhaps a hearth (1531:01), another one from occupation debris (1527:19), and a third also contained fish remains (1533:12). The other three samples (1512:11, 1530:12 and 1536:01) were from indeterminate layers. The samples were floated using the Siraf-type flotation machine (Nesbitt 1993, 20) and produced small flots (40–100 ml) with 60 to 70% char-coal in them. The residues were checked on site. The flots were sorted with a low power binocular microscope at a magnification of x12 and the sorted items were identified at x12–x50 magnification.

Composition of the samples

Most of the samples included mainly date stones, but other types of charred plant remains were also recovered, and even dominated the small assemblages. Cultivated

	CONTEXT	1533	1536	1512	1527	1530	1531
		PHASE 0.1		PHASE 0.2			
	Volume of flot (ml)	15	40	30	20	<10	15
SPECIES	TYPE						
Triticum sp.	grains			2 [2]			
	rachis				1		
Hordeum sativum	total grains	4 (2)	[3]	26 [20]	2 [1]		[1]
	straight			17			
	twisted			5			
	undecided			4 [20]			
	rachis segment		1				
Indeterminate cereal							[1]
Chenopodiaceae indet.	embryo				1		
Linum usitatissimum							1
Leguminosae	small seed		2				
Malva sp.					1		
Phoenix dactylifera	stones	***	***	[1]	**	**	****
	fleshy fruit	**					
	seed			1			
Lolium sp.						1	
Hordeum sp.		2	5 [1]				1
Phalaris sp.		1	4				

[75] **Plant remains from Test Pit 1**
Numbers in square brackets are the estimated number of seeds from fragments. Asterisks indicate relative abundance.

	ethmoid	prevomer	basioccipital	lacrimal	pterosphenoid	posttemporal	articular	dentary	maxilla	premaxilla	quadrate
Tylosurus crocodilus crocodile needlefish											
Carangidae (jacks, trevallies, yellowtails)	1						4	14	12	13	9
Haemulidae (grunts)		1			1		1	1			1
Lethrinidae (emperors)		1				41	57	50	47	77	34
Lutjanidae (snappers)							4	11	3	9	
Mullidae (goatfish)											
Platycephalidae (spiny flatheads)											
Pomocanthus maculosus (yellowbar angelfish)								1			
Rachycentron canadus cobia											
Scombridae (mackerals, tunas)											
Serranidae (groupers)		2		1		1	15	20	10	20	8
Siganidae (rabbitfishes)											
Sparidae (porgies, breams)							2	79	9	84	4
Sphyraenidae (barracudas)								1		1	
Vertebrae group											
Indeterminate			1					1			2
Total	**1**	**4**	**1**	**1**	**1**	**42**	**83**	**178**	**81**	**204**	**58**

hulled barley, *Hordeum sativum*, constituted the main item in one sample (1512:11), not a very common occurrence in the samples from Saar. Some of the barley was of the six-row variety, as attested by the presence of five twisted grains which would have been grains placed on either side of the spikelet of three. Some wheat, a few fragments of date pips and a seed of arable weed were also present in the sample. The remaining samples contained many fragments of date stones with some cultivated barley, a few seeds of wild barley, *Hordeum* sp. and canary grass, *Phalaris* sp. The seeds could have been the weed seeds of arable crops and may have come into the deposits with the barley grains. Some chaff was recovered: one rachis segment of barley and one basal rachis of indeterminate wheat. A single seed of cultivated flax, *Linum usitatissimum*, was present in one sample (1531:01), a species not previously reported from Saar. As it is only a single seed, it is not possible to speculate on whether it was grown under irrigation conditions at Saar or imported. There are examples from an Umm an-Nar tomb of flax used for bead string (Frifelt 1991, 117), but there is no record of flax seeds from sites in the Gulf.

Discussion

Nesbitt (1993) has explored the probable role of the date in the diet of the inhabitants of Saar. He also outlined possible reasons for the paucity of cultivated cereals and other plant remains in the archaeological record. One possible explanation for the scarcity of cereals is that they were not in fact cultivated at Saar, but imported. Using this model, these cereals would have been available only sporadically, as and when a cargo arrived. They could hardly, therefore, have formed a dietary staple. From the evidence available, the inhabitants seem to have relied mostly on fish and dates.

Another explanation for the lack of certain types of plant remains is that some preservation factor is involved: either charring was too fierce, especially in some of the ovens found in the houses, such as the *tannurs*. Or perhaps post-depositional conditions were such that remains were simply not preserved. Such conditions, which may have applied to the whole of the Gulf area, could be a combination of rainfall, seasonal desiccation and, in places, accumulation of salt. These factors may have contributed to breaking up the already fragile remains, which would then have been dispersed by erosional forces such as wind or rain.

The samples from Test Pit 1 would tend to support the supposition that the scarcity of plant remains can be attributed to post-depositional factors: although small by the standards of sites in other areas such as Mesopotamia, the sample includes a balance of different types of plant remains which are typical for a site of this period. Furthermore, the presence of weed seeds and chaff fragments in the assemblage increases the likelihood of local

[141] The north-west wall of the temple
The Phase 2 buttress is along the bottom of the mid-section of the wall, with associated benches to the right. Its demolition at the end of Phase 2 is marked, as elsewhere, by the superimposed foundation packing for the Phase 3 wall.

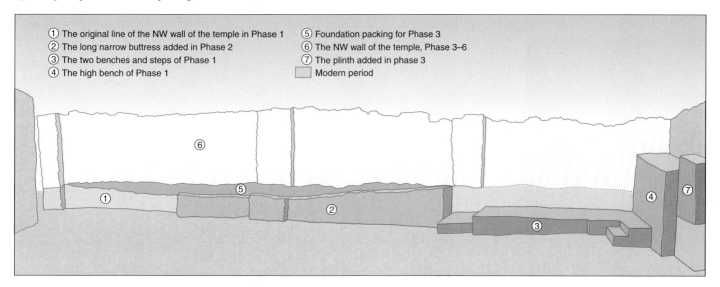

① The original line of the NW wall of the temple in Phase 1
② The long narrow buttress added in Phase 2
③ The two benches and steps of Phase 1
④ The high bench of Phase 1
⑤ Foundation packing for Phase 3
⑥ The NW wall of the temple, Phase 3–6
⑦ The plinth added in phase 3
▢ Modern period

[142] The western end of the temple
Circular plastered depressions are visible in the floor, with the two low stone walls, perhaps shelf supports, behind. The stone wall to the SW (left side) measured 36×160 cm. The NE wall (right side) was 30×170 cm.

[143] Footprints in the floor plaster
Embedded in the plaster of one of the floors (1785) were several footprints. The toe-impressions show up more clearly than those of the heels. The prints of two different individuals could be identified.

[144] The temple doorway
The superimposed thresholds can be seen across the temple doorway. The Phase 2 threshold is represented by the line of stones at the bottom of the doorway, with the Phase 3 and Phase 4 thresholds above. A pivot stone for the doorway is on the right.

[145] Stone bases outside the temple
These two stone bases, possibly offering tables, stood outside the temple in Phase 2. The one nearest the doorway (1783, seen on the left) was circular, and stood 3.6 m from the temple façade slightly south from the alignment of the doorway. The one on the right (1784) was located the same distance away from the temple and was half circular and half square.
Dimensions:
1783 (nearest the entrance) had a diameter of 106 cm and its extant height at the start of Phase 2 was 92 cm.
1784 measured 70×150 cm, with a height of 83 cm.

[146] Stone support
Against the façade of the temple was a shallow stone and mortar setting (1875) measuring 48×40 cm with a depth of 15 cm. It had a central depression 20 cm in diameter and 5 cm deep.

[147] Smashed pottery in the south-west corner of the storeroom (Area 220)
During the renovation work these pots had been carelessly thrown into the building debris within the storeroom (1750:07 and 08).

[148] The deep sand in-filling of Phase 3
Whether the sand fill brought into the temple between Phases 2 and 3 represents a purified ritual deposit is not clear, but two arguments militate against such a hypothesis. Firstly, no such deposit underlay the Phase 1 foundation of the temple and, secondly, the sand fill was confined to the main room of the temple, not being found in the storeroom.

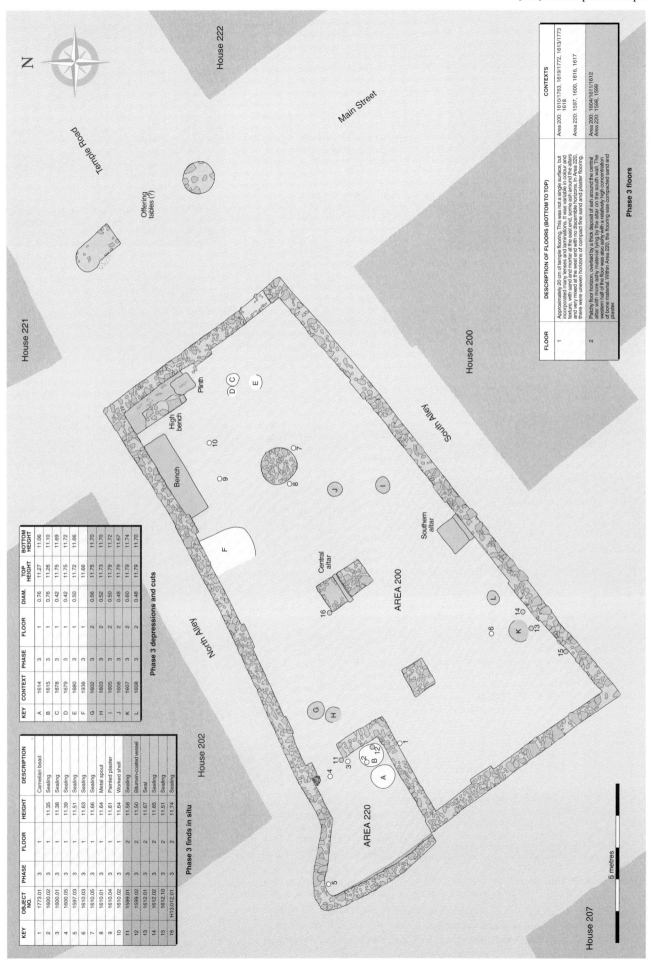

Phase 3 finds in situ

KEY	OBJECT NO.	PHASE	FLOOR	HEIGHT	DESCRIPTION
1	1773.01	3	1		Carnelian bead
2	1600.02	3	1	11.35	Sealing
3	1600.01	3	1	11.38	Sealing
4	1600.05	3	1	11.39	Sealing
5	1597.03	3	1	11.51	Sealing
6	1610.03	3	1	11.63	Sealing
7	1610.05	3	1	11.66	Sealing
8	1610.01	3	1	11.64	Metal spout
9	1610.04	3	1	11.61	Painted plaster
10	1610.02	3	1	11.64	Worked shell
11	1599.01	3	2	11.58	Sealing
12	1599.02	3	2	11.50	Bitumen-coated vessel
13	1612.01	3	2	11.67	Seal
14	1612.02	3	2	11.65	Sealing
15	1612.10	3	2	11.51	Sealing
16	H13.012.01	3		11.74	Sealing

Phase 3 depressions and cuts

KEY	CONTEXT	PHASE	FLOOR	DIAM.	TOP HEIGHT	BOTTOM HEIGHT
A	1614	3	1	0.76	11.27	11.06
B	1615	3	1	0.76	11.26	11.10
C	1678	3	1	0.42	11.75	11.69
D	1679	3	1	0.42	11.75	11.72
E	1680	3	1	0.50	11.72	11.66
F	1938	3	1		11.66	
G	1602	3	2	0.56	11.73	11.70
H	1603	3	2	0.52	11.73	11.70
I	1605	3	2	0.50	11.79	11.72
J	1606	3	2	0.48	11.79	11.67
K	1607	3	2	0.60	11.79	11.74
L	1608	3	2	0.48	11.79	11.70

Phase 3 floors

FLOOR	DESCRIPTION OF FLOORS (BOTTOM TO TOP)	CONTEXTS
1	Approximately 20 cm of temple flooring. This was not a single surface, but incorporated many lenses and laminations. It was variable in colour and texture, with sand and mortar at the east end, some ash around the altars and very mixed at the west end with no discernible horizons. In Area 220, there were uneven horizons of compact fine sand and plaster flooring.	Area 200: 1610/1763, 1619/1772, 1613/1773 1618; Area 220: 1597, 1600, 1616, 1617
2	Patchy floor horizon, overlaid by a thick deposit of ash around the central altar with more ashy material lying by the altar on the south wall. The western half of the floor was also ashy with a relatively high concentration of bone material. Within Area 220, the flooring was compacted sand and plaster.	Area 200: 1604/1611/1612; Area 220: 1598, 1599

N

House 222
House 221
House 202
House 207
House 200
Main Street
Temple Road
North Alley
South Alley
Offering tables (?)
AREA 200
AREA 220
Central altar
Southern altar
High bench
Bench
Plinth

5 metres

[150] Southern Altar
Phases 3–6
The front of the southern altar was continually being raised as the floor levels rose through Phases 3 to 6. Two of these rebuilds can be seen here, one marked by the small stone out of alignment on the left (NE) side, and the second by the top course of stones and pebbles. The back of the altar also showed evidence of renovation. Base of altar: 82×98 cm. Altar back: 87 cm across the top.

[151] Central Altar
The central altar was of similar size and dimensions to the southern altar and had the same curved device on the back. Base of altar: 63×100 cm. Altar back: 92 cm across the top.

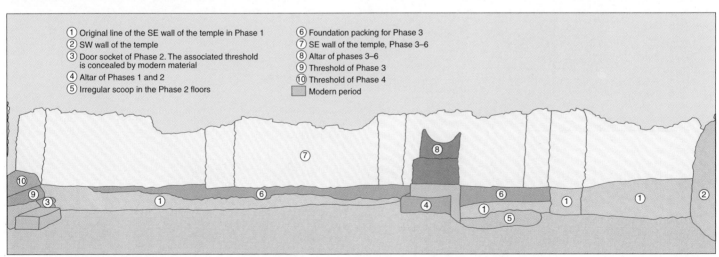

① Original line of the SE wall of the temple in Phase 1
② SW wall of the temple
③ Door socket of Phase 2. The associated threshold is concealed by modern material
④ Altar of Phases 1 and 2
⑤ Irregular scoop in the Phase 2 floors
⑥ Foundation packing for Phase 3
⑦ SE wall of the temple, Phase 3–6
⑧ Altar of phases 3–6
⑨ Threshold of Phase 3
⑩ Threshold of Phase 4
⬛ Modern period

[152] The south-east wall of the temple
The Phase 3 rebuilding is visible in the SE wall of the temple: the Phase 1/2 wall can most clearly be seen to the west (left side) of the altar, at the bottom. It is separated from the Phase 3 wall in this area by a packing of hard mortar used as foundation material. At both the west and east end, the original south wall was retained in the rebuild. Both the Phase 1/2 altar and the Phase 3 southern altar are shown, separated by our modern plasterwork which underpins the latter.

[153] Phase 3 bench in the north-east corner
The Phase 3 bench was built in the same position as the Phase 2 benches, but did not abut the high bench. Dimensions: 80x276 cm. Height: 30 cm.

[154] Impressions in the plaster of the high bench
On the north half of the high bench (towards bottom of picture) a lip of plaster formed two sides of a rectangle measuring at least 24x19 cm. Aligned with this impression on the southern half of the bench was a second plaster lip, 22 cm long. Between these two, and set further back, was a short 9 cm plaster line.

[155] Door threshold
The depressions in the Phase 3 threshold were perhaps where wooden planks or sections of palm trunks had been laid across to provide a more durable entrance. Note fragment of original plaster adhering to left side of doorway.

[156] Square plinth (side and top)
The plinth, underpinned by a modern breeze block, was slightly tapered, measuring 70 cm square at the bottom, reduced to 60 cm at the top. In the centre of the top was a raised area, 36x50 cm, with a ridge of plaster. Dimensions at base: 70x70 cm. Height at time of construction: 74 cm.

[157] External street surface and stone bases of Phase 3
The spread of mortar and plaster material in Phase 3 represented the only discernible surface within the continual build-up of sand in the street outside the temple. The Phase 1/2 stone bases were retained in Phase 3, presumably after being raised in height.

a

[158] Phase 4 bench
The stone superstructure of the Phase 4 bench was built directly on top of the plastered surface of its Phase 3 predecessor (demarcated in the detailed photograph by the white horizontal line which represents the top of the Phase 3 bench). The Phase 4 bench was originally constructed of a surround of large stone with a core of smaller stones and rendered with a gypsum plaster. Much of the core was accidentally removed by the previous excavators and was subsequently filled in again with sand.

b

Gypsum plaster from the bench, or possibly the wall, had collapsed on to the top of floor 4. With part of the core of the bench stripped away, the Phase 3 gypsum plaster, protected by the construction of the bench, has become visible on the rear wall.

a

[159] House 206 and door-jamb insertion
House 206 was wedged between the back wall of the temple and House 207 to the west. The doorway at the rear of the house was constructed by inserting masonry for one of the jambs into the rear wall of the temple.

b

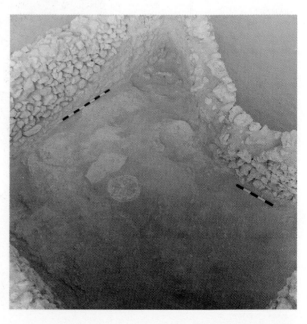

[160] Phase 4 Storeroom
During Phase 4, plastered depressions were found in the floors at the back of the storeroom. Plastered depressions V, X and Z, set into floor 5, are clearly visible within the storeroom. Door is on right-hand side.

DESCRIPTION OF FLOORS (BOTTOM TO TOP)

FLOOR	DESCRIPTION OF FLOORS (BOTTOM TO TOP)	CONTEXTS
1	Limited to NW and central area of the temple. Patchy, compacted floor of plaster and sand with several laminations. Ashy around the altars. The floor contains more plaster in Area 220.	Area 200: 1587, 1596 / Area 220: 1583
2	A patch of floor traced around the back of the central column. Compacted plaster with sand.	Area 200: 1581, 1582
3	Limited to central area and to a short stretch along south wall. Floor lenses of buff plaster and sand with concentrations of ash around altars. Along the south wall was a second area of ash and scorched earth.	Area 200: 1541, 1542, H13:009, H13:010
4	Several laminations of plaster and sand. This surface was fragmentary. In Area 220, patches of plaster were noted above a deposit of levelling debris (1550).	Area 200: 1529, 1539
5	Limited to an area around the altar on the south wall and to the western end of the temple. Laminations of compact plaster and sand.	Area 200: 1505, 1508, 1510, 1528, 1538 / Area 220: 1503

Phase 4 floors

KEY	CONTEXT	PHASE	FLOOR	DIAM.	TOP HEIGHT	BOTTOM HEIGHT
A	1586	4	1	0.58	11.75	11.70
B	1594	4	1	0.40	11.79	11.72
C	1595	4	1	0.56	11.79	11.70
D	1592	4	1	0.50	11.87	11.77
E	1593	4	1	0.26	11.85	11.80
F	1588	4	1		11.83	11.60
G	1585	4	2	0.56	11.82	11.78
H	H13:011	4	3	0.74		
I	H13:007	4	3	0.33		
J	1543	4	3	0.70	11.84	11.66
K	1584	4	3	0.50	11.87	11.80
L	1589	4	3	0.50	11.87	11.81
M	1590	4	3	0.52	11.86	11.80
N	1591	4	3	0.58	11.88	11.71
O	1549	4	3		11.91	11.74
P	1520	4	5	0.57	12.00	11.92
Q	1521	4	5	0.37	12.04	11.93
R	1522	4	5	0.35	12.05	12.01
S	1534	4	5	0.37	11.95	11.88
T	1535	4	5	0.67	11.91	11.83
U	1540	4	5	0.40	11.88	11.83
V	1544	4	5	0.48	11.87	11.83
W	1545	4	5	0.44	11.87	11.77
X	1546	4	5	0.48	11.86	11.79
Y	1547	4	5	0.38	11.85	11.76
Z	1548	4	5	0.44	11.83	11.79

Phase 4 depressions and cuts

KEY	OBJECT NO.	PHASE	FLOOR	HEIGHT	DESCRIPTION
1	1596.01	4	1	11.69	Sealing
2	1596.03	4	1	11.64	Sealing
3	1541.01	4	3	11.91	Fragment of pottery stem
4	1542.01	4	3	11.88	Sealing
5	1542.02	4	3	11.89	Sealing
6	1539.01	4	4	11.96	Sealing
7	1529.02	4	4	11.67	Copper tube
8	1529.03	4	4	11.97	Fragment of steatite vessel

Phase 4 finds in situ

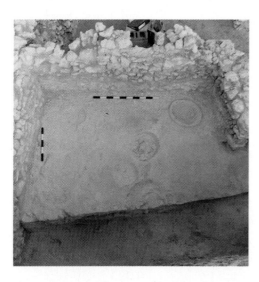

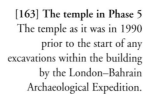

[162] **Plastered depressions in the south-west corner**
Plastered circular depressions were also present in the SW corner of the temple throughout the Phase 4 floor levels. In this photograph, the walls of the additional room (Area 221) constructed in Phase 5 have not yet been removed by excavation.

[163] **The temple in Phase 5**
The temple as it was in 1990 prior to the start of any excavations within the building by the London–Bahrain Archaeological Expedition.

[164] **The temple viewed from the south-west**
The new storeroom (Area 221) can be seen in the right-hand (SE) corner of the temple. The internal wall stands very low in comparison with its neighbours, but this may have been an accident of archaeological excavation. The line of the Phase 5 buttress is visible along the length of the SE wall of the temple.

[165] **The two altars**
By Phase 5, internal floor levels had risen so much that the altar tables were barely above the floor level. To the side of both altars can be seen patches of burnt material, the remains of whatever was burnt on them. The abutment between the central column and the Phase 5 stone skirt is clearly visible.

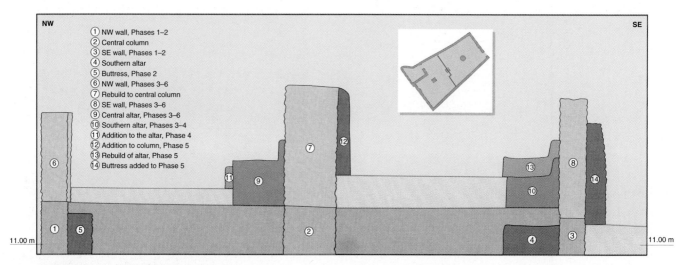

① NW wall, Phases 1–2
② Central column
③ SE wall, Phases 1–2
④ Southern altar
⑤ Buttress, Phase 2
⑥ NW wall, Phases 3–6
⑦ Rebuild to central column
⑧ SE wall, Phases 3–6
⑨ Central altar, Phases 3–6
⑩ Southern altar, Phases 3–4
⑪ Addition to the altar, Phase 4
⑫ Addition to column, Phase 5
⑬ Rebuild of altar, Phase 5
⑭ Buttress added to Phase 5

NW

SE

11.00 m

11.00 m

[166] **Schematic section through the temple**
The reconstructed section shows the relative heights of the superimposed alterations to the temple through Phases 1–5.

ceratohyal	hyomandibular	hypophal	opercular	cervical vetebra	abdominal vertebra	caudal veterbra	centrum	acanthotrich	otolith	cranial frag	tooth	fin spine	Total
				1									1
10	3	6											72
													5
43			30										380
1			1										29
							8						8
							1						1
													1
						4							4
						1	13						14
16	1	1	3						1				99
				3	1		4						8
14			3						4		2	15	216
						63	125						190
						1248							1248
	24						385	28		5152	13	2205	7811
84	**28**	**7**	**37**	**4**	**1**	**1316**	**536**	**28**	**5**	**5152**	**15**	**2220**	**10087**

[37] Fish remains by taxon and skeletal element

production of cereals. Although often tolerated in some populations, and not noxious, these weed seeds would normally be eliminated in the last stages of crop processing (Hillman 1981). Date-stone fragments, generally as common in the pre-temple levels of Test Pit 1 as elsewhere at Saar, were scarce in the sample which contained relatively abundant barley remains (1511/1512).

The plant samples from Test Pit 1 do not, of course, resolve all questions about plant material from Saar, but they do afford a glimpse of the kind of assemblages one would expect if preservation conditions were better, and show how important it is to continue sampling, especially in search of rapidly-sealed deposits, which could add substantially to our understanding of plant food production and diet on Bahrain in the second millennium BC.

Faunal Remains

Mammal and bird bones from the temple and the pre-temple levels of Test Pit 1 reflect in general the species which have already been found and studied from other contexts (Dobney and Jaques 1994). Some further identifications, mainly of fish, have been made (by Brian Irving), and some general comments can be assembled. Preservation of the bone was variable, but generally better

for material from the pre-temple levels: that from the temple itself had apparently suffered somewhat from trampling and reworking.

Fish

In all, 10,087 fragments of fish bone were recorded, of which 2,276 could be identified to family [37], using mainly bi-symmetrically paired cranial elements.

The assemblage of fish families from both the temple and the levels below it is broadly comparable with that reported from Qala'at al-Bahrain (Uerpmann *et al.* 1994). The latter assemblage lacked Mullidae, Haemulidae and Siganidae, which have been identified in the temple excavations at Saar, but were very rare. All are common in fish markets in Bahrain today, and *Siganus* (rabbitfish, Arabic *safi*) is in fact the most popular of the smaller fishes, commanding a high price. The other present-day favourite, *Epinephelus*, (grouper, Arabic *hammour*), which is even more expensive, is probably represented among the Serranidae from Saar, as it was at Qala'at al-Bahrain (*ibid.* 1994, 447). Other rare finds, not so far identified from Qala'at al-Bahrain were *Tylosaurus*, *Pomacanthus* (both sold today, but not popular) and *Rachycentron*.

Cartilaginous fish were represented in the Saar assemblage only by a single eroded shark vertebra fragment. Such fish do not survive well, though a few more were found at Qala'at al-Bahrain (Uerpmann *et al.* 1994, 446). Also present there, but not found in the temple assemblages, were catfish (*Arius thalassinus*), which again do not preserve well (*ibid.*). Parrotfish (family: Scaridae), often used as a cheap substitute for grouper today, is absent from both assemblages, though a few teeth have been found in another context at Saar. Another marine commodity very popular in the Gulf in modern times is shrimp, but no part of this creature would be expected to survive in the archaeological record.

Fish remains from Qala'at al-Bahrain were hand-collected rather than sieved, resulting in a smaller overall number of bones (4,227), but the total which could be identified at least to family was slightly greater (2,900) (Uerpmann *et al.* 1994). In some cases smaller sizes could be reconstructed for the Saar fish: 20–95 cm was the standard length for Serranidae, as opposed to a minimum of 30–40 at Qala'at al-Bahrain, and 10–50 cm standard length for Lethrinidae, rather than 20–25. These differences might well be due to the difference in recovery procedures. Clupeidae and Engraulidae (sardines and anchovies) which were assumed to be absent at Qala'at al-Bahrain on account of a lack of sieving procedures (Uerpmann *et al.* 1994, 452), were not found at Saar either.

Bones from a public building alone are obviously inadequate as a basis for a reconstruction of the ancient economy, and a couple of general observations must suffice for the present. The fish families represented in the temple excavations frequent a variety of habitats, so it is not possible at this stage to draw conclusions about fishing practices. The presence of large copper fish-hooks in the houses at Saar suggests, however, that deep-water fishing was done in addition, presumably, to netting and trapping. Large, static traps in shallow water (Arabic *hadrah*) are used today to catch fish going back out to sea with the ebb of the tide, as well as moveable wire traps. At Qala'at al-Bahrain it was possible to identify several of the Sparids as adult specimens of *Argyrops spinifer*, and some of the Scombrids as *Thunnus* sp., which frequent deep open water (Uerpmann *et al.* 1994, 449–50), but such identifications have not proved possible with the temple assemblages at Saar.

The four most important fish families from the Qala'at al-Bahrain excavations, Serranidae, Lethrinidae, Sparidae and Carangidae were also among the most common found in the temple excavations at Saar, with the difference that the Serranidae were not predominant, and Sphyrenidae outnumbered both them and the Carangids.

Distribution of fish remains

The number of identified fish fragments and the limited exposure of pre-temple levels in Test Pit 1 mean that no significant variations of families from one phase to another can be ascertained. Some of the highest concentrations of fish bone, however, do come from the pre-temple levels: 1,651 from the Phase 0.1 context 1533, for example. It should become possible to determine whether or not this is unusually high for domestic contexts at Saar when studies of more contexts have been completed.

For the temple itself, the less comprehensive excavation of the lower floors as opposed to the upper ones means no significant changes in quantities of fish through the lifetime of the building can be reconstructed with any certainty. Two observations can be made, however, about spatial distribution. Firstly, there is no concentration of identifiable fish remains in the storerooms. A certain amount of fish debris was incorporated in the fabric of some Phase 3 floors of Area 220, particularly the primary floor, 1750, while the corresponding level of Area 200 (1764) was clean. However, since the bones were actually mixed into the plaster floor, this probably means simply that less care was taken over preparing material to floor the storeroom than the main chamber. In Phase 5, rubble collapse in the new storeroom, Area 221, contained a few bones, but the general indications are that the storerooms were not full of fish. Secondly, there was a persistent concentration of fish bones on floors at the west end of the main chamber, immediately south of the storeroom (Area 220). If fish were being stored anywhere, presumably in a dried or salted condition, this is where they were kept. Or perhaps the sweepings from the central part of the chamber around the altars merely tended to accumulate in this far corner.

There were ashy patches with burnt fish remains around the altars, and some fragments of bones actually on the southern altar. They could not be identified even to family, but surely support the assumption that fish was being burnt on the altars as sacrificial offering. There is no corresponding occurrence of burning or animal debris for the benches at the north corner of the main chamber.

Mammal and bird remains

Small quantities of sheep/goat and cattle remains were found in both the temple and pre-temple deposits. None were burnt, and there is no convincing evidence that they were regular components of sacrificial offerings. Some sheep/goat ribs have knife marks close to the prox-imal articulation. Worthy of special remark are three tooth fragments of a female dugong (*Dugong dugon*) [77], a left proximal metacarpal of Arabian oryx (*Oryx leucoryx*) [78 & 79], two carpals of a dolphin (Delphinidae) which had acquired a high polish on the lateral and medial surfaces [80], and the left mandible of a mongoose [81]. This spec-imen was considered to belong to spotted mongoose (*Herpestes auropuntatus*), and it now seems probable that another specimen from Saar, previously published as Indian grey mongoose (*Herpestes Edwardsi*, Dobney and Jaques 1994, 116 & Fig. 16) should also be identified as spotted mongoose (Hans-Peter Uerpmann, personal communication). All these species are also found at Qala'at al-Bahrain (Uerpmann *et al.* 1994).

A complete femur of a cormorant (*Phalacrocorax nigrogularis*) was identified and a tarsometatarsus distal fragment of houbara bustard (*Chlamydotis undulata*) [82]. Most of the bird bones identified so far from Qala'at al-Bahrain were cormorant, perhaps caught accidentally in fishing nets (Uerpmann and Uerpmann 1994, 419). Houbara bustard has not yet, as far as we are aware, been reported from a comparable archaeological assemblage in the Gulf.

Molluscs

The marine and freshwater molluscs from the temple and from the small samples in Test Pit 1, which incorporate some of the temple floors as well as pre-temple deposits, are described here. New information on the use of shell in the temple as well as insights into the local marine and freshwater environments are presented.

Shells are found all over the surface of Saar, representing the discarded remains of shellfish that were part of the local diet in the early second millennium BC. Species that were eaten then included marine bivalves such as the venus clam (*Marcia* sp.) and pearl oyster (*Pinctada* sp.) with smaller numbers of marine snails such as Siratus sp. and conch (*Strombus* sp.). Domestic rubbish accu-mulated inside the houses and in the open areas at the back of them so that over time large numbers

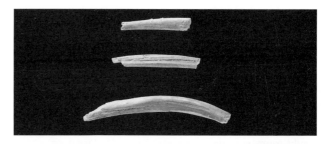

[77] Incisor tooth fragments of dugong (*Dugong dugon*). Largest 4.0 cm long.

[78] Proximal metacarpus fragment of Arabian Oryx (*Oryx leucoryx*). Scale 1:2

[79] Proximal metacarpus fragment of Arabian Oryx (*Oryx leucoryx*) showing dorsal surface.

[80] Two carpals of Dolphin (*Delphinidae*) showing highly polished surfaces. Scale 1:1

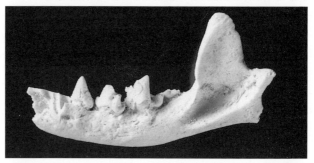

[81] Mandible of spotted mongoose (*Herpestes auropunctatus*). Scale 2:1

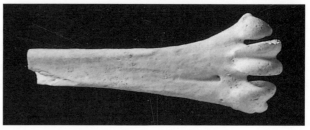

[82] Distal fragment tarsometatarsus of Houbara bustard (*Chlamydotis undulata*). Scale 2:1

of shells were incorporated into the archaeological layers. At the end of the 1993 season of excavation over 19,000 individual shells had been recovered and counted (Glover 1995).

Relative to the houses in the settlement the temple contains much less shell and there are also fewer species. Small, inedible, freshwater molluscs, on the other hand, are relatively more abundant compared to other areas of Saar. Thus, the distribution and abundance of species in the temple is not typical of the site as a whole. Below the temple, however, in Test Pit 1, the archaeological layers contain edible molluscs which are similar to those from the domestic houses. The basal layers have only a few edible species. Instead there are many small intertidal marine, freshwater and estuarine snails.

Methods

Shell was recovered from the deposit in four ways. Some larger fragments and whole shells were collected by hand during excavation and other shell fragments and smaller whole shells taken from the sieves. Hand collected and sieved shell were combined in each context. Small whole shells were also recovered from the whole earth samples by the flotation (Nesbitt 1993) and also from dry-sieving. The floated samples provided a different range of species compared to the dry-sieved and hand-collected samples which have added new evidence of local freshwater environments.

To determine the abundance of the different species a minimum number count was made for all taxa. In the case of gastropods all whole shells and largely intact shells were counted as one; the remaining fragments were sorted into different elements, including the aperture, body and apex and the largest figure taken as the number of individuals combined with the count of whole shells. Bivalves were sorted into left and right valves and the higher taken as the total number. The minimum number of individuals is based on the highest number of left or right examples of paired elements identified. Although Minimum Number counts have been widely used in archaeological study of animal remains they can be distorted by the sampling procedure (Glinsky 1995). This is particularly true when only a small number of samples is used to describe a larger feature. At Saar the extensive excavation of the temple means that this is less of a problem than at excavations where only a small number of samples have been taken. Nonetheless, the numbers of individual shells are only an approximation of the true figures.

SPECIES	HABITAT
Gastropoda	
Trochidae (trochus)	
Priotrochus kotschyi (Philippi 1849)	intertidal boulders
Turbinidae (turban shell)	
Lunella coronatus (Grnelin 1791)	intertidal boulders
Potamidae	
Cerithidea cingulata (Gmelin, 1791)	intertidal sand and mud
Planaxidae	
Planaxis sulcatus (Born 1788)	upper intertidal
Cerithiidae	
Clypeomorus bifasciata (Sowerby 1855)	intertidal
Rhinoclavis sp.	
Cerithium scabridum (Philippi 1848)	
Muricidae	
Siratus kuesterianus	
(Taperone-Canefri 1875)	intertidal
Thaididae (dog whelk)	
Cronia konkanensis (Melvill 1893)	intertidal boulders
Columbellidae	
Mitrella blanda (Sowerby 1844)	intertidal sand and mud
Bivalvia	
Glycymerididae (dog cockle)	
Glycymeris pectunculus (Melvill 1897)	shallow water and sand
Pteriidae (pearl oyster)	
Pinctada radiata (Leach 1814)	sub-tidal
Pectinidae (scallop)	
Chlamys ruschenbergerii (Tryon 1870)	sub-tidal
Spondylidae (spiny oyster)	
Spondylus cf. exilis (Sowerby 1895)	shallow sub-tidal
Veneridae (venus clam)	
Amiantis umbonella (Lamarck 1818)	intertidal, shallow water and sands
Marcia cf. flammea (Gmelin 1791)	
Circenita callipyga (Born 1778)	
Callista florida (Larnarck 1818)	
Freshwater species	
Thiaridae	
Melanoides tuberculata (Muller 1774)	freshwater & estuarine
Hydrobiidae	
Paludestrina sp.	freshwater
cf. *P. glaucovirens* (Melvill and Ponsonby 1896)	
Lymnaeidae	
Lymnea natalensis (Krauss 1848)	freshwater
Planorbidae	
Gyraulus piscinarum (Bourguignat 1852)	freshwater
Allopeas gracilis	terrestial

[83] Molluscan species from the temple and from pre-temple deposits in Test Pit 1

The Temple

Twenty-three species were found in the temple deposits, all of which were also found elsewhere in the site. The species from the temple are listed with their Linnaean and common names and habitats [83].

Pearl oyster (*Pinctada radiata*) live in shallow water up to 20–30 m in depth on gravel where they are attached by

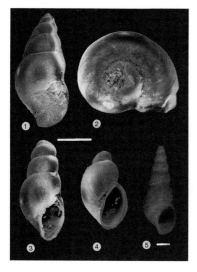

[84] **Small freshwater and terrestrial species**
1 *Paludestrina* cf. *glaucovirens*
2 *Gyraulus piscinarum*
3 *Allopeas gracilis*
4 *Lymnea natalensis*
5 *Melanoides tuberculata*
(Scales: 1 mm)

a byssus or cluster of 'threads' to stones and boulders. They are abundant around Bahrain where the warm, clear, nutrient-rich water provides the optimal conditions for growth. *Pinctada* was extensively fished up until recently. Although there are two species of *Pinctada* in the Arabian Gulf, *Pinctada radiata* is generally the more common species at present and the evidence from Saar suggests that this was true in the past as well.

Clams at Saar include *Marcia* cf. *flammea*, *Amiantis umbonella* and *Circenita callipyga*. These are intertidal to shallow sub-tidal species which live just below the surface of the sand or mud and feed by filtering food through their gills. They are common on the shore and easily collected for food. The species at Saar are all found in Bahrain at present particularly in the sheltered tidal flats such as those near Hidd.

Only two edible snail species are found in the temple: the small top shell Lunella coronatus and the spiny muricid snail *Siratus kuesterianus*. *Lunella* lives intertidally on mixed sand and boulder shores where it grazes on algae and Siratus is a predatory snail in intertidal and shallow sub-tidal water attacking a range of molluscan prey including pearl oyster. These species are still relatively common on Bahrain and like the clams are an easily collected food. The remainder of species in the temple are small inedible marine gastropods and freshwater species which can be useful indicators of prehistoric environments [205]. The freshwater species *Lymnea natalensis*, *Gyraulus piscinarum* and *Paludestrina* cf. *glaucovirens* are described for the first time from an archaeological context in the Arabian Peninsula.

The small, freshwater, thiarid snail *Melanoides tuberculata* occurs throughout the Indo-Pacific region in both

freshwater and partially saline habitats. In Bahrain it is abundant in irrigation ditches, springs and along muddy tidal channels such as Tubli Bay. The other freshwater species, *Gyraulus piscinarum*, *Lymnea natalensis*, *Paludestrina* cf. *glaucovirens*, are found in lentic freshwater habitats such as shallow ponds, pools and slow-flowing watercourses, where they live on muddy substrates or freshwater plants. They are not freefloating in the water column. *Lymnea* and *Paludestrina* were found in large numbers in slow-flowing irrigation ditches near springs during a survey in 1994 but *Gyraulus* was not recorded. Small, inedible marine species are also present in the temple. Cerithiidae typically inhabit intertidal rocky or sandy shores; the potamid snail *Cerithidea cingulata* lives on muddy upper to mid intertidal shores and among mangroves, and *Mitrella blanda* is found on intertidal sandy mud. The top shell *Priotrochus kotschyi* lives on boulders in the upper intertidal, and is very common throughout the Arabian Gulf.

A clear distinction exists between the molluscan fauna of the temple Phases 1–6 and the pre-temple building and associated layers of Phase 0 [85 & 86]. In the temple phases there are only a few shells of the larger edible species such as clam and pearl oyster. In contrast, edible species are much more abundant in the pre-temple phases, which supports other evidence that there were domestic houses here before the temple was built. Area 200, the main room of the temple, has the greatest diversity of species, but it is also the largest area sampled. On the whole, the numbers of shell are low in all the temple phases. Area 220 has relatively less shell than Area 200. The distribution and abundance of shells indicate that

[85] **Distribution of mollusca (MNI) from dry-sieved contexts**

PHASE	Melanoides	Marcia	Amiantis	Pinctada	Siratus	Glycymeris	Chlamys	Circenita	Priotrochus	Lunella	Spondylus	Total
4	96	41	15	18	2	1	2	1	0	1	0	177
3	267	28	23	25	1	1	0	0	1	0	1	347
2	97	9	2	2	2	0	0	0	0	0	0	112
1	31	4	1	1	1	0	0	0	0	0	0	38
6	0	1	1	0	0	0	0	0	0	0	0	2
5	56	20	4	6	2	0	0	0	0	1	0	89
4	7	0	0	0	0	0	0	0	0	0	0	7
3	18	5	1	2	0	0	0	0	0	0	0	26
2	0	0	0	1	0	0	0	0	0	0	0	1
1	1	1	0	1	0	0	0	0	0	0	0	3
0.4	165	69	22	8	1	0	0	0	0	1	0	266
0.2	0	215	23	31	32	0	0	0	0	12	0	313
0.1	3	15	1	2	0	0	0	0	0	6	0	27

▨ Pre-temple   ▨ Temple, Area 200   □ Temple, Area 220

[86] Distribution of mollusca (MNI) from flotation samples

Context	Phase	Floor	Melanoides	Lymnea	Paludestrina	Gyraulus	Allopeas	creithiids	Cerithidea	Mitrella	Planaxis	Marcia	Amiantis	Pinctada	Spondylus	Circenita	Lunella	Siratus	Priotrochus	Cronia	Weight of shell fraction (gm)	total MNI
H13:010	4	3	9	4	-	-	-	-	-	-	-	-	-	-	-	-	-	-	-	-	0.9	13
H13:024	1		235	300	10	60	-	-	-	-	-	1	-	1	-	-	-	-	-	-	n/a	607
H13:027	0	4	195	265	14	93	-	5	3	-	-	2	-	1	-	-	-	-	-	-	34.4	578
H13:028	0	4	15	45	3	30	-	-	-	-	-	1	-	-	-	-	-	-	-	-	1.7	93
1512	0	2	30	4	1	3	-	10	1	1	-	12	1	2	-	-	3	1	1	-	84.8	70
1516	0	2	30	3	3	5	-	16	2	1	1	27	2	-	1	-	-	-	1	-	25.9	92
1531	0	2	30	8	-	5	-	8	1	-	-	-	-	-	-	-	-	-	1	-	2.3	52
1533	0	1	35	4	-	2	-	20	-	1	-	2	2	-	-	-	-	-	1	-	19.3	67
1536	0	1	45	5	-	-	1	30	2	3	-	1	-	3	-	-	-	-	-	-	n/a	90
K16:049			15	-	-	-	-	1	-	-	-	-	2	-	-	1	-	-	-	-	9.8	19
K16:008			25	1	-	-	-	1	-	-	1	-	30	-	65	-	1	-	-	1	1	560.6	126
K16:051			16	21	4	2	-	-	-	-	1	-	-	-	-	-	-	-	-	-	-	2.2	44
K16:026			130	-	12	9	1	10	-	-	-	-	-	-	-	-	-	-	-	-	-	69.4	162
K16:053			115	8	6	7	4	-	-	-	-	3	1	2	-	-	-	-	-	-	-	18.4	146
K16:029			120	10	15	9	4	1	-	1	-	2	1	-	-	-	-	-	-	-	-	21.3	163

House 51   Pre-temple   Temple

there are somewhat higher numbers of freshwater shell such as *Melanoides* in Phases 1–3 compared to Phases 4–6. This data is suggestive of a more intensive use of water in the earlier phases

Sources of the shell in the temple

Edible shells may have found their way into the temple in a number of ways. Perhaps they were deliberate offerings in temple rituals. At present there is no evidence for this although it has been suggested that fish might have been used in temple ritual. Indeed, the very low numbers of edible shell suggest that it is unlikely that they were regularly brought to the temple as part of the ritual or as food. Additionally, there are no concentrations of shell around the altars or other features in the temple. However, shells deposited in Bronze Age burials in other areas of the Arabian Gulf indicate that shell sometimes had a symbolic significance. The evidence so far is limited to funerary deposits and often to more decorative species (Vogt & Franke-Vogt, 1987). It is much more likely that shell was unintentionally brought into the temple, probably during rebuilding and alteration of the structure. Undoubtedly shells were common all over the ancient settlement, just as they are on the surface of the site at present. Earth fill brought into the temple during rebuilding, of which there were several phases, must have contained varying amounts of shell.

Small freshwater species are relatively more abundant in the temple compared to other buildings at Saar [87]. The snail *Melanoides* is found in sieved deposits and flotation samples of all phases. *Lymnea* sp. and *Gyraulus* sp. are found in large numbers in flotation samples from Phases 1–2 of the temple. The flotation data shows that although

all these freshwater species occur in other parts of the site, the temple has unusually high concentrations of them. Not only are there more freshwater shells but their proportional abundance differs from other parts of the site. In the temple there are proportionately more *Lymnea* and *Gyraulus* compared to House 51 or the pre-temple Phase 0 layers. *Lymnea* is particularly abundant in the temple. *Melanoides* on the other hand is relatively more abundant in House 51 and in pre-temple deposits. *Lymnea* and *Gyraulus* are typical of freshwater springs or slow-flowing streams while *Melanoides* has a wider environmental tolerance, living in both fresh and slightly saline water.

Generally, *Lymnea* and *Paludestrina* shells found in the flotation samples are immature, less than 5 mm in length. It is probable that adult animals have not survived intact in the archaeological deposit. The shells are extremely fragile and were either crushed when the water was used or over the course of time in the deposit. A few fragments of shell of larger individuals survive in the flotation samples in support of this explanation.

How did freshwater snails get into the temple? Were they accidentally scooped up when water was collected from a spring or water channel? Were they collected as dead shells in mud from freshwater stream channels? There are several possible explanations. Mud, which is one of the possible constituents of plaster, would contain the dead shells of freshwater molluscs and, coincidentally, live animals may have been incorporated while the mud was collected. No analytical evidence is available yet for the composition of the plaster used at Saar but differences in colour suggest that different types of materials were used to prepare plaster. Mud may also have been used in

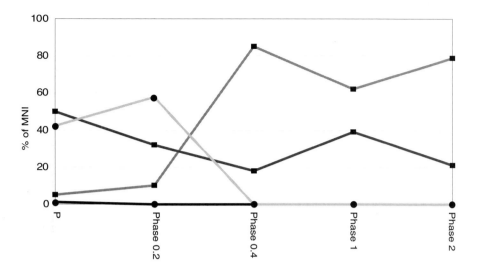
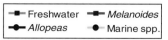

[87] Distribution (%) of fresh-water and marine molluscs and *Melanoides tuberculata*

levelling and raising floors although this has yet to be confirmed by soil micromorphology. Lambrick (1979) has suggested that much of the freshwater species at Harappa are derived from riverine soils brought in to either raise the site further above the flood-plain or simply to level floors after flood damage. Unlike the Indus valley, alluvial soils are absent in Bahrain, but the abundance of freshwater species in the site does suggest that there were several freshwater streams or channels nearby, including perhaps irrigation channels.

Water must also have been used in the mixing of the plaster constituents for the floors and walls and other installations and it is likely that freshwater snails were accidentally included. Indeed, this is likely to be the main source of freshwater snails in the deposit. Archaeological evidence shows that the temple was more carefully maintained than any other building at Saar. The altars, for example, have many layers of plaster renewal and the fine laminated stratigraphy of the floors indicates that they were frequently resurfaced and smoothed with fresh plaster. In other areas of Saar freshwater snails are also abundant in plastered floors and basins. For example, a plastered floor at the rear of House 56 contained large numbers of *Melanoides*. Water may have been important in rituals in the temple or for washing.

A third possibility is that snails were attached to freshwater vegetation which was brought to the site, perhaps as fodder or floor covering. At present, there is no corroborative evidence from either the plant remains or soil micromorphology, and it is difficult to envisage why freshwater plants should have been particularly common in the temple. Palm comprises the majority of phytoliths discovered in the analysis of soil micromorphology. It is

improbable that freshwater snails would be attached to palm leaves unless they were lying in water for some time.

The discovery of a well in the settlement during the 1995 season shows that springs and water courses were not the only source of water at Saar. Flotation samples from the well contained freshwater molluscs, predominantly *Melanoides tuberculata*, with small numbers of *Lymnea* sp., *Gyraulus* sp. and *Paludestrina* sp. There was also a single specimen of the terrestrial species *Allopeas gracilis* and of the small marine snail *Clypeomorus bifasciata*. However, at present, stratigraphic evidence does not show whether *Melanoides* and the other freshwater species were living in the well, or whether they are derived from the fill after abandonment of the well. The relative abundance of species is comparable to that found in many of the houses. Freshwater snails might possibly survive in a well provided that there was sufficient light for some freshwater vegetation to grow.

The temple is unique at Saar in having a particularly high proportion of *Lymnea* sp. and *Gyraulus* sp. compared to *Melanoides* sp. It is difficult to interpret this data on the present evidence. In particular there is little information on the modern ecology of these species in Bahrain. However, the data might indicate different sources of freshwater were used. Further research is planned to examine questions relating to the use of water within the settlement.

Test Pit 1

Test Pit 1 provides evidence for the layers beneath the temple down to bedrock (Phases 0.4–0.1) as well as samples from the temple floors themselves (Phases 1–5). The layers just below the temple (Phase 0.4) are generally similar in species abundance to the temple itself. There are fewer edible species and more freshwater species, although one deposit has rather more edible species (H13:25). On present evidence it is thought that Phase 0.4 is associated with the construction of the earliest temple rather than with pre-temple buildings.

There are no flotation samples from Phase 0.3, which contains a pre-temple building. The Phase 0.2 layers contain hearths and building debris. In this phase freshwater species decline markedly although they are still present in small numbers. Edible species increase here, particularly the small venus clams. The range of species of edible mollusc from Phase 0.2 and the relatively high abundance of *Melanoides* relative to other freshwater species compares closely with that of domestic houses in other areas of Saar. Phase 0.1 is dominated by small, non-edible marine, estuarine and freshwater species. A single terrestrial species, *Allopeas gracilis*, also occurs in Phase 0.1. This species is associated with cultivated fields or gardens. Typically the deposit contains mainly the marine family Cerithiidae with a few *Melanoides* and one or two shells of edible species. Cerithiids are commonly found in most areas of Saar accidentally taken to the site in beach sand or attached to other shells. The shell in Phase 0.1 is probably anthropogenic, associated with the first occupation of the site.

Summary

Analysis of the marine and freshwater shells have added to the extensive database of bio-archaeological information from Saar. The temple has an unusual distribution of mollusc species that differs from the domestic houses. The absence of edible species, for example, implies a different function for the temple but, unfortunately, does not provide further evidence which might help discriminate between a ritual or other use of the building. Comparison with modern fauna provides evidence that the marine environment of Saar was similar to that today. Thus, the common species in the site include the subtotal pearl oyster, clams from sheltered inter-tidal sand flats and inter-tidal marine snails such as *Siratus* and *Lunella*. All these species are still found in Bahrain.

The large numbers of freshwater shells in the temple provide evidence for a more extensive use of water compared to other areas of the site. Many of the shells may have been mixed with plaster, which was frequently renewed in the temple. Also, water was probably used for washing, perhaps in rituals and, although less likely, may have been carried in attached to freshwater vegetation.

The layers below the temple in Test Pit 1 show that domestic occupation preceded the temple, but the samples are too small to say much of that early period. But marine resources such as fish and shellfish were an important part in this early phase. At the base of Test Pit 1, edible species and artefacts are rare, but there are numbers of inter-tidal cerithiids and some *Melanoides*. The shell in these two basal layers is probably to be associated with the earliest human activity on the site.

Chapter 7.
The Temple: An Overview

The Saar temple is a unique construction, with no close parallels, but the architecture of the building, as well as the internal fittings and the objects found within, all suggest that it had a specialized function as a temple within the settlement.

The ancient inhabitants of Saar clearly considered the building to be special: they placed it at the heart of the settlement, on the highest spot, at the junction of the town's two major streets. The surrounding landscape is essentially flat and low-lying, apart from the long ridge on which the mound field developed, so the temple, on its modest elevation, must have been visible for quite some distance, perhaps even from the sea to the east. They emphasized its importance by projecting the facade into the street beyond the line of adjacent buildings. Furthermore, the temple is substantially larger than neighbouring houses, has a very different ground plan, and there are distinctions in the range and quantity of objects discovered inside.

Excavated religious structures rarely contain many finds: if such a building is abandoned by the people who used it, they tend to remove any sacred objects; if it is attacked and destroyed, then cult items are prized as plunder. What we did find, however, supports some differentiation from the ordinary houses round about. The pottery repertoire on the whole mirrors that of the houses, but the lack of ground-stone tools (only 3 from the temple) is in marked contrast to their ubiquity in domestic contexts: some 850 ground-stone tools have now been recorded from 30 fully excavated buildings and associated areas. The temple also contained far less shell material than other buildings and very few of the large edible shells so common elsewhere.

The general shape of the temple is architecturally chaotic. What is striking is the apparent lack of regularity: the main walls do not run parallel to one another, the buttresses on the walls, assumed to be supports for the roof beams, do not align well with their respective central

columns, and the looping wall of the NW corner almost fails to connect again with the main back wall of the temple. Some of this may be ascribed to poor surveying and building technique, but the predominant impression is that the temple was a building which was fitted awkwardly into the available space, sandwiched between adjacent houses. We do not, of course, have full evidence for the actual street pattern around the temple during Phase 1, when the temple was first constructed, as later buildings now obscure it. However, where we have investigated earlier buildings elsewhere in the settlement, we have noted that the original street pattern seems to be preserved through subsequent phases of rebuilding.

There is certainly an external coherence to the building, with the long walls running parallel to those of adjacent houses to create neat alleyways on either side, but this is at the expense of internal symmetry. This is unusual, as religious buildings so often assume a formalized, standard plan, as can be seen from prehistoric 'Ubaid temples, for example, and indeed from mosques and churches. But at Saar the actual form the building took was less important, perhaps because it was to serve a local cult, with no long history of monumental architecture to dictate its shape and style.

Internally, too, there is a lack of architectural standardization: round and square columns exist side-by-side. The round column is sited nearest the entrance, maybe visible from the street. Perhaps this earned it more complex architectural treatment than the square columns further in, which may have been half shrouded in gloom and less visible [211].

One further anomaly of the overall plan requires comment: the looping section of wall in the NW corner. The loop was an original feature of the temple, located in an area used at least partly as a storeroom, and thus probably roofed, however lightly. The only explanation that we can think of, is that it was necessary to build out the temple wall here to accommodate access to the roof, perhaps via a wooden ladder. But this is entirely speculative.

Thus the location and plan of the building, and the artefact distribution within it, shows that it is not a house, not even a superior one like House 53, further down Main Street. By process of elimination, the choice of function can be narrowed down to a building of major public, administrative or cultic significance, categories which need not be mutually exclusive. More detailed analysis of all artefact classes, and of the location and nature of the internal fittings, combined with the micro-morphological study, all help us to refine this analysis.

The concentration of plastered depressions observed in the floors at the back, western part of the temple, together with relatively unclean and poorly-swept floors, suggested at the time of excavation that this was the utilitarian end of the temple, where foodstuffs and incoming offerings

[88] A seated god
This detail from a seal found at Saar shows a horned god sitting on a stool and drinking through a long straw. The single scored line under his feet may represent a raised dais (P19:01:10).

were stored, presumably for later use in the temple rituals. This interpretation receives support from the micromor-phological analysis, which revealed a complete lack of microscopic residues in the depressions. The suggested explanation for this is that such depressions must have been covered by something, most likely a pot.

The function of the western end as a storage area is supported also by the other finds, notably broken seal impressions, presumably discarded when the containers they sealed were opened. Examination of the sealing backs has shown that pottery jars and other containers such as boxes were broached, even if not stored, in the temple. Fishbone, too, was noted as being concentrated at this western end of the temple.

The separate room in the NW corner (Area 220) was also thought to have been a storage area. Here were more plastered depressions. The contents of the storeroom are noteworthy on two counts: a relatively large proportion of the bitumen fragments found in the temple came from this room, and it was the only part of the temple where sherds of large storage-jars were found. Preliminary analysis of the bitumen suggests it was imported from Khuzestan in western Iran, and raises the interesting and neglected question of trade between Dilmun and Susa (Potts 1990a, 226). The storeroom had a door, as is shown by the series of door-sockets that were found, and it can be suggested that it provided a more secure area than the main room for the storage of valuable goods or cultic paraphernalia. Some of the broken sealings may, indeed, have been door sealings from this room.

The principal focus of ceremony within the temple appears to have been the group of installations in the NE corner. This area received preferential treatment: the floor was kept very clean; some surfaces may have been covered with matting; and it was here that the fragments of crimson-painted plaster were found.

The high bench was the only internal fitting to survive intact the demolition of Phase 2, and subsequent recon-struction of the temple in Phase 3, so it must have been carefully protected during this process. It seems to have been an immutable part of the temple furnishings. Obviously it was important not in itself, but because of whatever sat on top, the only traces of which were frag-mentary indentations in the plaster, suggesting that one or more objects with rectangular bases had been posi-tioned there.

It is known from texts that, in the cities of Southern Babylonia contemporary with Saar, statues of gods in

[89] Symbols of worship
Standards and altars such as these are commonly depicted on
Dilmun seals as objects of veneration.

human form, and cultic symbols, were placed inside the
temples (Postgate 1992, 117). The statues could be made
of precious materials and lavishly decorated and, though
for obvious reasons none have been found in position,
they were apparently set on a brick dais raised above the
level of the temple floor.

The iconography of cultic scenes on Dilmun seals
borrows much from their Babylonian counterparts. In
both traditions gods appear in human form, wearing
similar dress, with a horned helmet, and sometimes seated
on a raised dais [88]. That similar cultic scenes appear on
both seal groups suggests at least some shared cultic practices and it seems a reasonable assumption that in the Saar
temple the high bench in the NE corner was in fact an
emplacement for the statues, or perhaps cultic symbols, of
whatever deities were worshipped within.

The altars were a second focus of cultic activity. The
two altars present from Phase 3 onwards appear to have
served similar functions: material was being burnt on
them, as evidenced by the presence of ash both on top
and dumped at the side, and of fragments of burnt fish
bone. There were tentative indications that aromatics
were also consumed. A standard may have been set into
the floor next to the southern altar. Why two similar
altars were required is not known, but there are many
possible explanations: perhaps the level of offerings and
rituals grew to the extent that one altar alone was insufficient; or perhaps it became necessary for a second deity to
have a dedicated altar.

The curious shape of the altar backs requires further
comment, and again the seals provide the best parallels. A
fairly common theme on Dilmun seals is of men with
hands raised (i.e. worshipping) before a pole on top of
which is set a crescent symbol. Sometimes these so-called
standards are placed on top of a stylized podium or altar.
In at least one case, the crescent is rendered in stylized

fashion within a rectangle [89]. Sometimes within the
crescent is a second symbol usually interpreted as a sun
burst. Here then, on the Dilmun seals contemporary with
the temple, there is clear evidence that men worshipped
before symbols which, on very good analogy with
Babylonian religion, appear to represent the crescent of
the moon and the orb of the sun, and thus the deities
associated with them. It seems possible, therefore, that a
moon god was worshipped in the Saar temple [212]. To
the Babylonians, the crescent horns of the moon god Sin
also appear to be linked with cows (Postgate 1992, 132),
so the same secondary association may have existed at
Saar.

The small size and awkward internal space of the
temple precludes the notion of a large congregation
worshipping inside, and the temple may have been the
exclusive domain of the priests. On the other hand, Saar
was a relatively small community, with an estimated 50-
60 houses, so that it can also be imagined that the temple
was large enough to accommodate the worship of small
groups and individuals. There was, of course, a public
space outside, where, at the intersection of the two main
streets were two, and later five, low stone features. These
were set into the loose sand of the street, without any
associated burnt debris or signs of scorching, suggesting
that they did not fulfil the same function as the internal
altars. If they were indeed offering tables, as we have
suggested on our plans, it was in the sense of being where
individuals placed their private donations and offerings to
the temple. An alternative interpretation is that they were
supports which bore for public display, either permanently or on special occasions, the statues and symbols of
the gods.

The increase in the number of these outdoor features
in Phase 5, coupled with the addition of the second storeroom, might be taken as indications that the temple's
activities were expanding at this time. But did these activities ever spread beyond the ordering of the religious and
ceremonial life of the settlement? There is no real
evidence that the temple was also vital to the administrative life of the settlement, or that it was concerned with
the redistribution of goods on any significant scale. The
presence of broken clay sealings within the temple is
taken as an indication merely that containers were stored
in the temple and that the contents of those containers
were broached for use within the temple. Nor does it
seem that the temple (or indeed the settlement) had any
particular connection with the nearby mound fields.

Obviously, the latter served as the burial ground for the inhabitants of Saar and nearby settlements, but there are no indications that Saar or its temple provided special facilities for mortuary rites. The temple and the settlement did not grow up because of the burial fields, but *vice versa*, and the inhabitants of Saar were not preoccupied either with building tombs or servicing them.

The settlement of Saar should be seen rather as a collection of fairly modest houses, whose inhabitants were engaged primarily in the ordinary pursuits of life, such as fishing, cultivating dates, and a little local trading. At the centre of this settlement was the temple, certainly a small, rather rustic building when compared to that of Barbar, but nevertheless adequate for the spiritual needs of the Saar community. Our evidence also suggests that the temple continued in use after many, but not necessarily all, of the neighbouring buildings had fallen in decay. It

may be imagined that the temple was kept going as long as there was some community, however small, for it to serve, but ultimately it did not escape the gradual decay which, for whatever reason, afflicted the entire settlement and led to its eventual abandonment.

Whether there was a temple at Saar from the very beginning remains a question that cannot be answered definitively. The results of Test Pit 1 show that the settlement had a considerable history prior to the establishment of the temple, and that the earliest deposits in the area are domestic in nature. We can be certain, therefore, that there was *not* an earlier temple on the same site as the later one, nor, as far as we can tell, in the immediate neighbourhood. The construction of a new religious building was therefore an innovation, a reflection of Saar's participation in the growing prosperity that was to be Dilmun's Golden Age.

BIBLIOGRAPHY

AAE: Arabian Archaeology and Epigraphy.

BBVO: Berliner Beiträge zum vorderen Orient.

BTTA: Khalifa, H.A. Al & M. Rice (eds.) 1986: *Bahrain through the Ages: the Archaeology*. Kegan Paul International, London.

JASP: Jutland Archaeological Society Publications. Moesgaard, Aarhus.

JOS: Journal of Oman Studies.

PSAS: Proceedings of the Society for Arabian Studies.

al Nashef, K. 1986. The deities of Dilmun. In: *BTTA* pp. 335–339.

Amiet, P. 1986: Susa and the Dilmun Culture. In: *BTTA* pp. 262–268.

Bellefroid, B. forthcoming: 'An Early Flint Site at Saar, Bahrain'. To appear in *AAE*.

Beyer, D. 1986: Les Sceaux. In: *Calvet & Salles* 1986 pp. 89–103.

Beyer, D. 1989: The Bahrain Seals. In: *Lombard & Kervran 1989* pp. 135–164.

Bibby, T.G. 1970: *Looking for Dilmun*. Penguin, Harmondsworth.

Bibby, T.G. 1973: *Preliminary Survey in East Arabia 1968*. JASP 12.

Bibby, T.G. 1986: "The land of Dilmun is holy...". In: *BTTA* pp. 192–194.

Boardman, S. & Jones, G. 1990: Experiments on the effects of charring on cereal plant components. *Journal of Archaeological Science* 17 pp. 1–11.

Bullock, P., Fedoroff, N., Jongerius, A., Stoops, G. & Tursina, T. 1985: *Handbook for soil thin section description*. Waine Research, Wolverhampton.

Calvet, Y. & J. Gachet (eds.) 1990: *Failaka. Fouilles Françaises 1986–1988*. Travaux de la Maison de l'Orient 18. Lyon.

Calvet, Y. & J.-F. Salles (eds.) 1986: *Failaka. Fouilles Françaises 1984–1985*. Travaux de la Maison de l'Orient 12. Lyon.

Collon, D. 1987: *First impressions: Cylinder seals in the ancient Near East*. British Museum publications. London.

Courty, M.A., Goldberg, P. & Macphail, R.I. 1989: *Soils and micromorphology in archaeology*. Cambridge University Press, Cambridge.

Courty, M.A., Goldberg, P. & Macphail, R.I. 1994: Ancient people – Lifestyles and cultural patterns. In: Wilding, L. & Oleshko, K. (eds.): *Micromorphological indicators of anthropogenic effects on soils*. Symposium of the subcommission B. 15th International conference of Soil Science, Acapulco, Mexico, 1994.

Crawford, H.E.W. 1973. Mesopotamia's invisible exports. *World Archaeology* 5 pp. 232–241.

Crawford, H.E.W. 1991: Seals from the first season's excavations at Saar, Bahrain. *Cambridge Archaeological Journal* 1:2 pp. 255–262.

Crawford, H.E.W. 1993: London–Bahrain Archaeological Expedition: excavations at Saar 1991. *AAE* 4 pp. 1–19.

Dittman R. 1986. Seals, Sealings and Tablets: Thoughts on the Changing Pattern of Administrative Control from the Late Uruk to the Proto-Elamite Period at Susa. In: Finkbeiner, U. & Rollig, W. (eds.) 1986: *Gamdat Nasr. Period or Regional Style?* pp. 332–366. Beihefte zum Tübinger Atlas des Vorderen Orients Reihe B. Weisbaden.

Dobney, K.M. & Jaques, D. 1994: Preliminary report on the animal bones from Saar. *AAE* 5 pp. 106–120.

Doe, Brian 1986: The Barbar Temple: the masonry. In: *BTTA* pp. 186–191.

Doornkamp, J.C., Brunsden, D. & Jones, D.K.C. 1980: *Geology, geomorphology and pedology of Bahrain*. Geo Abstracts Ltd., Norwich.

Duistermaat, K. 1994: *The clay sealings from late Neolithic tell Sabi Abyad*. Leiden University. Unpublished dissertation.

Edens, C. 1988: Archaeology of the Sands and Adjacent Portions of the Sharqiyah. *Journal of Oman Studies Special Report* 3 pp. 113–130.

Englund, R. 1983: Exotic Fruits. In: *Potts 1983* pp. 87–89.

Fahn, A., Werker, E. & Baas, P. 1986. *Wood anatomy and identification of trees and shrubs from Israel and adjacent regions*. Israel Academy of Sciences and Humanities, Jerusalem.

Feriola, P. & Fiandra, E. 1983: Clay sealings from Arslantepe VIA: administration and bureaucracy. In: Frangipane, M. & Palmieri, A. (eds.): Perspectives on Protourbanism in Eastern Anatolia. *Origine* XII, pp. 455–509.

Frankfort, H. 1939: *Cylinder Seals. A Documentary Essay on the Art and Religion of the Ancient Near East*. London.

Frifelt, K. 1986: Burial mounds near Ali excavated by the Danish Expedition. In: *BTTA* pp. 125–134.

Frifelt, K. 1991: *The Island of Umm an-Nar. Vol. 1. Third Millennium Graves*. JASP 26:1.

Frifelt, K. 1995: *The island of Umm an-Nar. Vol. 2. The Third Millennium Settlement*. *JASP* 26: 2.

Frohlich, B. 1983: The Bahrain Burial Mounds. *Dilmun. Journal of the Bahrain Historical and Archaeological Society* 11, pp. 5–9.

Frohlich, B. 1986: The human biological history of the Early Bronze Age population in Bahrain. In: *BTTA* pp. 47–63.

Gé, T., Courty, M.A., Matthews, W. & Wattez, J. 1993: Sedimentary formation processes of occupation surfaces. In: Goldberg, P., Nash, D.T. & Petraglia, M.D. (eds.): *Formation processes in archaeological context*. Monographs in World Archaeology No. 17. Prehistory Press. Madison.

Gelb, I. J., Steinheller, P. & Whiting, R.M. (eds.) 1991: *Earliest land tenure systems in the Near East*. Chicago.

Gibson, McG. (ed.) 1981: *Uch Tepe I. Tell Razuk, Tell Ahmed al-Mughir, Tell Ajamat*. The Chicago–Copenhagen Expedition to the Hamrin. Chicago and Copenhagen.

Glinsky, N. *et al.* 1995: Estimating numbers of whole individuals from collections of body parts; a taphonomic limitation of palaeontologicaly record. *Paleobiology* 20, 2 pp. 245–258.

Glob, P.V. 1954: The Flint Sites of the Bahrain Desert. *Kuml* 1954 pp. 106–115.

Glob, P.V. 1955: The Danish Archaeological Bahrain–Expedition's Second Excavation Campaign. *Kuml* 1955 pp. 178–193.

Glover, E, 1991: The Molluscan fauna from Shimal, Ras al-Khaimah, United Arab Emirates. *Internationale Archéologie 6 Golf-Archaeology* pp. 205–220.

Glover, E. 1995: Molluscan evidence for diet and environment at Saar in the early second millennium BC. *AAE* 6 pp. 157–179.

Glover, E. in press: In: Yule, P. (ed.): *Die Gräberfelder in Damad al Shan (Sultanate Oman): Materialien zu einer Kulturgeschichte*. ABADY. Philipp von Zabern, Mainz.

Groneberg, Brigitte 1992: Le Golfe Arabo-Persique vu depuis Mari. In: J-M. Durand (ed.): *Florilegium marianum. Receuil d' études en l'honneur de Michel Fleury*. Paris.

Groom, N. 1981: *Frankincense and myrrh. A study of the Arabian incense trade*. London, Longman.

Heinz, M. 1994: Die Keramik aus Saar/Bahrain. *Baghdader Mitteilungen* 25 pp. 119–308.

Hillman, G. 1981: Reconstructing crop husbandry practices from charred remains of crops. In: R. Mercer (ed.): *Farming Practice in British Prehistory* pp. 123–162.

Hodgson, J.M. 1976: *Soil Survey field handbook*. (Soil Survey Technical Monograph 5). Harpenden, Soil Survey.

Højgaard, Karen 1986: Dental anthropological investigations on Bahrain. In: *BTTA* pp. 64–72.

Højlund, F. 1987: *Failaka/Dilmun The Second Millennium Settlements, Vol. 2. The Bronze Age Pottery*. JASP 17: 2.

Højlund, F. 1989. The Formation of the Dilmun State and the Amorite Tribes. *PSAS* 19 pp. 45–59.

Højlund, F. 1992: Holy Architecture in Bronze Age Bahrain. Dilmun. *Journal of the Bahrain Historical and Archaeological Society* 15 pp. 73–79.

Højlund, F. 1995: Bitumen-coated basketry in Bahraini burials. *AAE* 6 pp. 100–102.

Højlund, F. & Andersen, F.H. 1994: *Qala'at al-Bahrain I The Northern City Wall and the Islamic Fortress*. JASP 30: 1.

Hurley, W.M. 1979: *Prehistoric cordage. Identification of impressions on pottery*. Aldine manuals on Archaeology 3. Washington.

Ibrahim, M. 1982: *Excavations of the Arab Expedition at Sar el-Jisr, Bahrain*. Ministry of Information, Bahrain.

Kandil, H. n.d.: *Report on the excavations at Saar*. Unpublished manuscript in Arabic, National Museum of Bahrain.

Kapel, H. 1967: *Atlas of the Stone-Age Cultures of Qatar*, Reports of the Danish Archaeological Expedition to the Arabian Gulf 1. *JASP* 6.

Killick, R.G. *et al.* 1991: London–Bahrain Archaeological Expedition: 1990 excavations at Saar. *AAE* 2 pp. 107–137.

Kjærum, P. 1980: Seals of "Dilmun-Type" from Failaka, Kuwait. *PSAS* 10 pp. 45–53.

Kjærum, P. 1983: *Failaka/Dilmun. The Second Millennium Settlements Vol.1, The Stamp and Cylinder Seals*. Plates and Catalogue Descriptions. *JASP* 17: 1.

Kjærum, P. 1986: The Dilmun Seals as evidence of long distance relations in the early second millennium BC. In: *BTTA* pp. 269–277.

Konishi, M. A. 1994: *Ain Umm es-Sujur, An interim report 1993/4*. Center for Asian Area Studies, Rikkyo University, Japan.

Kramer, C. 1979: An archaeological view of a contemporary Kurdish village: domestic architecture, household size, and wealth. In: Kramer, C. (ed.): *Ethnoarchaeology. Implications for ethnography for archaeology*. New York, Columbia University Press.

Kramer, S. N. 1963: Dilmun: quest for Paradise. *Antiquity* 37 pp. 111–115.

Lambrick, H.T. 1979: The Indus flood plain and the Indus Civilization. In: G. Possehi (ed.): *Ancient Cities of the Indus*. Vikas.

Larsen, C.E. 1983: *Life and Land Use on the Bahrain Islands. The Geoarchaeology of an Ancient Society*. Prehistoric Archeology and Ecology Series. University of Chicago Press.

Leemans, W.F. 1960: *Foreign Trade in the Old Babylonian Period*. Studia et Documenta ad Iura Orientis Antiqui Pertinentia 6. Leiden.

Limbrey, S: 1975. *Soil science and archaeology*. Academic Press, London.

Lombard, P. & M. Kervran (eds.) 1989: *Bahrain National Museum Archaeological Collections. Vol. I*. Ministry of Information, Bahrain.

Mackay, E.J.H., Harding, G.L., & Petrie, F. 1929: *Bahrain and Hamamieh*. Publications of the British School of Archaeology in Egypt Vol. 47.

Martin, Harriet P. 1988: *Fara: A Reconstruction of the Ancient Mesopotamian City of Shuruppak*. Chris Martin & Associates, Birmingham.

Martin, H. P. & Matthews, R. J. 1993: Seals and sealings. In: Anthony Green (ed.): *The 6G Ash-Tip and its contents: cultic and administrative discard from the temple?* pp. 23–81. Abu Salabikh Excavations Vol. 4. London.

Masry, Abdullah H. 1974: *Prehistory in Northeastern Arabia: The Problem of Interregional Interaction*. Ph.D. Dissertation 1973, Dept. of Anthropology, University of Chicago, Illinois. Coconut Grove, Miami Florida, Field Research Projects.

Matthews, R. J. 1991: Fragments of officialdom from Fara. Iraq 53 pp. 1–15.

Matthews, R. J. 1993: *Cities, seals and writing: Archaic seal impressions from Jemdet Nasr and Ur*. Gebr. Mann Verlag, Berlin.

Matthews, W. 1992: *The micromorphology of occupational sequences and the use of space in a Sumerian city*. Unpublished Ph.D. thesis, University of Cambridge.

Matthews, W.1994: Micromorphological characterization and interpretation of occupational deposits and microstratigraphic sequences at Abu Salabikh, Iraq. In: Barham, T., Bates, M. & Macphail, R.J. (eds): *Archaeological sediments and soils: analysis, interpretation and management*. Archetype Books, London.

Matthews, W., and Postgate, J.N, with Payne S., Charles, M.P. & Dobney, K. 1994: The imprint of living in a Mesopotamian city: questions and answers. In: Luff, R. & Rowley-Conwy, P. (eds.): *Whither environmental archaeology?* Oxbow Monographs 38. Oxford.

McAdams, H. *et al.* 1977: Saudi Arabian Archaeological Reconnaissance 1976. The Preliminary Report on the First Phase of the Comprehensive Archaeological Survey Program. *Atlal* 1 pp. 21–40.

McNicoll, A. n.d.: *Archaeological Investigations in Bahrain 1973–4*. Unpublished Manuscript for Bahrain Department of Antiquities.

McNicoll, A. & M. Roaf 1975: *Archaeological Investigations in Bahrain 1973–1975*. Unpublished manuscript.

Mitchell, T.C. 1986: Indus and Gulf type seals from Ur. In: *BTTA* pp. 278–285.

Moon, J.A. & Killick, R.G. 1995: A Dilmun Residence on Bahrain. In: Finkbeiner, U., Dittmann, R. & Hauptmann, H.: *Beiträge zur Kulturgeschichte Vorderasiens*. Festschrift R.M. Boehmer pp. 413–438. Von Zabern, Mainz.

Moorey, P.R.S. 1994: *Ancient Mesopotamian materials and industries*. Clarendon Press, Oxford.

Mortensen, P. 1971: On the date of the temple at Barbar. *Artibus Asiae* 33:4 pp. 299–302.

Mortensen, P. 1986: The Barbar Temple: its chronology and foreign relations reconsidered. In: *BTTA* pp. 178–185.

Mughal, M.R. 1983: *The Dilmun Burial Complex at Sar. The 1980–82 Excavations in Bahrain*. Ministry of Information, Bahrain.

Nesbitt, M. 1993: Archaeobotanical evidence for early Dilmun diet at Saar, Bahrain. *AAE* 4 pp. 20–47.

Nielsen, K. 1986: *Incense in ancient Israel*. Leiden, E.J. Brill.

Nissen, H.J. 1977: Aspects of the development of early cylinder seals. In: Gibson, M. & Biggs, R. (eds.) *Seals and Sealings in the Ancient Near East*, pp. 15–23. Bibliotheca Mesopotamica VI. Undena Publications, Malibu.

Nissen, H.J. 1985: Ortsnamen in den archäischen Texten aus Uruk. *Orientalia* 54 pp. 226–233.

Norton, J. 1986: *Building with earth. A handbook*. Salvo Print, Leamington Spa.

Parr, P. *et al.* 1978: Preliminary Report on the Second Phase of the Northern Province Survey 1397/1977. *Atlal* 2 pp. 29–50.

Pic, M. 1990: Quelques éléments de glyptique. In: *Calvet & Gachet 1990* pp. 125–140.

Piesinger, C.M. 1983: *Legacy of Dilmun: The Roots of Ancient Maritime Trade in Eastern Coastal Arabia in the 4th/3rd Millennium B.C.* Ph.D. dissertation. University of Wisconsin-Madison.

Plenderleith, H.J. 1934: Metals & Metal Technique. In: Woolley, C. L.: *Ur Excavations II: The Royal Cemetery* pp. 284 ff. London & Philadelphia.

Pongratz-Leisten, B. 1988: Keramik der frühdynastischen Zeit aus den Grabungen in Uruk-Warka. *Baghdader Mitteilungen* 19 pp. 177–320.

Popenoe, P. 1973: *The Date Palm*. Miami Field Research Projects.

Porada, E. 1971: Remarks on Seals Found in the Gulf States. *Artibus Asiae* 33:4 pp. 331–338.

Postgate, J. N. & Moon, J. A. 1982: Excavations at Abu Salabikh 1981. *Iraq* 44 pp. 103–136.

Postgate, J. N. 1992: *Early Mesopotamia, Society and Economy at the Dawn of History*. Routledge, London.

Potts, D.T. (ed.) 1983: *Dilmun. New Studies in the Archaeology and Early History of Bahrain*. BBVO 2.

Potts, D.T. (ed.) 1988: *Araby the Blest*. Carsten Niebuhr Institute Publications 7. Copenhagen.

Potts, D.T. 1990a: *The Arabian Gulf in Antiquity, vol. I–II*. Clarendon Press, Oxford.

Potts, D.T. 1990b: *A Prehistoric Mound in the Emirate of Umm al-Qaiwain, U.A.E. Excavations at Tell Abraq in 1989*. Munksgaard, Copenhagen.

Ratnagar, S. 1981: *Encounters. The Westerly Trade of the Harappa Civilization*. Oxford University Press, Delhi.

Reade, J. & R. Burleigh 1978: The Ali Cemetery: Old Excavations, Ivory and Radiocarbon Dating. *JOS* 4 pp. 75–83.

Roaf, M. 1974: Excavations at Al Markh, Bahrain. A fish midden of the fourth millennium B.C. *Paléorient* 2 pp. 499–501.

Roaf, Michael 1976a: *The Work of the British Archaeological Expedition to Bahrain 1976*. Unpublished manuscript in the library of the Bahrain Historical and Archaeological Society library.

Roaf, M. 1976b: Excavations at Al Markh, Bahrain. *PSAS* 6 pp. 144–160.

Rosen, A.M. 1986: *Cities of clay. The geoarchaeology of tels*. University of Chicago Press, Chicago.

Schiffer, M.B. 1987: *Formation processes of the archaeological record*. University of New Mexico Press, Albuquerque.

Smith, G.H. 1978: Two prehistoric sites on Ras Abaruk, Site 4. In: de Cardi, B. (ed.): *Qatar Archaeological Report, excavations 1973* pp. 80–106.

Sollberger, E. & J-R. Kupper 1971: *Inscriptions Royales Sumeriennes et Akkadiennes*. Paris.

Tomlinson, P.B. 1961: *Anatomy of the monocotyledons, II Palmae*. Clarendon Press, Oxford.

Uerpmann, H.-P., Uerpmann, M. & Van Neer, W. 1994: Animal Bones. In: *Højlund and Andersen 1994* pp. 417–454.

van de Mieroop, M. 1992: *Society and Enterprise in Old Babylonian Ur*. BBVO 12. Berlin.

Vine, P. 1993: *Bahrain National Museum*. State of Bahrain, Ministry of Information & Immel Publishing. London.

Vogt, B. & Franke-Vogt, U. 1987: *Shimal 1985/1986: Excavations of the German Archaeological Mission in Ras Al-Khaimah, U.A.E.: A preliminary report*. BBVO 8. Berlin.

Weingarten, J. 1990: The sealing structure of Karahöyük. *Oriens Antiquus* XXIX 1–2 pp. 63–95.

Winton, A.L. *et al.* 1916: *The microscopy of vegetable foods*. New York, John Wiley.

Woodburn, M.A. & Crawford, H.E.W. 1994: London–Bahrain Archaeological Expedition: 1991–2 excavations at Saar. *AAE* 5 pp. 89–105.

Zettler, R. L. 1987: Sealings as artifacts of institutional administration in ancient Mesopotamia. *Journal of Cuneiform Studies* 39 pp. 197–240.

Appendices

1. Notes on the Recording System

For the first two seasons, recording of excavation layers and finds was carried out within a 10 metre grid, oriented north to south and labelled alpha-numerically. The temple lay mostly within squares G13 and H13 (see Killick *et al.* 1991, Fig. 4). Context numbers, from one to infinity, were initially allocated according to grid square and were applied to every discrete 3-dimensional space *within each square,* be it an archaeological layer, a wall or other feature. Thus H13:02 was the second archaeological layer within the 10 m square H13. Object numbers were allotted as sub-divisions of the context, so H13:02:09 would be the 9th object found in context H13:002.

The system is an adaptation of the Wheeler–Kenyon system, commonly used on the vertical excavations of complex tell sites where the staff usually encompass a range of abilities and experience. It provides sufficient sections to keep a reasonably close check on the progress of the excavations (especially with a 5 m grid), but tends to result in fragmentation of the archaeological record. The stratigraphy of adjacent grid squares, dug one after the other, perhaps in different years by different staff, are often impossible to match up accurately.

At Saar, where we have been excavating well-defined buildings horizontally, the system was unsatisfactory. Where a context crossed the main grid line into adjacent 10 m squares, it had to be given as many as three new numbers. This made the recording system cumbersome and prone to error. So, in the third season, we in effect abandoned the grid except as a surveying tool, and switched to a variant of the single-context numbering system widely used within British archaeology. In this system, each archaeological layer, or feature, is given only a single unique number no matter where it goes on the site.

The grid square designation was therefore dropped from the context designation in favour of a single 3 or 4 figure number, e.g. 1589. To avoid duplication, one supervisor used numbers 1500–1599, another 1600–1699, and so on. Objects continued to be numbered according to context number, so 1654:02 would be the second object found in context 1654. There is no difference in meaning, therefore, between numbers of the type '1654' and numbers of the type 'H13:02' encountered in this volume.

Bone fragments from a context were usually given a single number between them, though exceptional pieces, such as groups of articulated bones were sometimes given separate numbers. The same applies to the shells, and small amorphous fragments of copper, bitumen, plaster, and unworked flint or stone. Objects of the same material found together, such as groups of beads or sealing fragments, were sometimes given a single number between them, especially if it seemed likely they might join. The earth taken from a context to be water-sieved was also given an object number. The miscellaneous potsherds found in a context were *not* given an object number, but individual pieces such as whole vessels or sherds with exceptional decoration were.

2: Context List

Notes

Each context is assigned a one-word description such as 'floor' or 'collapse'. These labels are used as an initial filter for the database so that researchers can quickly pull out the most discrete contexts and discard, where appropriate, secondary or contaminated material. However, they serve only as a rough guide to the nature of each context and interpretation is refined by using detailed sheets filled in at the time of excavation.

For the phases of the temple (Phases 1–6), the first number of the phase designation refers to the phase, the second to the floor level within the phase. For the pre-temple phase (Phase 0), the subdivisions are broader and are used to delineate the major phases of activity. Some contexts are phased only to level and not to floor.

CONTEXT	TYPE	AREA	PHASE	DESCRIPTION
1500	COLLAPSE	221	5	Layer of rubble and collapsed plaster
1501	COLLAPSE	220	5	Rubble and plaster wash from wall collapse
1502	FLOOR	220	6.1	Friable, off-white plastery deposit
1503	FLOOR	220	4.5	Patches of very compact off-white plaster flooring
1504	OCCUPATION	200	6.1	Mixed deposit full of fish bone
1505	FLOOR	200	4.5	Plastery floor
1506	FLOOR	221	5.1	Series of plaster floors
1507	FLOOR	200	6.1	Floor laminations
1508	FLOOR	200	4.5	Compact pale yellow/brown gritty sand
1509	FLOOR	200	5.2	Buff-coloured hard plaster floor
1510	FLOOR	200	4.5	Compact plaster floor
1511	SAND	200	3.1	Sand in-fill
1512	LAYER	TP1	0.2	Mortar and sand south of pretemple wall
1513	LAYER	TP1	0.2	Mortar and plaster south of pre-temple wall
1514	FLOOR	221	6.1	Mottled sand with ashy patches
1515	FLOOR	200	5.1	Compact sandy floor with patches of ash around the altars
1516	LAYER	TP1	0.2	Sand and plastered surfaces with hearth
1518	FEATURE	221	5.1	Circular depression
1519	FEATURE	221	5.1	Circular depression
1520	FEATURE	200	4.5	Circular depression
1521	FEATURE	200	4.5	Circular depression
1522	FEATURE	200	4.5	Circular depression
1523	LAYER	TP1	0.2	Mixed material underlying pre-temple wall
1524	FEATURE	200	5.1	Circular depression
1526	FLOOR	200	5.1	Removal of floor 1515
1527	OCCUPATION	TP1	0.2	Occupation debris
1528	FLOOR	200	4.5	Compact, fine sandy plaster floor
1529	FLOOR	200	4.4	Mixed context of floors and sand
1530	FEATURE	TP1	0.2	Animal burrow
1531	FEATURE	TP1	0.2	Small hearth
1532	FLOOR	TP1	0.2	Patch of floor associated with hearth (1531)
1533	OCCUPATION	TP1	0.1	Loose matrix full of fish bone
1534	FEATURE	200	4.5	Circular depression
1535	FEATURE	200	4.5	Circular depression
1536	SAND	TP1	0.1	Sand overlying bedrock
1537	FEATURE	221	5.1	Foundation trench for walls of new storeroom, Area 221
1538	FLOOR	200	4.5	Laminations of floors of fine sand with occupation debris

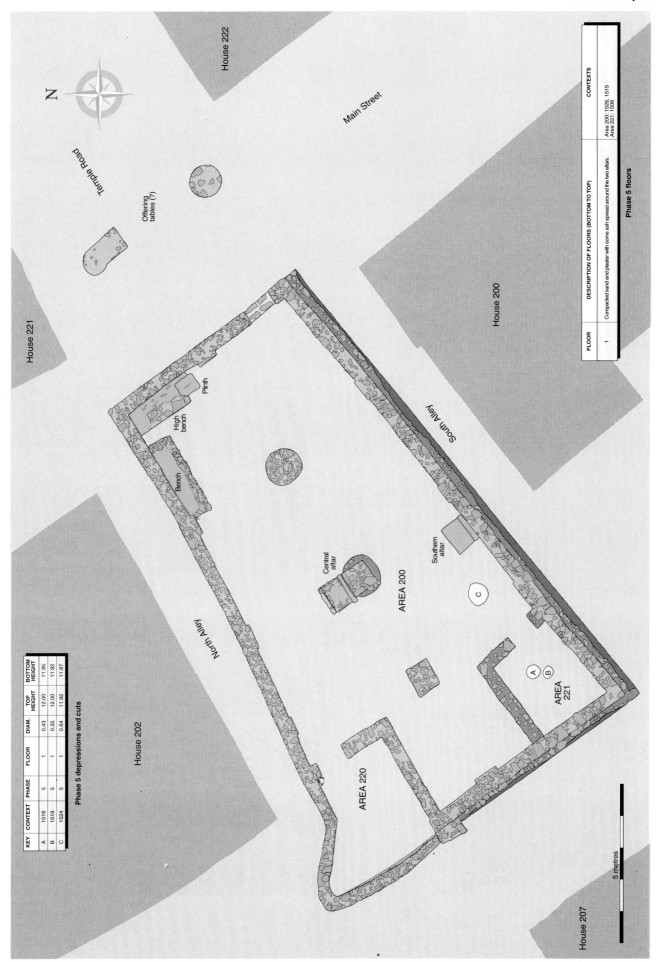

N

House 222

Main Street

Temple Road

Offering tables (?)

House 221

House 200

Plinth

High bench

Bench

South Alley

North Alley

House 202

Central altar

Southern altar

AREA 200

C

AREA 220

A
B

AREA 221

House 207

5 metres

Phase 5 depressions and cuts

KEY	CONTEXT	PHASE	FLOOR	DIAM.	TOP HEIGHT	BOTTOM HEIGHT
A	1518	5	1	0.43	12.00	11.95
B	1519	5	1	0.35	12.00	11.92
C	1524	5	1	0.64	11.92	11.87

Phase 5 floors

FLOOR	DESCRIPTION OF FLOORS (BOTTOM TO TOP)	CONTEXTS
1	Compacted sand and plaster with some ash spread around the two altars.	Area 200: 1526, 1515 Area 221: 1506

[168] The southern altar in Phase 5

[169] The central altar in Phase 5

[170] **Additions to the south-west corner**
The SW corner of the temple appears to have suffered constantly from instability. A final attempt to shore it up was made in Phase 6 when a second buttress was wrapped around the corner (seen here in the foreground).

[171] **Phase 6 of the temple as excavated in 1984**
This photograph shows the highest floor in the temple sequence as excavated by the previous expedition. Three circular pits, possibly vessel depressions, are visible next to the central altar and there is one more in front of the southern altar. The excavators recorded that the pit next to the central column was 28 cm deep, with a diameter of 70 cm.

[172] **South Alley**
The Phase 5 external buttress on the SE wall sloped down towards the back of the temple. This can be seen here where the street level in South Alley has been taken down to the base of the buttress.

[173] **Buttress on south-east corner**
This view of the temple wall next to the entrance shows the skin added in Phase 5 and the corner buttress of Phase 6, both marked by vertical cracks.

[174] **Phase 6 Offering tables**
These five circular stone bases, set at the front of the temple in Phase 6, had diameters of 86–87 cm and survived to a maximum height of 75 cm. To the right (SE), the walls of House 222 can be seen breaking the surface and in section.

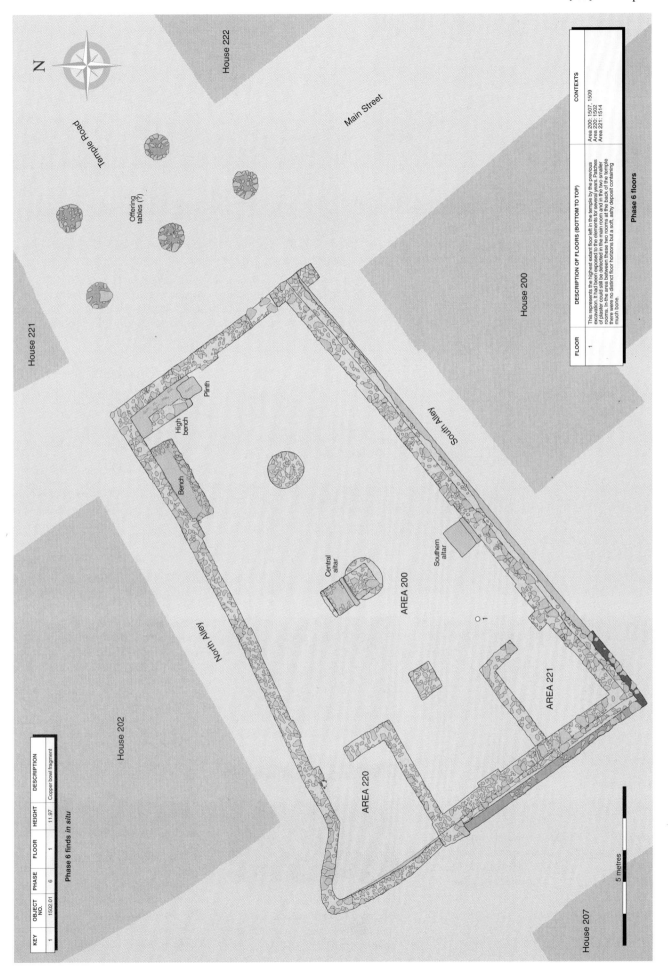

N

House 222

House 221

Temple Road

Offering tables (?)

Main Street

House 202

North Alley

Plinth

High bench

Bench

Central altar

AREA 200

Southern altar

South Alley

AREA 220

AREA 221

House 200

House 207

5 metres

Phase 6 finds *in situ*

KEY	OBJECT NO.	PHASE	FLOOR	HEIGHT	DESCRIPTION
1	1502.01	6	1	11.97	Copper bowl fragment

Phase 6 floors

FLOOR	DESCRIPTION OF FLOORS (BOTTOM TO TOP)	CONTEXTS
1	This represents the highest extant floor left in the temple by the previous excavation. It had been exposed to the elements for several years. Patches of plaster could still be detected in the main room and in the two smaller rooms. In the area between these two rooms at the back of the temple there were no distinct floor horizons but a soft, ashy deposit containing much bone.	Area 200: 1507, 1509 Area 220: 1502 Area 221: 1514

[176] Sand accumulating in Main Street
Throughout the life of the temple, sand accumulated rapidly in the street outside. The Phase 6 stone bases (seen here from the SE, looking up Main Street) sat on top of a sand deposit up to 75 cm deep.

a

[177] Layers in South Alley
In Phase 6 a large dump of plaster was heaped across South Alley, running over the by now abandoned House 200 and up against the temple wall. In places it had a width of 4.20 m, with a maximum depth next to the temple wall of 87 cm.

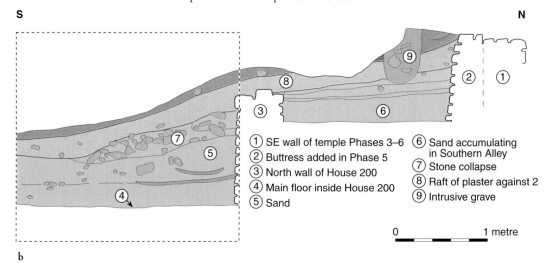

S   N

① SE wall of temple Phases 3–6
② Buttress added in Phase 5
③ North wall of House 200
④ Main floor inside House 200
⑤ Sand
⑥ Sand accumulating in Southern Alley
⑦ Stone collapse
⑧ Raft of plaster against 2
⑨ Intrusive grave

0   1 metre

b

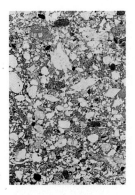

[178] Medium plaster Type 106
Side of southern altar. Thin-section 93.4, Unit 7. Plane polarized light. Frame height: 7.2 mm.

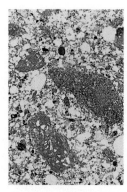

[179] Gritty plaster Type 107
Top of southern altar. Thin-section 93.79, Unit 29. Plane polarized light. Frame height: 7.2 mm.

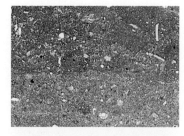

[181] Gypsum plaster Type 108
NE Area 200. Thin-section 93.86, Unit 11. Cross polarized light. Frame width: 7.2 mm.

[180] Fine plaster Type 105
Two layers of plaster lining a depression in Area 200. No microscopic residues between each layer of plaster. Thin-section 93.85. Plane polarized light. Frame width: 7.2 mm.

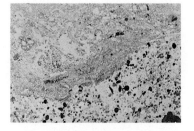

[182] Impression of base
Impression of the bottom of an object in a layer of sand at the side of the southern altar, perhaps from a standard. Overlain and in-filled with layers of burnt date-palm leaflets. Thin-section 93.4, Units 11.1–11.2. Plane polarized light. Frame width: 14.4 mm.

[183] Impression of knife
Impression of a tapering sharp object on the surface of a plaster on top of the southern altar, perhaps from a knife. Overlain and in-filled with a thin layer of silty clay and burnt date-palm fragments, and covered by another layer of plaster. Thin-section 93.84, Units 5–7. Plane polarized light. Frame width: 4.4 mm.

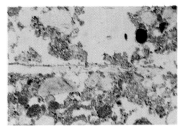

[184] Gramineae in a layer of moist sediments/plaster
At the side of the southern altar. Thin-section 93.4, Unit 8.4. Plane polarized light. Frame width: 7.2 mm.

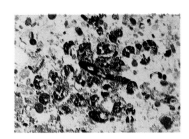

[185] Charred date-palm vascular bundles
Perhaps a fragment of string. Side of the southern altar. Thin-section 93.4, Unit 11.1. Plane polarized light. Frame width: 4.4 mm.

[186] Well-preserved date-palm leaflets
Date-palm leaflets with spherical silica bodies articulated in the plant tissue. Side of the southern altar. Thin-section 93.4, Unit 6.1. Plane polarized light. Frame width: 1.3 mm.

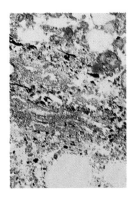

[187] Burnt date-palm leaflet
Fragments between two layers of plaster on top of the southern altar, second series. Thin-section 93.79, Units 19–21. Plane polarized light. Frame height: 1.3 mm.

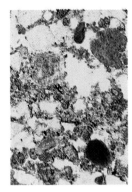

[188] Fragments of bone on top of the southern altar Thin-section 93.79, Unit 26. 1. Plane polarized light. Frame height: 1.3 mm.

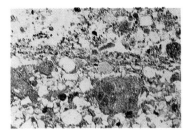

[189] Date-palm matting
Layer of date-palm matting/loose leaflets on top of a plaster floor at the side of the southern altar. Thin-section 93.4, Unit 9.5. Plane polarized light. Frame width: 4.4 mm.

[190] Date-palm ash
Layers of date-palm ash and leaflets. Front of the central altar. Thin-section 93.13, Unit 12. Plane polarized light. Frame width: 2.2 mm.

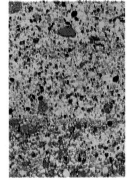

[191] Clean sandy deposits on top of a plaster floor
In the NE of Area 200, with a lens of fine compacted deposits which may have accumulated below the base of a mat or rug. Thin-section 93.86, Units 2–3. Plane polarized light. Frame height: 7.2 mm.

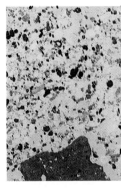

[192] Wind-blown sand and fragment of bedrock
In Test Pit 1 Phase 1. Thin-section 93.1, Unit 1. Plane polarized light. Frame height: 7.2 mm.

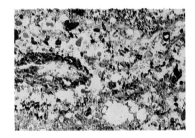

[193] Layer of *in-situ* burning
In Test Pit 1 Phase 0.1. Thin-section 93.2, Unit 1. Plane polarized light. Frame width: 7.2 mm.

[194] Deposits on the top of the southern altar
Ash and scorched clay lenses on top of the altar, evidence for the recurrent burning of material.

[195–201]
Abundance of plant types
Abundance of plant types as a percentage of deposit area in occupation deposits from the southern and central altars, Area 200 NE corner, and Test Pit 1, Phase 0.1.

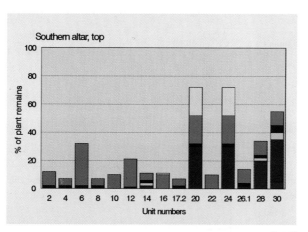

[195]

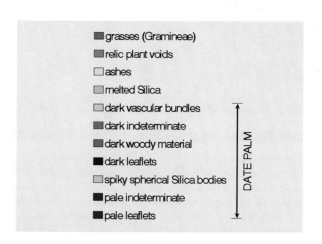

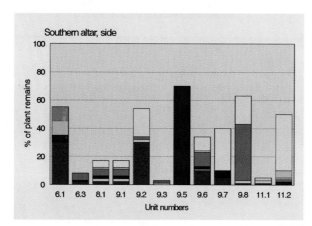

[196]

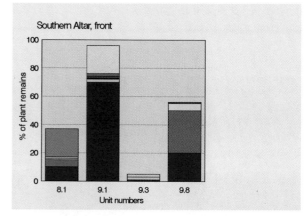

[197]

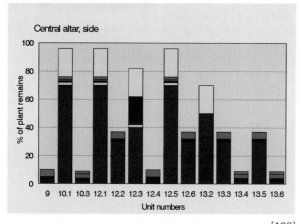

[198]

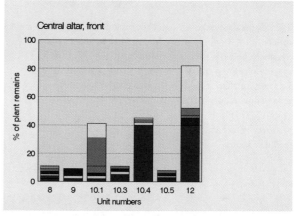

[199]

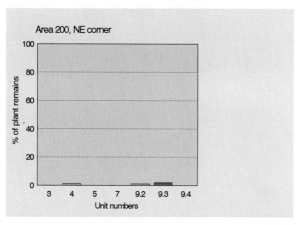

[200]

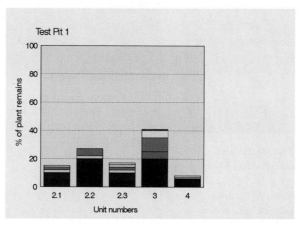

[201]

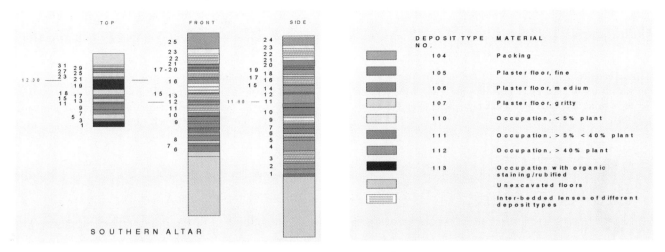

[202] Microstratigraphic columns from sections from the southern and central altars

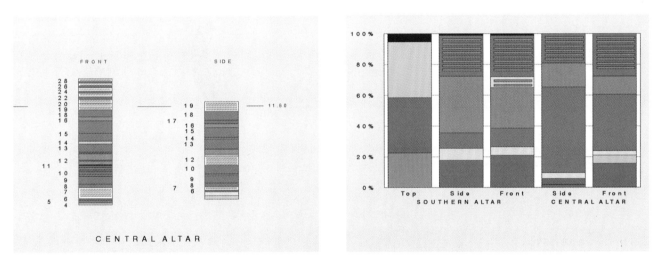

[203] Percentages of deposit types in microstratigraphic sequences from the altars

[204] Floor and occupation deposits running up to the front of the southern altar
A block of flooring was left against the altar so that vertical sections could be sampled.

[205] Ritual activity
On this seal, dating to 3200 BC, a *lugal* (literally, a 'big man') is making an offering in front of an altar with a bull figure on it (after Frankfort 1939, Pl. 3e).

[206] Temple industry
This heavily-drilled seal of similar date shows women at work and was probably used by an official within a temple administration (seal originally in the Erlenmeyer collection).

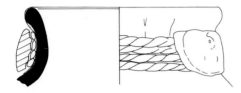

[207] Sealing on neck of jar
The jar was sealed by placing a covering over the mouth, tied around the neck by string. A lump of wet clay was applied over the string and then impressed with a seal. Jar diameter is approx. 17 cm.

 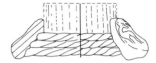

[208] Sealing on reed
Striated indentations on the reverse of an impression indicate that it was attached to a reed peg.

 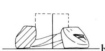 
 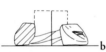 

[127] Peg sealings
Boxes and containers were fastened shut with a wooden peg which was sometimes sealed. Door fastenings too could be made secure in a similar fashion.

[210] Disk-shaped sealing attached to jar

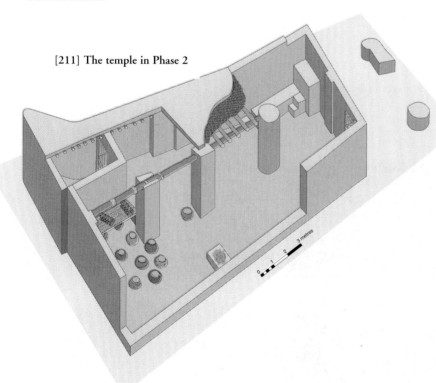

[211] The temple in Phase 2

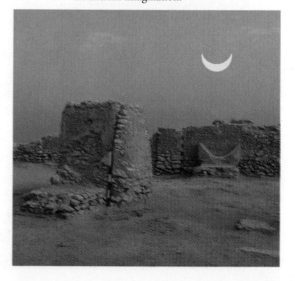

[212] The temple by night
The moon hangs in the sky above the altars. Does this modern imagery reflect an ancient imagination?

CONTEXT	TYPE	AREA	PHASE	DESCRIPTION
1539	FLOOR	200	4.4	Very compact smooth plaster floor
1540	FEATURE	200	4.5	Circular depression
1541	FLOOR	200	4.3	Compacted sandy floor
1542	FLOOR	200	4.3	Very compact plaster floor
1543	PIT	200	4.3	Circular pit
1544	FEATURE	220	4.5	Circular depression
1545	FEATURE	220	4.5	Circular depression
1546	FEATURE	220	4.5	Circular depression
1547	FEATURE	220	4.5	Circular depression
1548	FEATURE	220	4.5	Circular depression
1549	PIT	200	4.3	Linear cut
1550	MAKE-UP	220	4.4	In-filled material between floors
1581	FLOOR	200	4.2	Very compact off-white plaster floor
1582	FLOOR	200	4.2	Patchy floor of compacted sand, silt and ash
1583	FLOOR	220	4.1	Uneven patch of floor
1584	FEATURE	200	4.3	Circular depression
1585	FEATURE	200	4.2	Circular depression
1586	FEATURE	220	4.1	Circular depression
1587	FLOOR	200	4.1	Sandy plaster floor
1588	PIT	200	4.1	Linear cut
1589	FEATURE	200	4.3	Circular depression
1590	FEATURE	200	4.3	Circular depression
1591	FEATURE	200	4.3	Circular depression
1592	FEATURE	200	4.1	Circular depression
1593	FEATURE	200	4.1	Circular depression
1594	FEATURE	200	4.1	Circular depression
1595	FEATURE	200	4.1	Circular depression
1596	FLOOR	200	4.1	Compact mottled plaster and sand floor
1597	FLOOR	220	3.1	Mixed material
1598	FLOOR	220	3.2	Floor lensing of compact sand and plaster
1599	FLOOR	220	3.2	Compact off-white plaster floor
1600	FLOOR	220	3.1	Patches of fine sand and plaster
1601	FEATURE	220	3.2	Door-socket
1602	FEATURE	200	3.2	Circular depression
1603	FEATURE	200	3.2	Circular depression
1604	FLOOR	200	3.2	Very hard floor of sand and plaster
1605	FEATURE	200	3.2	Circular depression
1606	FEATURE	200	3.2	Circular depression
1607	FEATURE	200	3.2	Circular depression
1608	FEATURE	200	3.2	Circular depression
1609	FEATURE	200	3.1	Stone setting
1610	FLOOR	200	3.1	Well-preserved, hard buff-coloured plaster floor
1611	FLOOR	200	3.2	Same as 1604 but richer in fish bone and softer texture
1612	FLOOR	200	3.2	Hard floor, same as 1604
1613	FLOOR	200	3.1	Floor lenses with some sand and ash
1614	FEATURE	220	3.1	Circular depression
1615	FEATURE	220	3.1	Circular depression
1616	FLOOR	220	3.1	Patchy off-white plaster floor
1617	FLOOR	220	3.1	Patchy off-white plaster floor
1618	FLOOR	200	3.1	Compact sand and gypsum with ashy patches
1619	FLOOR	200	3.1	Several floor lenses
1620	MAKE-UP	220	2.1	Compact coarse sand and grit
1652	BENCH	200	4.1	Bench in NE corner

CONTEXT	TYPE	AREA	PHASE	DESCRIPTION
1653	BENCH	200	3.1	Bench in NE corner
1654	PLINTH	200	3.1	Plinth abutting high bench, 1653, in NE corner
1655	COLUMN	200	1.1	Circular column in temple
1656	FEATURE	200	5.1	Circular skin around central column
1657	FEATURE	200	4.1	Additional length added to front of central altar
1658	FEATURE	200	3.1	Central altar
1659	COLUMN	200	1.1	Central column
1660	COLUMN	200	1.1	Square column, SW end
1661	ALTAR	200	1.1	Southern altar
1662	WALL	200	3.1	SE wall, Phases 3-6
1663	WALL	200	5.1	Buttress added to SE wall
1664	WALL	200	6.1	Small buttress on E corner
1665	WALL	200	6.1	Buttress added to SE wall
1666	WALL	200	6.1	Buttress added to SW wall
1667	WALL	200	6.1	Second buttress built against 1665
1668	WALL	200	1.1	SW wall, Phases 3-6
1669	WALL	200	1.1	Irregular loop of wall, NW corner
1670	WALL	200	3.1	NW wall
1671	WALL	200	1.1	NE wall
1672	FEATURE	200	4.1	Threshold of temple entrance
1673	WALL	220	3.1	Wall with doorway into Area 220, Phases 3-6
1674	WALL	220	3.1	SE partition wall between Areas 220 and 200, Phases 3-6
1675	WALL	221	5.1	Partition wall between Areas 221 and 200
1676	WALL	221	5.1	Door-jamb of storeroom, Area 221
1678	FEATURE	200	3.1	Circular depression
1679	FEATURE	200	3.1	Circular depression
1680	FEATURE	200	3.1	Circular depression
1681	PLASTER	200	3.1	Wall plaster
1682	PLASTER	200	3.1	Wall plaster
1683	FEATURE	200	3.1	Bench in NE corner
1684	WALL	221	5.1	Partition wall between Area 200 and storeroom Area 221
1685	FEATURE	220	3.2	Door-socket rebuild
1686	FEATURE	220	3.2	Door-socket rebuild
1687	FEATURE	220	3.1	Door-socket rebuild
1730	BEDROCK	TP1	0.1	Bedrock
1750	MAKE-UP	220	3	Deposit of crushed mortar. Packing for Phase 3 rebuild
1752	FLOOR	220	2.2	Sequence of hard plaster floors
1756	SAND	200	3	Mixed context of sand and occupation material
1763	FLOOR	200	3.1	Series of laminated floors
1764	MAKE-UP	200	3	Deep deposit of sand in-fill
1770	FLOOR	220	1.1	Laminated plaster floors
1772	FLOOR	200	3.1	Area of laminated flooring
1773	FLOOR	200	3.1	Patch of floor at SW end of temple
1774	MAKE-UP	200	3	Mortar packing to support rebuild to SE wall
1775	FEATURE	220	1	Stone pivot wedged with potsherd
1776	FLOOR	220	1.1	Plaster floor
1778	COLLAPSE	200	2.3	Limestone rubble over shelf walls
1779	MAKE-UP	200	3	Small area of compact mortar

CONTEXT	TYPE	AREA	PHASE	DESCRIPTION
1780	MAKE-UP	200	3	Mottled soft sand
1781	FOUNDATION	200	3	Packing for rebuild in NW wall
1782	MAKE-UP	200	3	Packing material for construction of central altar
1783	FEATURE	201	2	Offering table
1784	FEATURE	201	2	Offering table
1785	FLOOR	200	2.3	Mud plaster floor
1810	OCCUPATION	200	2.3	Dump of flooring excavated out in antiquity
1811	PIT	200	2.3	Irregular pit in floor
1812	FEATURE	200	2.2	Circular depression
1813	FEATURE	200	2.2	Circular depression
1814	FEATURE	200	2.2	Circular depression
1815	FEATURE	200	2.2	Circular depression
1816	FEATURE	200	2.2	Circular depression
1817	FEATURE	200	2.2	Circular depression
1818	FEATURE	200	2.2	Circular depression
1819	FEATURE	200	2.2	Circular depression
1820	FEATURE	200	2.2	Circular depression
1821	FLOOR	200	2.2	Compact floor, intact across temple
1822	MAKE-UP	200	3.1	Packing for altar 1661
1823	FEATURE	200	1	Southern altar, Phases 1-2
1824	FEATURE	200	1	Rectangular bench
1825	FEATURE	200	1	Steps to high bench
1826	FEATURE	200	1	Low square bench in NE corner
1827	WALL	200	2.1	Shelf support, NE wall
1828	WALL	200	2.1	Shelf support, SW wall
1830	WALL	200	1	Main NW wall, Phases 1-2
1831	WALL	200	1	Area 220 NE wall, Phases 1-2 (earlier build to 1673)
1832	WALL	200	1	Area 220 SE wall, Phases 1-2 (earlier build to 1674)
1833	WALL	200	1	Main SE wall, Phases 1-2
1834	FEATURE	200	3.1	Door threshold
1835	FEATURE	200	2.1	Door threshold of flat limestone slabs
1836	FEATURE	200	2.1	Door socket
1838	SURFACE	201	3	Street surface of sand, gypsum and stone chippings located outside temple entrance
1843	FLOOR	220	1	3-5 cm of laminated floor
1844	FLOOR	220	1	Series of fine floors overlying the construction horizon of the temple
1874	SAND	201	2.2	Sand in Main Street in front of the temple
1875	FEATURE	201	2.1	Small square feature, perhaps a post support, abutting the front wall of the temple
1896	FLOOR	200	1	Patchy plaster floor
1897	MAKE-UP	200	1	Construction horizon of compact mortar and rubble
1904	FLOOR	200	2.1	Four compacted fine floors
1905	FLOOR	200	2.1	Patchy flooring
1906	FLOOR	200	2.1	2-3 laminated surfaces
1907	FLOOR	200	1.3	Uniform mortary floor
1910	FLOOR	200	1.2	Compacted sand with plaster horizons
1911	FLOOR	200	1.1	Patchy floors
1915	FLOOR	200	1	Intact plastered floor
1916	FEATURE	200	1	Plastered scoop
1918	MAKE-UP	200	1	Construction horizon
1919	MAKE-UP	200	1	Mortary packing for floor
1923	FEATURE	200	1	Circular scoop in floor 1924
1924	OCCUPATION	TP7	0.3	Pre-temple occupation
1928	OCCUPATION	TP7	0.3	Pre-temple occupation
1929	OCCUPATION	TP7	0.3	Pre-temple occupation
1930	OCCUPATION	TP7	0.3	Laminated floors of grey plaster
1932	FEATURE	220	4.1	Door-jamb inserted for House 206
1934	WALL	TP2	0.3	Pre-temple wall, partially re-used
1935	WALL	TP2	0.3	Pre-temple wall
1936	WALL	200	2.2	Buttress to wall 1830
1938	FEATURE	200	3.1	Linear cut
5007	FEATURE	201	6	Offering table outside temple, inner row, north
5008	FEATURE	201	6	Offering table outside temple, outer row, north
5009	FEATURE	201	6	Offering table outside temple, inner row, middle
5010	FEATURE	201	6	Offering table outside temple, outer row, south
5011	FEATURE	201	6	Offering table outside temple, inner row, south
5033	SAND	201	6	Windblown sand in street
H13:000	SAND	200	6	Top layer of windblown sand
H13:005	SAND	200	6	Light grey yellow-brown fine sand with grit and small stone inclusions
H13:006	FLOOR	200	5.2	Several layers of thin plaster floors with lenses of occupation
H13:007	FEATURE	200	4.3	Circular pit in floor
H13:008	FEATURE	200	4.3	Circular pit in floor
H13:009	FLOOR	200	4.3	Layers of plaster with lenses of occupation
H13:010	FLOOR	200	4.3	Ash and plaster to west of altar
H13:011	FEATURE	200	4.3	Circular cut in floor
H13:012	OCCUPATION	200	3.2	Mixed ashy material and plaster lenses
H13:013	FEATURE	200	5.2	Linear cut in front of central altar
H13:014	OCCUPATION	200	3.2	Compact sand with some ash and mortar
H13:015	FEATURE	200	3.1	Southern altar in temple
H13:016	FEATURE	200	3	Plaster depression
H13:017	FEATURE	200	3	Plaster patch
H13:020	MAKE-UP	200	3	Sand in-fill
H13:021	MAKE-UP	200	3	Sand in-fill
H13:022	MAKE-UP	200	3	Sand in-fill
H13:023	FEATURE	200	1	Circular pit
H13:024	MAKE-UP	200	1	Levelling material, mortary
H13:025	MAKE-UP	TP1	0.4	Sand and mortar
H13:026	FEATURE	200	1	Linear plaster feature, possibly foundation for temple wall
H13:027	MAKE-UP	TP1	0.4	Sand and mortar in-fill
H13:028	MAKE-UP	TP1	0.4	Sand
H13:029	MAKE-UP	TP1	0.4	Sand
H13:030	COLLAPSE	TP1	0.3	Rubble patch
H13:031	MAKE-UP	TP1	0.4	Sand and plaster fragments
H13:032	MAKE-UP	TP1	0.4	Sand and mortar
H13:033	MAKE-UP	TP1	0.4	Sand and plaster fragments
H13:034	COLLAPSE	TP1	0.3	Sand and mortar off wall H13:035
H13:035	WALL	TP1	0.3	Pre-temple wall in sounding
H13:036	COLLAPSE	TP1	0.3	Sand and mortar

3: Index of Contexts Arranged by Phase

PHASE 0.1
1533
1536
1730

PHASE 0.2
1512
1513
1516
1523
1527
1530
1531
1532

PHASE 0.3
1924
1928
1929
1930
1934
1935
H13:30
H13:34
H13:35
H13:36

PHASE 0.4
H13:25
H13:27
H13:28
H13:29
H13:31
H13:32
H13:33

PHASE 1
1775
1823
1824
1825
1826
1830
1831
1832
1833
1843
1844
1896
1915
1916
1918
1919
1923
H13:23
H13:24
H13:26
1897

PHASE 1.1
1655
1659
1660
1661
1668
1669
1671
1770
1776
1911

PHASE 1.2
1910

PHASE 1.3
1907

PHASE 2
1783
1784

PHASE 2.1
1620
1827
1828
1835
1836
1875
1904
1905
1906

PHASE 2.2
1752
1812
1813
1814
1815
1816
1817
1818
1819
1820
1821
1874
1936

PHASE 2.3
1778
1785
1810
1811

PHASE 3
1750
1756

1764
1774
1779
1780
1781
1782
1838
H13:16
H13:17
H13:20
H13:21
H13:22

PHASE 3.1
1511
1597
1600
1609
1610
1613
1614
1615
1616
1617
1618
1619
1653
1654
1658
1662
1670
1673
1674
1678
1679
1680
1681
1682
1683
1687
1763
1772
1773
1822
1834
1938
H13:15

PHASE 3.2
1598
1599
1601
1602
1603
1604

1605
1606
1607
1608
1611
1612
1685
1686
H13:12
H13:14

PHASE 4.1
1583
1586
1587
1588
1592
1593
1594
1595
1596
1652
1657
1672
1932

PHASE 4.2
1581
1582
1585

PHASE 4.3
1541
1542
1543
1549
1584
1589
1590
1591
H13:07
H13:08
H13:09
H13:10
H13:11

PHASE 4.4
1529
1539
1550

PHASE 4.5
1503
1505
1508
1510

1520
1521
1522
1528
1534
1535
1538
1540
1545
1546
1547
1548

PHASE 5
1500
1501

PHASE 5.1
1506
1515
1518
1519
1524
1526
1537
1656
1663
1675
1676
1684

PHASE 5.2
1509
H13:06
H13:13

PHASE 6
5007
5008
5009
5010
5011
5033
H13:00
H13:05

PHASE 6.1
1502
1504
1507
1514
1664
1665
1666
1667

4. Catalogue of Finds Arranged by Context

Notes

This is a catalogue of finds from the temple, extracted from the excavation database. Entries for shells and bones have been omitted, unless worked or of individual interest. Flotation and carbon samples are also omitted.

Abbreviations

di.   diameter
sd. di.   strand diameter
sg. di.   string diameter
TP   twist period
SSD   string spin direction

All measurements are in centimetres. Where no measurements are given, none were taken. This applies particularly to fragments of bitumen and corroded copper.
Illustration numbers are given in square brackets.

Area designations

Area 200: the main room of the temple
Area 220: the storeroom in the NW corner
Area 221: the storeroom in the SW corner (Phase 5 onwards)
Area 201: the street immediately outside the temple entrance
Test Pit: for locations see [123]

Catalogue

1500:01 Flint.
1) End-scraper, utilized wide cortical flake. Good-quality, dark brown flint with creamy-white cortex. Sub-rectangular/oval. Prepared striking-platform is scarred/faceted with hinged distal termination. Previous strikes on dorsal face from distal and side. Left edge fairly straight with use-wear. Distal edge has 7 cm of retouch/use-wear from ventral surface. Intact. Length 4.2–3.4 (max., platform to distal), width 4.6, thickness 1.26.
2) Flake. Mottled brown-grey flint with creamy-white cortex at both ends. Sub-rectangular/oval flake. Prepared striking-platform (one strike) with scars on dorsal side of edge, with plunging distal termination. Previous strikes from proximal end: one is hinged. Right edge is uneven, being naturally denticulated due to hinged scar. Left edge is gently concave and has possible use-wear. Its lower distal corner has retouch or use-wear with two chips flaked out from the ventral side. Length: 3.0, width 2.7.
Area 221 Phase 5.

1502:01 Copper bowl. [29]
Fragments of a copper bowl or plate, with bitumen still adhering to the inside. Impression of woven or knitted textile in parts of the corroded surface. Very fragile. Di. of the bowl 7.0. Area 220 Phase 6.1.

1502:02 Copper fragment.
Small oval shaped piece of copper. Badly corroded. Dimensions 1.4x1.0x0.6. Area 220 Phase 6.1.

1504:01 Bitumen fragments.
Tiny, shattered fragment of bitumen, part of a basket-lining. Dimensions of largest fragment 1.5x1.1x0.2. Area 200 Phase 6.1.

1505:01 Bitumen fragments.
Several fragments of bitumen, some with basket impressions. Dimensions of largest 4.6x3.3x1.0. Area 200 Phase 4.5.

1505:03 Copper strip. [34]
With notched end, perhaps a graving tool. Length 2.5. Area 200 Phase 4.5.

1505:04 Bitumen stopper.
Bitumen jar stopper. About half extant. Probably had a flat, circular top, to fit into the mouth of a jar. Di. 5.5. Area 200 Phase 4.5.

1505:05 Painted plaster.
Small piece of painted plaster, one end painted red. Dimensions 3.6x2.0x1.5. Area 200 Phase 4.5.

1505:08 Bitumen sealing.
Bitumen sealing. Irregular, flattish piece of bitumen. One side smooth with a flat surface, the other irregular. On one edge of this side are parallel concave impressions. Dimensions 8.4x4.3x1.1. Area 200 Phase 4.5.

1506:01 Copper fragments.
Two small pieces of copper, one round in shape, the other crescent-shaped. Dimensions 1) 1.1 di. 2) 1.2x0.7x0.4. Area 221 Phase 5.1.

1507:02 Bitumen fragment.
Fragment of bitumen with basket impression on one side. Dimensions 2.0x2.0x0.5. Area 200 Phase 6.1.

1508:03 Clay sealing.
Two small fragments of yellow/green unbaked clay.
1) Small fragment, irregular, unclear string impression on reverse. Dimensions 1.5x0.9x0.6.
2) Obverse: figure in net pattern skirt. To the left he holds a long straw which leads into a pot at his feet. Reverse lost. Segment of edge remains. Dimensions 1.7x1.4x0.6. Area 200 Phase 4.5.

1510:04 Copper fragments.
Two small fragments of badly corroded copper, irregular in shape. Dimensions 1) 1.3x0.8x0.3. 2) 0.3x0.6x0.4. Area 200 Phase 4.5.

1511:01 Copper fragment.
Fragment of badly corroded copper, irregular in shape. Dimensions 1.4x0.8x1.2. Area 200 Phase 3.1.

1512:01 Bitumen fragments.
Large quantity of small fragments of bitumen, all with basket-weave impressions on them. Two larger lumps. Dimensions of lumps 3.5x2.8x2.0, 3.0x3.0x1.5. Test Pit 1 Phase 0.2.

1512:02 Palm wood and dates.
Nineteen carbonized date-stones and one whole date. Three small

pieces of carbonized wood, and one larger piece. Dimensions of larger piece 6.0x3.6x1.0. Test Pit 1 Phase 0.2.

1512:03 Flint.
Cortical flake, possibly from pounder. Possibly utilized as scraper. Oval flake of mottled grey-brown flint with creamy-white/grey cortex. A red flaw on the ventral surface caused the flake to be concave rather than convex. Striking-platform is the cortex of nodule, with previous scars on its left side and a slightly plunging distal termination. Previous strikes on the dorsal surface from the proximal end and the side. The right edge is chipped from possible use-wear on either side of a small pointed nose/tip. Length 2.86, width 3.34, thickness 0.94. Test Pit 1 Phase 0.2.

1512:04 Stone tool. [55]
Pounder/smoother. Light brown quartz. Sub-triangular trapezoid, with sub-rectangular flattish base and rounded apex. One side almost vertical, the other convex. Base and apex are abraded, as well as parts of the concave side and the edges. The flat vertical side is fairly smooth and possibly worn that way. The edges of the base and the surface near the apex are partly scarred. Intact. A compact tool or object possibly used for other purposes. Height 5.5, width 5.0, thickness 4.0. Base 5.0x3.3–4.0. Test Pit 1 Phase 0.2.

1512:05 Stone tool. [56]
Pounder, possibly also smoother. Dark, grey-black, close-grained stone. Sub-cuboid with convex ends. Natural surfaces flat to concave with partial desert varnish. One convex surface, and the edges of the other surfaces are abraded. Pounding concentrated at each end, with partial scarring on the edges. The ends are pentagonal and trapezoid. The latter has an adjoining narrow, smooth, angled surface, which may be from use. Intact. Trapezoid end 5.0–3.6x4.3–3.4 (with/without angle). Pentagonal end 4.3x3.8. Total dimensions 7.1x5.2–4.4x4.7–4.4. Test Pit 1 Phase 0.2.

1512:06 Flint. [60]
Sub-ovoid nodule of mottled brown-grey flint, with rough surface and partial creamy-grey cortex. Several areas of the surface are abraded, particularly the zone of maximum di. One flatter end is deeply scarred, probably due to pounding. Individual scars not easily distinguishable. Dimensions 7.35x5.96x5.40. Largest scar: length 2.4, width 2.36. Test Pit 1 Phase 0.2.

1512:07 Fossil.
Fossilized shell. Test Pit 1 Phase 0.2.

1512:10 Stone tool.
Smoother, possibly also pounder. Utilized fragment of grey, fossiline limestone. Sub-square with one edge pointed near the centre. One flattish face which is partially worn smooth to a dark-grey surface colour. The opposite face is irregular and pitted. The edges are near-vertical and slightly-worn. The pointed edge is narrower, scarred, and partially abraded. This is possibly due to natural causes, coarse retouch or pounding. Length 5.5, width 4.9, thickness 2.0. Test Pit 1 Phase 0.2.

1513:02 Bitumen fragments.
Several crumbling pieces of bitumen with basket impressions, and one possible cloth impression. Dimensions of largest piece 1.2x1.6x0.3. Test Pit 1 Phase 0.2.

1513:03 Flint.
1) Possible bipolar core fragment or punch. Mottled, light brown-grey flint with remnant of creamy, light grey cortex. Scarred striking-platform with slightly concoidal distal fracture and scarred distal end. Previous scars on the dorsal surface from the proximal end. One of these was from the production of a blade-flake. Flake scar: length 0.95, width 0.9. Blade scar: length 2.2, width 0.65. Total length 2.2, width 1.4, thickness 1.0.
2) Pointed, wide flake, possible awl. Slightly mottled, light brown flint. Scarred striking-platform with hinged distal termination. Previous strikes on the dorsal surface from the sides. One strike with the aid of central flaw has created one side of the tip, the other from a probable retouch strike from the ventral surface. Length 1.5, width 2.22, thickness 0.36.
Test Pit 1 Phase 0.2.

1513:05 Dates.
Twelve carbonized date-stones. Test Pit 1 Phase 0.2.

1513:07 Metal ore.
Piece of black/brown iron(?) ore, irregular in shape. Dimensions 3.5x2.8x1.3. Test Pit 1 Phase 0.2.

1514:01 Copper fragment.
Fragment of badly corroded copper, roughly rectangular in shape. Dimensions 3.3x1.8x1.1. Area 221 Phase 6.1.

1516:02 Dates.
Large quantity of carbonized date-stones, with three whole dates. Test Pit 1 Phase 0.2.

1516:03 Copper slag.
Lump of copper or copper slag. Fracture shows a purplish core inside. Very roughly rectangular in shape. Dimensions 2.0x1.5x1.1. Test Pit 1 Phase 0.2.

1516:06 Stone tool.
Possible fragment of smoother/grindstone, or possibly just natural. Sub-rectangular fragment of brown sedimentary stone, possibly coarse mudstone. One flat face has brown smoothed patches on the surface, particularly on a small raised area. The opposite face is flattish, with small, raised, rounded bumps. All edges are near-vertical, with three being fairly straight and the other broken and concave. Due to the nature of the stone it is difficult to see signs of working. Dimensions 8.2x5.7x2.6. Test Pit 1 Phase 0.2.

1516:09 Pearl. [40]
Tiny, irregular, yellowish pearl found in flotation residue. Di. c. 0.15. Not measured as very fragile. Test Pit 1 Phase 0.2.

1516:10 Flint.
Three flakes, and two fragments from flotation residue 1516:07.

1) Broken flake of light brown flint. Broken proximal end, and hinged distal termination. Numerous scars on the dorsal surface, and one edge is very scarred or worn. Length <1.5, width 2.2, thickness 0.4.
2) Semi-circular sliver (broken flake) of brown flint. The convex striking-platform is scarred and worn. The distal end is broken. Dimensions 2.1x0.6x0.4.
3) Elongated chip of brown flint with creamy-white cortex. Dimensions 1.0x0.5x0.3.
4) Small flake of grey flint. Slightly scarred striking-platform and feather distal termination. Length 0.9, width 1.0, thickness 0.3.
5) Small pyramidal chip of grey flint. Dimensions 1.0x0.6x0.3. Test Pit 1 Phase 0.2.

1523:01 Dates.
Over thirty carbonized date-stones. Test Pit 1 Phase 0.2.

1523:02 Bitumen fragment.
Small lump of bitumen possibly a piece of a stopper. One side smooth and domed, the other angular and irregular, and broken off round the edges. Dimensions 3.0x2.7x2.0. Test Pit 1 Phase 0.2.

1523:04 Flint.
1) Retouched blade. [57n] Light brown flint, with creamy-white blotches and red speckles. Focal striking-platform, faceted to one side, and feather distal termination. The distal end is partly broken. The centre of the right edge is roughly bifacially retouched, denticulated, from the ventral surface. There is use-wear on either side along the same edge. The other edge also has retouch/use-wear. Length 3.68, width 2.0, thickness 0.53.
2) Awl. Sub-triangular, irregular flake of grey flint with dark stain (soot?) on dorsal surface. Possibly heat-affected or flawed stone. The irregular tip has been formed by a strike on either side from the ventral surface, and has subsequent retouch or use-wear.
Dimensions 3.0x1.92x0.99.
3) Possible pounder/core fragment or possible punch. Sub-cuboid fragment of grey flint. Possibly heat-affected, as the dorsal is darker than the grey fractured interior.
Dimensions 2.49x1.50x0.95. Test Pit 1 Phase 0.2.

1524:01 Bitumen fragments.
One large lump of bitumen and four tiny pieces, one showing evidence of basket-weave impression. Dimensions of lump 4.0x2.0x1.3. Area 200 Phase 5.1.

1526:01 Bitumen fragments.
Twelve small fragments of bitumen, four showing basket impressions. Dimensions of largest 3.2x3.0x0.4. Area 200 Phase 5.1.

1526:04 Copper fragments.
Two small copper fragments of irregular shape.
Dimensions 1) 1.4x0.8x0.4. 2) 1.5x1.3x0.5. Area 200 Phase 5.1.

1527:01 Bitumen fragments.
Six lumps of bitumen. One large, thick piece, showing possible impressions of wood. Dimensions 8.0x4.4x2.3. Test Pit 1 Phase 0.2.

1527:04 Flint.
Twenty-one fragments in all, some of which can be joined to make 13 artefacts.
1) Exhausted core or core fragment. [57a] Pointed ovoid piece of brown flint with whitish blotches. Single platform. Range of flake scars with feather-hinged terminations. Blade scar: length 1.95, width 0.97. Flake scar: length 1.44, width 1.3. Total length 3.1, width 1.66, thickness 1.50.
2) Scraper. [57i] Thick, chunky flake of brown flint with sooty/heat-affected surface. Raised strike on scarred platform with reworked distal end. All edges retouched. Big strike (accidental?) from the ventral surface has formed a thick, sloping, concave right edge. The flint here is layered and cracking. Other edges except the distal are steeply retouched from the dorsal surface forming a notch (left), a concave edge (top right) and a rounded corner that leads to a straight proximal edge. Length 2.50, width 2.35, thickness 1.1.
3) Awl. [57b] Mottled and blotchy brown-pink flint with worn, thin, dull dark pinky-brown cortex and some thin white patina. A probably naturally-shattered fragment that has been reworked after the patina was formed. Irregular, faceted, cortical striking-platform with irregular, concoidal fracture and hinged distal termination. The tip formed on the right dorsal edge by two side-strikes, both from the ventral surface. The top right strike is small and from near the tip, the lower one is big and wide. The dorsal surface near the tip is scarred and heat cracked. The tip has possible use-wear. Intact. Length 2.4, width 3.3, thickness 1.1.
4) Wide flake possibly utilized as awl. Mottled, brown-pink flint with dark grey flaw or cortex. Focal striking-platform with hinged distal termination at dark flaw. Previous strike on the dorsal surface from the distal end. A small tip (possibly utilized) has been formed on one side by a strike on the proximal edge. The other side on the top of the right edge has either retouch or wear from the dorsal surface. The rest of the right edge is slightly worn. Length 1.75, width 2.3, thickness 0.5.
5) Possible utilized flake or broken awl. Light-brown cherty flint with creamy-white cortex on proximal edge. The striking-platform is plain with an irregular, concoidal fracture and a slightly hinged distal termination. The right edge is broken or reworked. The left and the distal edges are worn, and the left distal tip has been broken off.
Length 1.65, width <1.55, thickness 0.44.
6) Possible utilized flake, possible scraper. [57l] Poor quality, dark grey-brown cherty flint. Brittle, and probably heat-affected. Broken into two adjoining flakes at the dorsal side of the striking-platform. Scarred striking-platform with hinged distal termination. Previous strikes on the dorsal surface from the proximal end (3 hinged). Distal edge has retouch or use-wear from the dorsal surface. Total length 4.1, width 3.38, thickness 0.9.
7) Flake. Broken into two adjoining flakes at the ventral side of the striking-platform. Poor quality, dark brown cherty flint. Brittle and probably heat-affected. Scarred striking-platform with hinged distal termination. The distal surface is potlidding and the lower left corner has two broken edges. Length 3.15, width <3.2, thickness 0.5.
8) Flake or naturally heat-fractured fragment. Broken into two adjoining flakes at the proximal end of the ventral surface. Poor quality dark brown cherty flint with a thin creamy-white cortex. Brittle and probably heat-affected. Prepared scarred striking-platform

and plunging distal termination with cortex. Length 1.5, width 2.3, thickness 1.0.

9) Flake. Broken into two adjoining flakes. Grey banded chert with smooth, almost shiny surfaces. Rough striking-platform, partly scarred, with slightly hinged distal termination. Previous strikes on the dorsal surface from the proximal end. Left edge has thin light grey cortex and two large chips, possibly deliberate denticulated retouch, from the ventral surface. The right edge has broken off. Total length 2.8, width <3.4, thickness 1.1.

10) Broken flake. White-grey banded chert with smooth, shiny surfaces. Scarred striking-platform with broken, hinged, distal termination. Length <2.1, width <1.65, thickness 0.6.

11) Small flake. Possibly natural pot lid, or broken off flakes 9–10 above. Rough surface where broken off, otherwise similar white-grey chert. Dimensions 1.75x1.0x0.35.

12) Fragment. Flattened, faceted spheroid, probable naturally-fractured piece. Light grey, cherty flint with duller surface than interior. Dimensions 2.3x1.9x1.4.

13) Piece of possible core fragment. Multi-pointed, sub-ovoid fragment of brown flint with creamy-white cortex. Dimensions 2.1x1.6x1.6. Test Pit 1 Phase 0.2.

1527:05 Dates.
Large quantity of date-stones, and two whole dates. Test Pit 1 Phase 0.2.

1527:07 Metal ore.
Small piece of metallic ore. Dimensions 2.8x2.0x2.2. Test Pit 1 Phase 0.2.

1527:08 Metal slag.
Small piece of metallic slag. Test Pit 1 Phase 0.2.

1527:10 Flint. [57f]
Bifacially retouched awl. Diamond-shaped thin flake of good-quality, brown, translucent flint. Striking-platform bifacially reworked with a plunging distal termination. The platform and one proximal edge were bifacially retouched to form one side of the point, the other formed by a side-strike from the ventral surface. The tip is slightly broken/worn. Length 1.76, width 1.37, thickness 0.38. Test Pit 1 Phase 0.2.

1527:12 Worked shell.
Shell with hole, possibly worked. Shell dimensions 4.1x3.9. Hole dimensions 1.3x1.0. Test Pit 1 Phase 0.2.

1528:01 Bitumen fragments.
Six small fragments of bitumen, the two largest with basket-weave impressions. Dimensions of largest 1.8x1.4x0.6. Area 200 Phase 4.5.

1528:04 Copper fragments.
Five badly corroded fragments of copper. All irregular in shape. Dimensions 1) 2.2x1.7x0.6. 2) 1.7x1.2x0.7. 3) 1.5x1.2x0.4. 4) 0.9x0.6x0.5. 5) 0.8x0.5x0.4. Area 200 Phase 4.5.

1529:02 Copper fragment.[35]
Tubular length of copper with longitudinal split. One end slightly splayed. Length 3.4, di. 0.6. Area 200 Phase 4.4.

1529:03 Steatite rim. [53a]
Fragment of well-made stone vessel, perhaps a lid or plate with a flange round the edge. Dark, green-grey steatite. Sub-triangular fragment, original surfaces polished smooth. Fits 6025:16. Dimensions 2.5x2.1x1.0–0.7. Rim thickness 0.7. Area 200 Phase 4.4.

1529:04 Stone object.
Small piece of worked stone. Two broken edges, one finished. Now triangular. Perhaps a segment from a disk-shaped tool or object. Dimensions 2.4x2.0x0.7. Area 200 Phase 4.4.

1529:06 Bitumen fragments.
Large quantity of bitumen fragments, many with reed and basket impressions. Several pieces are very thick, and obviously from a very robust vessel. Typical dimensions 4.0x2.4x1.7, 3.7x2.0x2.0. Area 200 Phase 4.4.

1529:07 Copper fragments.
Two small copper fragments. Dimensions 1) 2.0x1.0x0.5. 2) 1.3x1.1x0.3. Area 200 Phase 4.4.

1529:08 Copper slag.
Two lumps of possible copper slag. Dimensions 1) 2x1x0.5. 2) 1.5x0.6x0.5. Area 200 Phase 4.4.

1529:09 Copper fragments.
Ten pieces of irregularly-shaped, badly corroded copper. One larger, roughly rectangular piece. Dimensions of large piece 2.5x1.5x0.7. Area 200 Phase 4.4.

1529:10 Copper slag.
Lump of slag. Irregular in shape. Dimensions 3.0x2.4x1.0. Area 200 Phase 4.4.

1533:05 Flint.
Large awl/borer. Irregular flake of brown flint with whitish blotches. Flint is poor quality and breaking into odd planes. The striking-platform is plain, with a feather/slightly hinged distal termination. The previous strikes on the dorsal surface are from the proximal and left side. The long-angled tip has been formed on either side by a strike from the ventral surface. Length 5.48, width 3.87, thickness 1.60. Test Pit 1 Phase 0.1.

1533:06 Date.
Carbonized date. Test Pit 1 Phase 0.1.

1533:08 Copper fragment.
Small copper fragment. Test Pit 1 Phase 0.1.

1536:02 Dates.
Thirty carbonized date-stones. Test Pit 1 Phase 0.1.

1536:04 Flint.
1) Awl/point. [57d] Small triangular flake of brown flint with creamy-white cortex. Focal striking-platform and feather distal termination.

Side-strike near platform from ventral surface to form point. This created a right edge which is worn, or has use-wear from the ventral surface. Intact. Length 1.8, width 0.95, thickness 0.31.

2) Scraper/utilized large cortical flake. [58] Sub-oval flake of brown banded flint below a grey chert band below creamy-white cortex. Scarred striking-platform (cortical surface) with plunging distal termination. There is use-wear on a steeply-angled, straight edge towards the distal end. Intact. Length 6.15, width 5.53, thickness 1.23.

3) Large cortical flake. Oval flake of banded grey-white flint below a red thin band, below a grey chert band, below a light brown-grey cortex. Scarred striking-platform with a slightly-plunging, distal termination. Previous strikes on the dorsal surface/cortex from the proximal and both sides. Abrading marks, or use-wear, and large scars at proximal end of cortex on the dorsal surface/cortex. Possibly broken off a pounder. Intact. Length 6.39, width 5.58, thickness 1.50.

4) Scraper or utilized flake. [59] Large, fan-shaped, cortical flake of brown banded flint below a thin red band, below a grey-brown cortex. Scarred, almost faceted, striking-platform with hinged distal termination. Previous scars on the distal surface/cortex from the proximal end. The distal edge has been discontinuously bifacially, and unifacially, retouched and/or shows use-wear. A small section of the edge is denticulated. Intact. Length 4.83, width 5.80, thickness 2.03.

5) Sub-ovoid fragment of grey-brown flint with whitish blotches. One end has possible use-wear on the edge and the opposite point is similarly worn. No obvious striking-platform, and it may have been naturally broken off. The flint is brittle and appears heat-affected. Possibly utilized as a punch or awl. Dimensions 2.01x0.87x0.78. Test Pit 1 Phase 0.1.

1536:06 Bitumen fragment.
Piece of bitumen with reed impressions on one side. Dimensions 3.3x1.9x0.8. Also some small fragments, some with basket-weave impressions. Test Pit 1 Phase 0.1.

1538:02 Bitumen fragments.
Bitumen fragments, two with basket impressions. Dimensions of largest piece 4.0x3.2x0.6. Area 200 Phase 4.5.

1538:03 Copper fragments.
Four badly corroded copper fragments. All irregular in shape. Dimensions 1) 2.9x1.5x1.2. 2) 1.8x1.5x0.5. 3) 2.1x0.8x0.5. 4) 1.4x0.8x0.6. Area 200 Phase 45.

1539:01 Clay sealing. [9]
Complete sealing. Roughly circular lump of yellow/green unbaked clay, with complete impression of stamp seal with an estimated di. of 2.2. Smoothed edges with fingerprints visible. Obverse: hatched rectangle down the centre with a seated bearded figure to the right, hands outstretched towards it. On the left of the rectangle, an unidentified motif, possibly an animal head. Small circular hole, di. 0.2, in the centre of the rectangle punched from the front. Reverse: disk-shaped piece with slight curve to reverse face, di. ca. 10.0, generally smooth surface crossed by three rows of string impressions. Sd. di. 0.25, sg. di. 0.3, TP 0.8, SSD Z-spun, medium/coarse fibres. Traces of possible fold impressions from a covering, perhaps leather. Disk on string. Dimensions 3.0x3.2x1.1. Phase 4.4.

1539:02 Date.
One carbonized date-stone. Area 200 Phase 4.4.

1539:05 Clay sealing.
Four fragments of unbaked yellow/green clay, string marks on one, remains of design on a second.
1) Reverse: string impressions. Sd. di. 0.3, sg. di. 0.35, TP 0.65, SSD S-spun, medium/coarse fibre. Dimensions 2.2x1.7x0.6.
2) Obverse: Edge of seal impression showing human arms, torso, legs. Fingerprints also visible. Dimensions 1.3x0.9x0.7.
3) Dimensions 1.4x0.9x0.6.
4) Dimensions 2.0x1.2x0.8.
Area 200 Phase 4.4.

1541:01 Pottery object. [74]
Stemmed pottery object. Both ends probably broken. Buff coloured, powdery- textured fabric. Solid stem with a flared, rimmed depression at one end. Overall length15.1. Di. of stem 4.1. Di. of rim 8.8. Depth of depression 4.0. Area 200 Phase 4.3.

1541:02 Copper fragment.
Small copper fragment. Irregular in shape. Dimensions 1.6x1.0x0.2. Area 200 Phase 4.3.

1541:03 Bitumen fragments.
Nine pieces of bitumen, all irregular in shape and of varying sizes. Largest two pieces are adhering to the inside of pottery sherds. Small fragments have basket impressions. One thin, curved sliver may be part of a pot lining. Dimensions of largest 4.2x3.3x1.0. Area 200 Phase 4.3.

1542:01 Clay sealing. [10]
Fragment of yellow/green unbaked clay. Obverse: a horned animal, couchant, looking back over its shoulder to the left. Behind it are three vertical motifs, the middle one appears to be a leg or snake. A horizontal line runs under the scene. Reverse broken away. Dimensions 2.4x1.8x0.7. Area 200 Phase 4.3.

1542:03 Clay sealing.
Five small pieces of yellow/grey clay.
1) Fragment of yellow clay. Obverse: part of an impression showing two lines at right angles, with hatched squares in the angles. Irregular in shape. Dimensions 1.6x1.2x0.4.
2) Obverse: clear fingerprints, but no trace of impression.
3–5) Fingerprints, but otherwise featureless.
Area 200 Phase 4.3.

1542:04 Clay sealing.
Fragment of soft grey clay. Smooth edge. Obverse illegible. Reverse: smooth curved surface. Di. 2.8. Possible peg impression. Dimensions 2.5x1.5x1.7. Area 200 Phase 4.3.

1543:03 Clay sealing.
Dark grey clay. Fragment of clay with fingerprint impressions. Very flaky damaged sealing. Dimensions 2.5x1.5x2.1. Area 200 Phase 4.3.

1543:04 Bitumen fragments.
Two tiny bitumen fragments. No evidence of any weave impressions. Not measured. Area 200 Phase 4.3.

1543:05 Metal slag.
Three pieces of slag. Dimensions 1) 2.2x1.0x0.6. 2) 1.5x1.8x0.9. 3) 1.3x1.5x0.7. Area 200 Phase 4.3.

1543:06 Clay sealing. [11]
Hard white clay. Obverse: a standing figure in a net skirt, one hand outstretched to the left towards perhaps a tree. Unidentified motif to the right. Reverse: smooth curved peg impression, di. 1.6, crossed by 2 rows of string impressions. Sd. di. 0.3, sg. di. 0.35, TP 0.7, SSD S-spun, medium/coarse fibres. Peg and string. Dimensions 2.5x1.4x0.7. Area 200 Phase 4.3.

1549:03 Bitumen fragments.
Eight small pieces of bitumen, all irregular in shape, three with basket-weave impressions. Dimensions of largest 1.2x0.8x0.2. Area 200 Phase 4.3.

1549:04 Nut.
Fragment of nut shell. Area 200 Phase 4.3

1550:04 Bitumen fragments.
Four pieces of bitumen, no evidence of basket impressions. Dimensions of largest 2.1x1.6x1.0. Area 220 Phase 4.4.

1550:05 Copper fragments.
Three irregular copper fragments. Dimensions 1) 1.7x0.9x0.8. 2) 1x0.8x0.5. 3) 0.7x0.2. Area 220 Phase 4.4.

1550:06 Clay sealing.
Nine pieces of yellow/green unbaked clay and one of grey/white clay.
1) Obverse: a hatched square, perhaps a fish, and a palm tree/standard. Reverse: smooth impression of circular peg, di. 1.2, length >1.4. Peg bound by 3 rows of string impressions. Sd. di. 0.3, sg. di. 0.35, TP 0.9, SSD S-spun, medium/coarse fibres. Peg and string. Dimensions 2.6x1.8x1.0.
2) Pale green clay, fingerprints on two surfaces. Obverse: faint remains of seal impression. Reverse: no clear markings. Dimensions 2.4x2.0x1.5.
3) Pale yellow/green clay. Obverse: no clear markings. Reverse: unclear string impressions. Dimensions 1.9x1.8x1.1.
4) Pale yellow/green clay. Reverse: unclear string impressions. Dimensions 1.7x1.4x0.6.
5) Pale yellow/green clay. Reverse: string impressions. Sd. di. 0.3, sg. di. 0.35, TP 0.7, medium/coarse fibres.
6) Pale yellow/green clay. Reverse: very unclear string impressions, medium/coarse fibres. Dimensions 1.7x0.8x0.3.
7) Yellow/grey clay. Reverse: very unclear string impressions. Dimensions 1.3x0.9x0.6.
8) Yellow/grey clay, no clear markings on either face. Dimensions 1.2x0.8x0.7.
9) Grey/white clay. Obverse: possible traces of seal impression. Reverse: one surface flat and smooth, second surface at right angles to it has

unclear string impressions. Dimensions 1.7x1.2x0.9. Area 220 Phase 4.4.

1581:03 Bitumen fragment.
Tiny, flat bitumen fragment, no evidence of basket or reed impressions. Roughly square in shape. Dimensions 1.2x1.1x0.3. Area 200 Phase 4.2.

1581:04 Clay sealing. Three pieces of yellow/green, unbaked clay.
1) Obverse: no seal impression, but clear fingerprints. Hole, di. 0.15, pierced through sealing from obverse to reverse. Reverse: two smooth flat surfaces, rest broken. Possibly a tag/label. Dimensions 2.1x1.4x1.4.
2) Obverse: no seal impression, smooth surface. Reverse: slight curve to reverse face, three rows of string impressions. Sd. di. 0.3, sg. di. 0.3, SSD S-spun, medium/coarse fibres. Perhaps a pot and string. Dimensions 1.8x1.2x0.6.
3) Obverse: no seal impression. Single incised line. Reverse: no clear details. Dimensions 2.1x1.3x0.5.
Area 200 Phase 4.2.

1587:01 Flint. [57g]
Backed awl, also possibly small scraper. Flake of light brown, good-quality chert struck off a naturally-shattered fragment. Scarred, almost focal, striking-platform and plunging distal termination. Remnant desert-polished surfaces at both ends. The tip at the distal end has been formed by a small strike to the left from the dorsal surface, and, to the right, by a longer side-strike from the ventral. Both edges on either side of the tip have been retouched from the ventral surface. The left proximal edge is straight and continuously finely retouched, or backed from the ventral surface. The tip is slightly worn. Intact. Length 2.88, width 2.62, thickness 0.71. Area 200 Phase 4.1.

1587:02 Clay sealing.
Three fragments of hard, gritty, greenish clay.
1) Reverse: small area of flat surface, perhaps from peg. Scattered string impressions, medium/coarse fibre. Dimensions 2.0x1.7x0.8.
2) No markings on either side. Dimensions 1.8x1.6x0.6.
3) Obverse: possible impression of animal head. Fingerprints on both sides. Dimensions 1.7x0.9x0.6.
Area 200 Phase 4.1.

1587:03 Copper fragments
Two pieces of copper. 1) Roughly round in shape. Di. 0.6. 2) Irregular in shape. Dimensions 2.1x0.8x0.6. Area 200 Phase 4.1.

1587:05 Clay sealing.
Fragment of hard yellow/green clay. Obverse: left edge of impression. Design shows the net skirt of a standing figure facing right and holding perhaps a spear in one hand. Reverse: 2 faces at right angles. One shows unclear string impression, the other an impression of a smooth curved peg with di. 1.6, length >0.8. Peg and string. Dimensions 1.3x1.2x0.7. Area 200 Phase 4.1.

1588:02 Bitumen fragments.
Five small pieces of bitumen, one with a basket-weave impression. Less than 1.0 square. Area 200 Phase 4.1.

1588:05 Clay sealing.
Clay impression fragment. Piece of seal impression in hard yellow clay. Reverse has been stuck in something flat. Obverse has left edge of seal impression showing the net skirt of a standing figure and one arm holding a bow. Crude and deeply cut. Dimensions 1.4x1.5x0.7. Area 200 Phase 4.1.

1593:01 Clay sealing. [12]
Soft grey clay, originally disk shaped but now broken in half. Obverse: standing male animal, body, hind legs and tail extant, the rest broken with a rosette or plant below its belly. Another illegible motif behind it. Probably from the same seal as 1622:02 (from House 203). Reverse: faint string impressions. Disk on string(?). Dimensions 1.7x1.6x0.7. Area 200 Phase 4.1.

1596:01 Clay sealing. [13]
Yellow/green hardened clay with complete circular seal impression. Di. of seal 2.14. Obverse: a hatched rectangle down the centre, with a schematic human figure seated either side, arms outstretched to hatched rectangle, which is outlined by a post(?) on either side. Perhaps a weaving or netting scene. Reverse: disk-shaped piece with tangled mass of string impressions on reverse. Sd. di. 0.3, sg. di. 0.35, TP 0.8, SSD S-spun, medium/coarse fibres. String is probably in form of loose knot. May originally have been disk on string. Fingerprints round the edge of the disk. Dimensions 3.0x2.6x1.2. Area 200 Phase 4.1.

1596:02 Clay sealing. [14]
Four fragments of yellow/green hardened clay, all with fragmentary seal impressions. Three fragments join and are from the same, almost complete sealing.
1–3) Obverse: three standing human figures, wearing flounced dresses, and facing left. The seal is the same as that used on 1596:03. Reverse: scattered string impressions. Disk on string. Fingerprints round edge. Overall di. (reconstructed) 2.7. Actual dimensions 2.9x2.7x0.6.
4) Obverse: feet of a human and the rest is lost. Reverse: string impressions. Sd. di. 0.25, sg. di. 0.3, TP 0.7, SSD S-spun, medium/coarse fibres. Dimensions 1.7x1.3x0.6.
Area 200 Phase 4.1.

1596:03 Clay sealing. [15]
Yellow/green hardened clay with most of an impression preserved. Estimated di. of seal 2.3. Obverse: two standing human figures and the faint outline of a third, with flounced skirts standing in a row facing left, the central figure holds a jar to the left. From the same seal as 1596:02. Reverse: string impressions. Sd. di. 0.25, sg. di. 0.3, TP 0.8, SSD S-spun, medium/coarse fibres. Angle of reverse suggests a jar sealing. Dimensions 2.5x2.2x1.5. Area 200 Phase 4.1.

1596:04 Copper fragments.
Two badly corroded fragments of copper. Both irregular in shape, both recovered from a floor context. Dimensions 1) 2.5x1.8x1.3. 2) 1.3x1.2x0.6. Area 200 Phase 4.1.

1596:08 Bitumen fragments.
Ten fragments of bitumen, three with basket-weave impressions.

Typical dimensions 2.7x2.0x0.4, 2.2x1.6x0.4. Area 200 Phase 4.1.

1596:09 Flint. [57m]
Scraper, also possible burin. Large sub-trapezoidal flake of light brown flint with white blotches and dark brown speckles. Translucent at edges. Striking-platform reworked, and the probable distal end is plunging. Previous scars on the dorsal surface are from the proximal end. The tool has been bifacially shaped and retouched. Some of the retouching is shallow and invasive. The two distal edges are heavily worked and retouched. The edge to the left is concave and that to the right notched. Two blunt points have use-wear, which may indicate that it was possibly utilized for chiselling (burin). Intact. Length 4.29, width 5.08, thickness: 0.98. Area 200 Phase 4.1.

1597:01 Clay sealing. Three fragments of yellow/green clay.
1) Obverse: no impression. Fingerprint. Reverse: unclear string impression. Dimensions 1.6x1.5x1.3.
2) Obverse: smooth. Reverse: parallel impressions of fibrous vegetal matter. Dimensions 1.6x1.5x0.7.
3) Small edge piece of an impression. Reverse: two faces at right angles, one has clear string impressions. Sd. di. 0.25, sg. di. 0.3, TP 0.5, SSD S-spun, medium/coarse fibres. Other face has clear impression of peg shaft, with di. 1.3, length >1.1, and with parallel striated impressions. Clearly a length of reed used as a peg and bound with string. Dimensions 1.4x0.9x0.8.
Area 220 Phase 3.1.

1597:02 Clay sealing. [16]
Yellow/green unbaked clay. Obverse: traces of hatched triangle. Reverse: no clear markings. Dimensions 2.2x2.1x1.2. Area 220 Phase 3.1.

1597:03 Bitumen stopper. [47]
Bitumen lid or stopper. Cylindrical, with one end flat, and probably originally circular. Length 3.7, overall di. 11.4, di. of cylindrical part 4.8. Area 220 Phase 3.1.

1597:05 Clay sealing.
Two fragments of grey unbaked clay.
1) Obverse: edge of an impression showing a man on the right, with arms raised, in front of a crescent-topped(?) standard. Rosette within arms of the standard. Reverse: no clear impressions. Dimensions 1.2x1.2x0.5.
2) Edge of a sealing, with fingerprints. Reverse: 3 or 4 rows of unclear string impressions, medium/coarse fibres. Dimensions 1.6x1.2x0.8.
Area 220 Phase 3.1.

1597:08 Copper slag.
Two lumps of copper slag. Both irregular in shape.
Dimensions 1) 3.4x2.9x2.1. 2) 1.5x1.2x1.0. Area 220 Phase 3.1.

1597:09 Bitumen fragments. [43]
Large quantity of bitumen fragments. Some join to form a thick, rounded base of a vessel or vessel lining, and pieces of rim. All have weave impressions on one side and some have straw and date-stone imprints on the other side. Dimensions of largest piece 8.1x4.6x1.4. Area 220 Phase 3.1.

1597:10 Clay sealing.
Yellow/green unbaked clay. Hemispherical, broken in half, originally with string through centre. Obverse: smoothed with traces of triangle enclosing hatched lines. All other surfaces lost. Di. 2.4, height 1.0. Area 220 Phase 3.1.

1598:01 Clay sealing.
Five pieces of light grey unbaked clay.
1) Obverse: triangular hatched design, next to a standing figure(?) Reverse: impressions of two surfaces at right angles, one smooth, perhaps from peg. Details unclear. Dimensions 1.7x1.1x1.3.
2) No seal impression, but reverse has very faint string impression. Dimensions 1.3x1.3x0.9.
3) No impression. Dimensions 1.3x0.8x0.6.
4) No impression. Dimensions 0.9x0.8x0.6.
5) No impression. Dimensions 1.2x0.8x0.5.
Area 220 Phase 3.2
.

1598:04 Bitumen fragments.
Two small lumps of bitumen, with no evidence of basket impressions. Dimensions 1) 1.4x1.2x0.7. 2) 1.8x1.2x0.8. Area 220 Phase 3.2.

1598:05 Stone fragment.
Irregularly-shaped piece of possible tool. No evidence of working. Dimensions 3.0x1.5x1.0. Area 220 Phase 3.2.

1599:01 Clay sealing. [17]
Complete sealing. Yellow/orange clay. Di. of seal: 2.2. Obverse: the design is obscured by a rectangular hole in the centre of the scene punched from the front. There is a seated(?) insect or monkey-like figure on the left, with a hatched rectangle on the far right-hand side. Reverse: gently curving surface with two rows of string impressions. Sd. di. 0.3, sg. di. 0.35, TP 0.8, SSD S-spun, medium/coarse fibres. Jar sealing(?). Dimensions 3.9x3.2x1.1. Area 220 Phase 3.2.

1599:02 Bitumen vessel. [44]
Cup or small bowl. A little of rim extant, about half of body, base complete. Rim folded in, probably originally oval or sub-rectangular in plan. Sides slightly convex, base square. The interior has basket-weave impressions all over. The outer surface is smooth. Di. of the rim 7.7, depth 4.2, thickness 0.3, base 4.5 cm square. Area 220 Phase 3.2.

1599:05 Copper slag.
Lump of orange, brown and green slag. Irregular in shape. Dimensions 3.3x2.3x1.5. Area 220 Phase 3.2.

1599:06 Bitumen fragments.
Three small bitumen fragments, all with basket-weave impressions. 1) Dimensions 2.4x1.4x0.8. 2) Dimensions 1.4x1.1x0.5. 3) Piece of rim, 1.3x1.1x0.7. Area 220 Phase 3.2.

1599:07 Clay sealing.
Grey/green unbaked clay. Obverse: the upper torso of a male figure, holding a long shield(?). Now irregular in shape. Reverse: no clear details. Dimensions 1.3x1.0x0.4. Area 220 Phase 3.2.

1599:08 Flint.
Flake. Possibly utilized flake or worn, naturally-fractured piece. Elongated sub-rectangular flake of brown flint with whitish blotches and creamy-white cortex. The dorsal surface is abraded and irregular, the ventral is rough and the stone is more cherty. The cortical striking-platform is at an angle to the flake and the concoidal fracture is long and concave. The distal termination is plunging. All the edges on the ventral surface are worn, possibly through use. Length 2.8, width 1.0, thickness 0.75. Area 220 Phase 3.2.

1599:09 Clay sealing.
Grey unbaked clay. Obverse: circular impression with the head of an animal facing left towards two curved lines, possibly the horns of a second animal. Reverse: unclear string impression. Fingerprints on the edge. Dimensions 1.9x0.9x0.5. Area 220 Phase 3.2.

1599:10 Clay sealing.
Grey clay lump with fingerprint impressions. Edge of seal visible on one surface, possible string marks on reverse. Dimensions 3.0x1.9x1.2. Area 220 Phase 3.2.

1599:11 Clay sealing.
Grey clay fragment, probably from sealing. Reverse: smooth and concave. Irregular in shape. Dimensions 2.1x1.5x0.4. Area 220 Phase 3.2.

1599:12 Clay sealing.
Dark grey clay fragment. No design, fingerprints are visible along one edge. Hole made by stick(?) jabbed into obverse. Hole: 0.35 in di., 0.4 deep. Dimensions 2.8x2.2x0.8. Area 220 Phase 3.2.

1599:13 Clay sealing.
Light grey lump of hardened clay. No design visible. Reverse: unclear string impression. Dimensions 2.7x2.1x1.0. Area 220 Phase 3.2.

1600:01 Clay sealing. [18]
Dark grey unbaked clay, about half of impression extant comprising right and lower left of design. Obverse: seated, bearded, nude figure, with arms held up to either side. To the right he touches caduceus-like symbol, perhaps twisted palm leaves, with an animal leg hanging from the top. To the left of the symbol are the hind quarters of an animal. Above the back of the animal is a fish(?). From the same seal as 1763:09 and 1853:95. Reverse: sub-circular piece with impression of smooth curving surface, di. 4.1, surrounded by 3 or 4 rows of string impressions. Sd. di. 0.3, sg. di. 0.35, TP 0.8, SSD S-spun, medium/coarse fibres. Disk on string. On the edges of the clay are fingerprints. Overall di. 2.8. Area 220 Phase 3.1.

1600:02 Clay sealing. [19]
Light pinkish unbaked clay. About half of disk-shaped piece extant. Obverse: a central 'standard' topped with a crescent, with a horned animal on either side of it. Both animals are looking back over their shoulders at each other. In the left field, above the animal's head, is a branch(?). There is a pinhole, di. 0.1 through the rump of the right-hand animal. Reverse: part of disk-shaped piece, with 3 or 4 rows of string impressions. Sd. di. 0.3, sg. di. 0.35, TP 0.7, SSD S-spun,

medium/coarse fibres. Disk on string. Fingerprints on edge. Dimensions 2.3x2.2x0.9. Area 220 Phase 3.1.

1600:04 Bitumen fragments.
Two tiny pieces of bitumen, no evidence of basket-weave impressions. Not measured. Area 220 Phase 3.1.

1600:05 Clay sealing.
Yellowish unbaked clay. Obverse: on the left a standing animal facing right, but looking back over its shoulder. On the right, a standing figure in a net skirt, probably facing left. A vertical line appears between the figures, perhaps a spear. Very worn. Reverse: faint string impressions, SSD S-spun, medium/coarse fibres. Dimensions 2.2x1.6x0.7. Area 220 Phase 3.1.

1604:04 Bitumen fragments.
Twelve irregular pieces of bitumen. All have been stuck to something, but do not appear related. One fragment has basket-weave impression. One sliver has impression of wood(?) or flattened reed/palm leaf. One thick blob has a right-angled turn as though stuck to a corner. One may be a rim fragment from a vessel. Dimensions of largest piece 3.8x2.5x1.2. Area 200 Phase 3.2.

1604:05 Copper fragments.
Seven pieces of copper.
1) Roughly triangular in shape. Dimensions 2.9x2.5x1.0.
2) Irregular fragment. Dimensions 3.3x2.2x1.3.
3) Irregular. Dimensions 1.4x1.0x0.8.
4) Crescent shaped piece, with what could be a tanged point at one end. Overall dimensions 1.9x0.6x0.3.
5) Irregular-shaped, flattened piece. Dimensions 1.2x0.8x0.2.
6) Rough crescent shaped piece. Dimensions 2.1x1.0x0.5.
7) A piece that looks roughly arrowhead-shaped, but is badly corroded. Overall dimensions 2.8x1.9x0.3.
Area 200 Phase 3.2.

1610:01 Copper artefact. [31]
Copper object, shaped like a long pouring lip, as on a modern Arabian coffee pot, but not obviously broken off. One end narrower than the other. Width at wide end 2.8. Width at narrow end 1.0. Area 200 Phase 3.1.

1610:02 Worked shell. [39]
Glycymeris pectunculus. Edges smoothed and a large hole cut into the body of the shell. Di. 3.8. Area 200 Phase 3.1.

1610:03 Clay sealing. [20]
Yellow/green unbaked clay fragment. Obverse: an erotic scene, the frontal view of a figure with widely splayed legs, a crescent below one arm, and part of a male figure, perhaps engaged in sexual intercourse. Various illegible motifs in the field. Reverse: unclear string impression, medium/coarse fibres. Dimensions 2.4x1.7x1.4. Area 200 Phase 3.1.

1610:04 Painted plaster.
Six pieces of painted plaster. One side of each fragment is flattened and

painted with a red-coloured substance, possibly ochre. Largest piece measures 6.5x4.0x1.4. Area 200 Phase 3.1.

1610:05 Date.
Two calcified date-stones. Dimensions 2.0x0.9x0.8, 1.4x0.8x0.7. Area 200 Phase 3.1.

1611:01 Bitumen stopper.
Stopper fragment, cylindrical with flattened, circular end. Also several fragments, seven with basket-weave impressions.
Extant height 0.6, di. of circular end 1.7x1.2. Area 200 Phase 3.2.

1611:02 Copper fragments.
Three fragments.
1) Long, thin curved piece, possibly the end of a fish-hook, but broken in antiquity. Length 2.1, thickness 0.2.
2) Irregular fragment. Dimensions 1.5x0.3.
3) Tiny, thin strip. Length 1.0, thickness 0.1.
Area 200 Phase 3.2.

1612:01 Steatite seal. [21]
Creamy soft stone. Obverse: a standing, nude male figure, looking to the right. In his right hand he holds a shield, in his left the horns of a long horned animal which looks back over its shoulder at him. An oblong symbol appears in the left field and a crescent in the right, behind the head of the animal. Reverse: standard Dilmun type, with three incised parallel lines across the boss at right angles to the perforation and four incised circles with central dots equally spaced around the edge. Edge: Failaka Variant 2 (Kjaerum 1983). Di. 1.9, height 1.2, weight 5.7 gm. Area 200 Phase 3.2.

1612:02 Clay sealing.
Irregular-shaped piece of yellow/orange, hardened clay. Probably used for sealing. One side is flattened and there is a thumb print on the edge, but no evidence of any impression on front or back. Dimensions 3.3x2.0x1.5. Area 200 Phase 3.2.

1612:07 Bitumen fragments.
Two tiny pieces of bitumen, with no evidence of impressions. Dimensions 1) 1.3x1.0x0.5. 2) 1.3x0.8x0.2. Area 200 Phase 3.2.

1612:08 Copper fragments.
Six pieces of copper.
1) Long, narrow, flattened strip. [36] Dimensions 3.3x0.5x0.2.
2) A flattened fragment with two grooves on one side.
Dimensions 2.2x2.1x0.5.
3) Small segment from probably tubular object. [37] Very thick and heavy, with 3 longitudinal facets on outer surface. About half of width preserved. Dimensions 1.7x0.6.
Three other pieces, irregular in shape.
Area 200 Phase 3.2.

1612:09 Clay sealings.
1) [22] Obverse: the head of a horned animal on the right, looking towards a 'ladder' motif. To the left of the ladder a human figure crouches, one arm outstretched towards the 'ladder'. Behind him is an illegible motif. Reverse: smooth curved surface, di. 1.5, with vegetal

striations from reed peg and one row of unclear string impressions, medium/coarse fibres. Reed peg and string. Dimensions 1.9x1.6x1.0.

2) Piece of clay with one flattened and smoothed surface, but no impression. Reverse: faint string impressions, medium/coarse fibre. Dimensions 1.1x1.0x0.4.

Area 200 Phase 3.2.

1612:10 Clay sealing. [23]
Fine pale grey clay. Obverse: a hatched rectangle, probably originally horizontally across the centre of the design. On one side is a row of bearded human heads facing left, the necks touching it at right angles. Three are preserved, with traces of a fourth. On the opposite side of the rectangle is part of a different, unidentifiable motif. Reverse: two faces at right angles, on one there is a string impression. Sd. di. 0.3, sg. di. 0.5, TP 0.9, SSD S-spun, medium/coarse fibres. The second face is smooth and flat. String and wall or container. Dimensions 2.8x2.0x1.3. Area 200 Phase 3.2.

1612:11 Clay sealing.
Dark grey unbaked clay. Fingerprints on one side. Irregular in shape. Dimensions 2.0x1.3x0.9.
Area 200 Phase 3.2.

1617:01 Copper fragment.
Irregular, very badly corroded piece of copper. Overall dimensions 3x1.7x0.8. Area 220 Phase 3.1.

1618:03 Copper fragments.
Two very badly corroded pieces of copper. Totally irregular in shape. Dimensions 1) 1.4x1.1x1.0. 2) 1.2x0.9x0.6. Area 200 Phase 3.1.

1661:04 Copper fragment.
One tiny ovoid fragment of copper. Dimensions 0.3x0.2x0.2. Area 200 Phase 1.1.

1662:01 Bitumen stopper. [48]
Bitumen stopper or plug. Cone shaped, with flattened tip. Height 3.9, di. at widest end 4.6, at narrow end 2.0. Area 200 Phase 3.1.

1750:02 Bitumen fragments. [42]
Numerous fragments of bitumen, some with impressions of a woven basket/vessel, perhaps all from the same one. Some pieces thicker, one with sherd on inside. Dimensions of largest piece 4.7x3.5x0.6. Area 220 Phase 3.

1750:03 Copper fragments. 3 copper fragments, the first two badly corroded and breaking up.
1) Sub-ovoid. Dimensions 1.4x1.4x1.1.
2) Sub-ovoid. Dimensions 1.5x1.4x1.4.
3) Sub-ovoid lump of copper with small curved tail. Dimensions 1.7x1.1x0.9.
Area 220 Phase 3.

1750:04 Flint.
1) Awl. Also possible small scraper. Dark brown flint with coarser mottling and light grey thin cortex. Wide retouched flake with wide,

concave, scarred striking-platform and slightly hinged distal termination which has been reworked. Convex distal edge, which has been discontinuously bifacially retouched. A small awl tip to the right of the distal edge was formed by a strike on either side from the dorsal surface. One shallow invasive scar runs across the centre of the ventral surface, possibly from the original flake strike. The proximal edge to the right of the striking-platform is straight. Intact. Length 1.8, width 2.53, thickness 0.8.

2) Awl. Blade-flake of brown flint with creamy-white cortex. Plain, cortical striking-platform with a hinged distal termination. The tip has been formed to the left by a side-strike from the ventral surface, and to the right by one from the dorsal. The tip and the side edges are worn, possibly through use. Intact. Length 2.5, width 1.05, thickness 0.6.

3) Awl. Blade-flake of brown mottled flint with creamy-white cortex. Scarred, near-focal, striking-platform with a broken or reworked distal end. Previous strikes on the dorsal surface from the proximal end. The tip at the distal end formed to the left by a wide side-strike and to the right by a shorter one, both from the ventral surface. The tip and the distal edges are worn, possibly through use. Length 2.45, width 1.3, thickness 0.8.

4) Retouched flake, possibly broken off a tool. Sub-oval flake of brown flint with creamy-white cortex. Focal, cortical striking-platform with a hinged distal termination. Previous strikes on the dorsal surface from the distal end. The right edge has been retouched, or has possible heavy use-wear, from the ventral surface. Length 1.25, width 0.05, thickness 0.35.

5) Flake. Fan-shaped flake of dark brown flint with creamy-white cortex. Focal, cortical striking-platform with hinged distal termination. Previous strikes on the dorsal surface from the proximal end. Length 1.23, width 1.65, thickness 0.25.

6) Possible scraper. [57k] Retouched flake, possibly a coarse convex scraper, or backed broken tool. Chunky, triangular flake of mottled light grey-brown chert. Scarred wide flattish striking-platform with plunging distal termination. Coarse, steep retouch on the right edge from the ventral surface. Possible retouch or use-wear towards the proximal end of the left edge. Length 1.97, width 2.25, thickness 0.94.
Area 220 Phase 3.

1750:05 Clay sealing. [24]
Fine light grey unbaked clay with salt crystals visible. Obverse: lower half of a seal impression. Standing nude male figure, head missing, facing left, holding a male horned animal by its head. Animal looks back over its shoulder towards him. Possibly from the same seal as H13:12:01. Reverse: impressions on two faces at right angles. On one face is the impression of a smooth curved peg, di. 1.2, length >1.2. On the second face are string impressions. Sd. di. 0.25, sg. di. 0.3, TP 0.7, SSD unclear, medium/coarse fibres. Also on a small part of this face is an impression of a flat surface with clear striated grain, probably from wood. This suggests the peg was inserted into a wooden door or container. Area 220 Phase 3.

1750:07 Pottery jar. [70a]
Pottery jar with bitumen lining. Restored from sherds: rim and neck missing, and a few small gaps in body. Pinky buff clay, grit temper. Body long, tapering to small, thickened flat base. Body ridged all over outside. Thickly crusted with bitumen inside and over broken upper

edge. Obviously used as a bitumen container. On breakage, bitumen has seeped through hole in base, and swollen along a large vertical crack in body, so that although bitumen 'sherds' join, they had to be removed to allow the pot to be put together. Found beside jar 1750:08. Preserved height 37.0, base di. 8.0, max. width 30.4. Area 220 Phase 3.

1750:08 Pottery jar. [70c & 72]
Pottery jar. Restored from sherds: much of body missing, and base does not fit. Red clay, buff patches on outer surface, sparse grit temper. Rim everted, short neck, shoulder and body round and with shallow ridges. Lower body tapers to thickened flat base. Small hole mended with bitumen in antiquity. Found beside jar 1750:07. Preserved height 32.6, rim di. 12.0, max. width (reconstruc.) c. 30.0. Original height probably c. 36. Area 220 Phase 3.

1750:09 Stone tool.
Possible smoother. Oval, water-formed pebble of light grey, close-grained stone, probably limestone. One face is very smooth around a slight central hollow. As this is more polished than the opposite concave surface it may have been worn during some kind of use. Intact. Dimensions 3.1x2.3x1.0. Area 200 Phase 3.

1750:10 Clay sealing.
Light grey clay lump, uneven. Surfaces smoothed. One surface shows possible impression of wood/leaf. Dimensions 2.6x1.8x1.5. Area 220 Phase 3.

1752:01 Pottery jar. [70b & 73]
Small jar, intact. Red clay, numerous exploded white grits. Wide mouth with gently angled rim, wide neck, globular body. Narrow flat base. Exterior and around rim covered with an uneven horizontal wash of dark red slip. Height 14.5, rim di. 9.6–9.7, base di. 5.5, max. di. approx. 15.0. Area 220 Phase 2.2.

1752:02 Bitumen vessel. [46]
Bitumen vessel/basket, crushed, but with half extant. Interior has basket-weave impressions. The exterior is smooth with a slight horizontal indentation below the rim, corresponding to the position of the original, woven-rim edge. Dimensions 9.5x6.5x3.0. Area 220 Phase 2.2.

1752:03 Bitumen vessel. [45]
Bitumen vessel/basket. Intact, except for rim damage. Badly cracked in all planes. Circular at rim, square at base with cross-shaped stitching. Bitumen-lined both the interior and exterior of the woven basket, as is clearly seem from the impressions. Slight horizontal indentation below the rim due to the lower edge of the woven rim. Di. 5.5–7.4.(distorted), approx. height 6.0. Area 220 Phase 2.2.

1752:04 Bitumen vessel.
Numerous bitumen fragments, probably from a single vessel, with impressions of basket-weave. Some rim and thicker walled fragments. Base was square, with pointed corners. Dimensions of large rim fragment 4.2x4.1x0.9. Area 220 Phase 2.2.

1752:06 Clay sealing.
Three possible sealing fragments of light grey clay.

1) Burnt. No clear markings apart from finger prints. Dimensions 1.9x1.9x1.3.
2) No visible markings. Dimensions 1.7x1.6x1.1.
3) No visible markings. Dimensions 1.6x1.4x0.8.
Area 220 Phase 2.2.

1752:07 Flint. [57]
Micro-awl. Small blade-flake of brown chert. Missing (broken) striking-platform and reworked distal end. Tip formed at the distal end by a strike to the left from the ventral surface, and one to the left from the dorsal. Intact. Length 1.23, width 0.65, thickness 0.3. Area 220 Phase 2.2.

1752:11 Clay fragments.
Twenty fragments of light grey-green silty clay with numerous, small gastropod shells within. From sieved fill of small jar, 1752:01. Probably originated from flooring material. Largest 4.6x4.1x2.5. Area 220 Phase 2.2.

1763:01 Plaster fragments.
Seven fragments of gypsum plaster, 6 painted with a crimson-red substance, possibly ochre.
1) Trapezoid decorated with a narrow curved line in reserve. Dimensions 7.8x7.1x1.6.
2) Sub-oval with possible reserved decoration. Dimensions 7.9x4.6x2.3.
3) Triangular with possible reserved decoration.
 Dimensions 2.6x2.1x0.9.
4) Triangular: 3.6x3.4x1.5.
5) Diamond shaped. Dimensions 1.8x1.3x0.9.
6) Sub-rectangular. Dimensions 6.3x4.4x2.1.
7) Diamond shaped with painted areas. Dimensions 1.0x6.0x1.3.
Area 200 Phase 3.1

1763:04 Possible bitumen sealings.
Eleven fragments of bitumen, perhaps from pot sealings. Varied shapes, some with folds and faint, illegible impressions of something. Dimensions of largest fragment 4.1x3.3x3.2. Area 200 Phase 3.1.

1763:05 Clay sealings.
Twelve fragments of light green sandy clay, including two definite sealings.
1) Obverse: no impression. Reverse: stretch of curved peg, di. 3.8, with unclear string impressions of medium/coarse fibres. Reed(?) peg and string.
2) Obverse: no impression. Reverse: two rows of string impressions. Sd. di. 0.2, sg. di. 0.25, TP 0.6, SSD S-spun.
The remaining fragments have no markings.
Area 200 Phase 3.1.

1763:07 Copper fragments.
Four fragments of copper. Nos.1–2 have brown staining (perhaps iron rust).
1) Irregular ovoid lump. Probably from the end of an object with a broken stem/shaft. Dimensions 2.3x2.1x1.2.
2) Sub-ovoid lump. Dimensions 1.3x0.9x0.8.
3) Sub-ovoid lump including part of a stem/shaft with a rectangular

section. Dimensions 1.7x1.1x0.9.
4) Irregular ovoid lump. Dimensions 1.7x1.0x1.0.
Area 200 Phase 3.1.

1763:08 Clay sealing.
Fine light grey clay. Obverse: upper central part of a seal impression preserved but the design is illegible with the exception of a possible animal head. Reverse: four rows of string impressions. Sd. di. 0.3, sg. di. 0.35, TP 0.9, SSD S-spun. Jar sealing(?) Dimensions 2.5x1.9x0.5. Area 200 Phase 3.1.

1763:09 Clay sealing. [25]
Fine grey unbaked clay with salt crystals visible. Obverse: badly damaged human head and arm facing left and touching broken 'caduceus' with animal leg hanging from the top. Two small holes pierced from obverse over impression. Same seal as 1600:01 and 1853:95. Reverse: two parallel rows of string impressions. Sd. di. 0.3, sg. di. 0.35, TP 0.7, SSD S-spun. Dimensions 1.0x1.2x0.6. Area 200 Phase 3.1.

1763:10 Clay sealing.
Fine unbaked grey clay. Obverse: part of standing figure in long skirt with one arm raised to the right, perhaps holding a long shield. Reverse: part of smooth surface with faint string impressions. Dimensions 1.9x1.2x0.6. Area 200 Phase 3.1.

1763:11 Clay sealing. [26]
Fine grey clay. Two pieces joined together. One quarter of the seal impression is preserved, intact to the edge. Obverse: bottom left quadrant of a seal impression showing leaping(?) naked figure above a long, notched, curved object, like a long animal horn. Below this at an angle of 90 degrees is the head and ruffed neck of a short horned animal. For similar design see seal 2070:05. Reverse: part of disk with unclear string impression. Dimensions 2.3x1.5x0.7. Area 200 Phase 3.1.

1764:03 Bitumen fragments.
Three fragments of bitumen with impressions of basket-weave. Dimensions of largest fragment 2.4x2.1x0.3. Area 200 Phase 3.

1770:02 Stone tool. [54]
Pounder/smoother. Sub-cuboid fragment of brown sandstone. Almost all the faces are flattish. One large rectangular face is worn smooth and flat with its edges abraded and scarred, especially one beside a concave face. The opposite face is partly smooth and slightly concave, but has been subsequently abraded. Both sub-rectangular ends are very abraded and slightly scarred. One is flat and the other is concave. The latter is the most abraded and scarred, making it even narrower along the central axis. The other flat face on the side, and all the edges, are also abraded. Intact. Dimensions 8.0x5.6–6.5x3.6–4.1. Area 220 Phase 1.1.

1772:01 Bitumen bung. [49]
Fragmentary lid or stopper. Cylindrical, with disk-shaped end. Dimensions 4.7x3.3x2.5. Area 200 Phase 3.1.

1772:02 Bitumen fragments.
Six fragments of bitumen. All have basket-weave impressions on one side, the other side being smooth. Traces of thin, interior lining too. Largest fragment 3.4x3.1x0.4. Area 200 Phase 3.1

1773:01 Stone bead. [52]
Cylindrical bead of orange banded agate. Intact except for worn ends beside the holes. Polished surface. Di. max. 0.9, min. 0.7, length 3.3. Area 200 Phase 3.1.

1775:01 Stone socket.
Door socket. Large, rough chunk of angular limestone, sub-rectangular in plan. Utilized on one side as a door-socket. Light brown stone with numerous inclusions of many sizes. The upper side has light brown, earthy-plaster deposits in which a sunken, circular hollow has been continually worn over a long period of time by the door. Intact. Length 29.5, width 23.5, thickness 11.0. Circular hollow, di. 4.0. The hole appears to have shifted sideways through time. The wider compound hole is 5.0 in di., 3.0 deep. Area 220 Phase 1

1776:01 Bitumen fragments.
Three fragments of bitumen with basket-weave impressions. Dimensions of largest fragment. 2.7x2.5x1.2. Area 220 Phase 1.

1780:02 Bitumen bead. [51]
Squashed, ovoid bitumen bead. Large central hole. One small area shows impression of organic material inclusions, possibly straw. Surface is now pitted. Intact. Di. 2.7, length 1.5, di. of hole: 0.5x0.4. Area 200 Phase 3.

1785:01 Copper object.
Copper object, incomplete and extant as two adjoining fragments. Curved thick object with two flat surfaces. Dimensions 3.0x1.3x0.8. (Metal in section is 0.4 thick.). Area 200 Phase 2.3.

1785:02 Copper object.
Thick L-shaped fragment of copper. One surface is flat, the other is irregular. Broken off unknown object. Dimensions 3.1x2.0x1.0. Area 200 Phase 2.3.

1785:03 Copper object.
Sub-circular object or fragment of copper. Thick with two roughly flat surfaces. Dimensions 1.6x1.4x0.6. Area 200 Phase 2.3.

1785:04 Clay sealing. [27]
Dark grey clay with mineral inclusions. About three quarters of sealing preserved. Obverse: all but the top left of design preserved, showing stylized palm tree in the centre, seated figure with head missing to left, holding trunk of tree with both hands. Badly damaged motif to right of tree, possibly an animal. Reverse: almost complete disk with three overlapping rows of string impressions. Sd. di. 0.3, sg. di. 0.4, TP 0.9, SSD Z-spun. Unusual string and clay suggest origin outside Saar. Dimensions 2.2x2.3x1.1. Estimated di. of seal 1.8. Area 200 Phase 2.3.

1785:05 Latex impression of footprint.
Latex rubber impression of a group of footprints in temple floor. Adjacent to matting impression 1785:08. Dimensions 127x80. Area 200 Phase 2.3.

1785:06 Latex impressions of footprints.
Latex rubber impression of a group of footprints in the temple floor. Near the central column of the temple. Dimensions 80x36. Area 200 Phase 2.3.

1785:07 Latex impression of footprints.
Latex rubber impression of a group of footprints in the temple floor. Near bench and impression 1824:01.Dimensions 92x76. Area 200 Phase 2.3.

1785:08 Latex matting.
Latex rubber impression of matting seen impressed on surface of temple floor. Beside footprints 1785:08. Dimensions 85x82. Area 200 Phase 2.3.

1785:09 Clay sealing.
Five fragments light grey sandy clay with inclusions. One fragment has illegible design on obverse. No clear impressions on reverse. Dimensions 1) 2.0x1.1x0.9. 2) 1.6x0.9x0.4. 3–5) <1.0. Area 200 Phase 2.3.

1821:01 Ivory object. [41]
Artefact of ivory. Cut length of flattened shaft, very cracked and broken pieces joined together. Both ends show where cut. Length 9.4, width 2.5–2.2, thickness 0.6. Area 200 Phase 2.2.

1824:01 Latex impression of matting.
Latex rubber impression of possible matting. Near to impression 1785:07. Dimensions 62.0x51.0. Area 200 Phase 1.

1843:02 Bitumen fragments.
Thirty-seven fragments of bitumen and numerous very small flakes. Only two small fragments have obvious impressions, one basket-weave, the other unidentifiable. Dimensions of the largest fragment 4.9x4.0x0.8. Area 220 Phase 1.

1843:04 Flint.
Light brown flint flake. Dimensions 1.3x1.2x0.1. Area 220 Phase 1.

1844:02 Bitumen fragments.
Thirty-six fragments of bitumen, of which thirteen have clear basket-weave impressions. Dimensions of the largest fragment 3.4x2.1x0.5. Area 200 Phase 1.

1874:01 Metal fragments.
Four copper fragments, one with iron adhering to all its surfaces, plus one iron fragment. Area 201 Phase 2.2.

1874:02 Copper nail. [32]
Copper nail, from street sand. Length 19.4, thickness 0.8. Di. across head 1.2. Area 201 Phase 2.2.

1896:03 Copper fragments.
Three fragments of copper.
1) Irregular-shaped fragment. Dimensions 0.9x0.8x0.6.
2) Copper loop or link. [159] Dimensions 1.5x0.6x0.3.
3) Irregular-shaped fragment. Dimensions 0.5x0.3x0.2.
Area 200 Phase 1.

1896:04 Pearl.
Possible pearl or fish tooth. Di. 0.4. Area 200 Phase 1.

1905:03 Copper fragments.
Two fragments of copper.
1) Elongated, irregular-shaped fragment. Dimensions 2.6x1.3x0.5.
2) Irregular-shaped, flat fragment. Dimensions 1.4x1.1x0.2.
Area 200 Phase 2.1.

1905:04 Flint. [57h]
Backed awl and possible notched scraper. Flake off a naturally weathered piece of brown flint with whitish blotches. Reworked striking-platform and hinged distal termination. Dorsal surfaces rough and weathered. The right edge is formed from a long side-strike from the dorsal surface which created one side of a tip at both ends. The notched long side of the proximal awl-tip was formed by unifacial shaping and retouch from the ventral surface. The continuous retouch (backing?) and/or use-wear is mostly from the dorsal surface. The right edge has similar retouch and/or use-wear done from the dorsal surface. Intact. Length 3.05, width 2.0. Area 200 Phase 2.

1906:03 Bitumen fragment.
Bitumen fragment with basket-weave impressions. Dimensions 1.7x1.2x0.2. Area 200 Phase 2.

1907:03 Glass beads.
Two glass beads.
1) Black, Woolley type 12. Length 0.5, di. 0.4.
2) Green, Woolley type 4. Length 0.5, di. 0.4.
Presumed intrusive.
Area 200 Phase 1.3.

1911:03 Copper fragment.
Copper fragment. Irregular-shaped. Dimensions 2.0x1.5x0.7. Area 200 Phase 1.1.

1915:03 Copper fragments.
Two fragments.
1) Irregular-shaped fragment, with traces of iron present. Dimensions 2.2x1.0x0.6.
2) Irregular-shaped fragment. Dimensions 1.0x0.9x0.5.
Area 200 Phase 1.

1915:04 Bitumen fragments.
Seven bitumen fragments. Dimensions of largest fragment 2.2x2.0x0.8. Area 200 Phase 1.

1919:03 Bitumen fragments.
Twenty fragments of bitumen. Dimensions of largest fragment 3.4x2.8x1.1.
Area 200 Phase 1.

1924:03 Bitumen fragments.
Twenty-two fragments of bitumen, some with faint impressions on. Dimensions of largest fragment 5.5x3.7x1.3. Test Pit 1 Phase 0.4.

1928:03 Copper fragments.
Three fragments of copper.
1) Irregular-shaped fragment. Dimensions 1.7x0.8x0.7.
2) Irregular-shaped, flat fragment. Dimensions 1.8x0.8x0.3.
3) Irregular-shaped fragment. Dimensions 1.5x1.3x0.9.
Test Pit 1 Phase 0.3.

1928:04 Bitumen fragments.
Numerous bitumen fragments. Dimensions of largest fragment 1.6x1.1x0.6. Test Pit 1 Phase 0.3.

1929:03 Copper fragment.
Copper fragment. Roughly circular/oval in shape. Dimensions 1.4x1.2x0.7. Test Pit 1 Phase 0.3.

1929:04 Bitumen fragments.
Numerous bitumen fragments. Dimensions of largest fragment 1.6x1.1x0.4. Test Pit 1 Phase 0.3.

1930:03 Clay fragments.
Twenty-four, hardened, yellow clay fragments. Dimensions of largest fragment 4.4x3.1x2.0. Test Pit 1 Phase 0.3.

H13:05:01 Copper fragments.
Two lumps of copper. One round and flat, di. c.1.5. One irregular, 2.2x0.9. Area 200 Phase 6.

H13:05:04 Bitumen fragments.
Eight fragments of bitumen, probably all part of a basket-lining. Dimensions of largest 2.7x1.7x0.5. Area 200 Phase 6.

H13:06:03 Bitumen fragments.
Many tiny fragments of bitumen, with basket-weave impressions. Dimensions of largest 1.3x1.5x1.3. Area 200 Phase 5.2.

H13:09:01 Copper link. [33]
Strip of copper wire, sharpened at both ends, bent to form a complex link, or clasp. One end is coiled into an irregular spiral ring, the other is bent nearly double to form a small hook, with the point bent again, away from the shaft. Restored from three broken pieces. Dimensions 7.7x3.6. Wire 0.2. thick. Area 200 Phase 4.3.

H13:09:05 Bitumen fragments.
Bitumen fragments with basket-weave impressions on one side. Dimensions of largest 2.2x1.3x0.7. Area 200 Phase 4.3.

H13:09:06 Copper fragments.
Four fragments of corroded copper. Dimensions of largest fragment 1.2x1.0x0.5. Area 200 Phase 4.3.

H13:09:07 Flint.
Flake, possibly utilized as end-scraper. Sub-rectangular flake of dark brown, mottled flint with creamy-white cortex. Plain striking-platform with plunging distal termination. Previous strikes on dorsal surface from the proximal end and the side. Possible use-wear on distal edge done from the ventral surface. Length 4.10, width 2.51, thickness 1.22. Area 200 Phase 4.3.

H13:11:03 Bitumen fragments.
Five small fragments of bitumen. Largest measures 1.3x1.5x1.1, and has impressions of string or reed. Area 200 Phase 4.3.

H13:12:01 Complete sealing. [28]
Pink clay. Obverse: oblong impression, the lowest part broken off, fingerprints on edge. Standing figure wearing a flounced skirt, arms up to either side. To the right he holds a shield(?), and on the right of that there is a hatched vertical oblong. To the left of the figure there is a horned animal facing left, with head turned to look back over its shoulder. Compare Kjaerum 1983, 201 and 202. Reverse: stretch of peg impression, di. 3.4, length >1.0 with parallel striations, clearly from a reed peg. Three rows of string impressions round peg. Sd. di. 0.25, sg. di. 0.3, TP 0.7, SSD S-spun medium/coarse fibres. Reed peg and string. Dimensions 2.5x2.2x1.0. Area 200 Phase 3.2.

H13:12:03 Bitumen fragments.
Several bitumen fragments, apparently part of a basket-lining. Dimensions of largest 1.4x1.6x0.5. Area 200 Phase 3.2.

H13:12:04 Copper fragments.
Four small fragments of badly corroded copper. Dimensions of largest fragment 1.5x1.0x0.6. Area 200 Phase 3.2.

H13:13:03 Bitumen fragment.
One fragment of bitumen with basket-weave impressions. Dimensions 1.1x1.2x0.8. Area 200 Phase 5.2.

H13:14:03 Bitumen fragments.
Four fragments of bitumen, three with basket-weave impressions on one side. Dimensions of largest 1.78x0.95x0.54. Area 200 Phase 3.2.

H13:14:04 Copper ring. [30]
One small copper link, badly corroded. Dimensions 0.9x0.9x0.4. Area 200 Phase 3.2.

H13:14:05 Copper fragment.
Badly corroded fragment. Dimensions 2.0x1.4x0.6. Area 200 Phase 3.2.

H13:14:08 Date.
Fragment of a carbonized date stone. Area 200 Phase 3.2.

H13:16:03 Bitumen fragments.
Very small fragments of bitumen, the larger pieces have basket-weave impressions on one side. Typical dimensions 1.3x1.3x0.3. Area 200 Phase 3.

H13:20:03 Bitumen.
Bitumen fragments, many with basket-weave impressions on one side. Dimensions of largest: 2.4x2.2x1.5. Area 200 Phase 3.

H13:20:04 Copper fragments.
Eleven fragments of copper. Dimensions of largest fragment 2.0x2.0x0.6.
Area 200 Phase 3.

H13:20:05 Flint.[57j]
Tool. Small scraper, or component tool such as a barb or sickle-blade. Triangular flake off a naturally-fractured piece of brown mottled flint with remnant creamy-white cortex. Focal striking-platform with plunging distal termination. Previous strikes on the originally-weathered dorsal surface from the distal and proximal ends. The distal edge has bifacial retouch and/or use-wear. Small area of retouch (backing?) on side and proximal end from the ventral surface. Intact. Dimensions 2.0x1.5x0.6. Area 200 Phase 3.

H13:22:03 Bitumen fragments.
Bitumen fragments with basket-weave impressions on one side. Typical dimensions 1.7x1.7x0.9, 4.1x2.0x0.7. Area 200 Phase 3.

H13:22:04 Copper fragments.
Two very badly corroded fragments of copper.
Dimensions 1) 2.2x1.6x1.2. 2) 0.7x1.1x0.6. Area 200 Phase 3.

H13:24:03 Bitumen fragments.
Quantity of bitumen fragments, some with basket-weave impressions. Dimensions of largest 2.1x2.0x1.9. Area 200 Phase 1.

H13:24:04 Worked bone.
Fragment of possibly polished bone. Area 200 Phase 1.
H13:24:05 Worked bone.
Fragment of possibly polished bone. Area 200 Phase 1.

H13:25:04 Bitumen fragments.
Bitumen fragments from basket lined both inside and out. Dimensions of largest fragment 3.2x2.8x0.8. Test Pit 1 Phase 0.4.

H13:27:04 Stone tool.
Sub-square piece of grey limestone with naturally worn, flattish faces that are slightly concave in the centre. One convex end has possibly been abraded. Possibly used briefly as a tool, but no real evidence of use. Dimensions 3.7x3.5x2.3. Test Pit 1 Phase 0.4.

H13:27:06 Copper fragments.
Three corroded fragments of metal. Dimensions 1) 2.0x1.6x1.0. 2) 1.4x1.0x0.8. 3) 1.8x1.5x0.5. Test Pit 1 Phase 0.4.

H13:29:01 Bitumen vessel.
Large quantity of bitumen fragments, all with clear basket impressions on one side. All apparently from one crushed vessel. Typical dimensions 3.0x2.5x0.15, 1.5x2.1x0.12. Test Pit 1 Phase 0.4.

H13:29:04 Bitumen fragments.
Large quantity of bitumen fragments, some with basket-weave impressions. Some thick and robust. Dimensions of largest 2.4x2.2x1.5. Test Pit 1 Phase 0.4.

H13:29:06 Bitumen fragments.
A number of small fragments of bitumen, at least one from a basket coated on both sides. Dimensions 1.5x1.4x0.4. Test Pit 1 Phase 0.4.

H13:31:04 Bitumen fragments.
Tiny fragments of bitumen. Dimensions of largest 1.6x1.4x1.3. Test Pit 1 Phase 0.4.

H13:32:03 Bitumen fragment.
Fragment of bitumen. Dimensions 2.0x1.3x0.9. Test Pit 1 Phase 0.4.

H13:32:04 Copper fragments.
Two corroded fragments of metal. Dimensions of largest fragment 2.0x1.0x0.8. Test Pit 1 Phase 0.4.

H13:33:03 Bitumen fragments.
Several fragments of bitumen, some of which are part of a basket coated inside and out. Dimensions of largest 2.4x1.8x0.9. Test Pit 1 Phase 0.4.

H13:33:04 Flint.
1) Awl or point. [57e] Triangular. Blade-flake of brown flint with grey chert mottling. Scarred striking-platform with reworked distal end. Tip formed at distal end by side-strike from ventral surface. The tip has broken. Possible use-wear on the right edge done from the ventral surface. Length <2. 15, width 0.81, thickness 0.51.
2) Possible utilized flake. Sub-triangular flake of light grey chert with scarred, near focal, striking-platform and plunging distal termination. Previous strikes on the dorsal surface from the sides. Two edges on either side of the distal end have retouch or use-wear done from the ventral surface. Length 2.01, width 2.82, thickness 0.81.
3) Flake. Sub-rectangular thin flake, of good-quality light brown flint (almost translucent) with whitish blotches. Scarred striking-platform and hinged distal termination. Length 0.90, width 0.77, thickness 0.25.
4) Flake. Sub-cuboid cortical flake of brown chert with creamy-white cortex. Focal striking-platform and plunging distal termination. Possibly broken off a pounder. Length 1.0, width 0.94, thickness 0.5.
5) Flake. Sub-rectangular cortical flake of mottled and banded brown flint, with thick, creamy-white cortex. Scarred or abraded, cortical striking-platform and hinged distal termination. Possibly broken off a pounder. Length 2.1, width 2.33, thickness 0.47.
6) Flake. Sub-rectangular cortical flake of coarse grey chert, with thick light grey cortex. Scarred or abraded, cortical striking-platform with feather distal termination. Two or three previous strikes on dorsal surface from proximal end. Possibly broken off a pounder. Length 1.75, width 2.48, thickness 0.75.
7) Flake. Narrow sub-triangular flake, of good-quality brown flint with whitish blotches. Focal striking-platform and feather distal termination. Length 1.28, width 0.57, thickness 0.28.
8) Flake or chip. Sub-oval flake of mottled and banded brown-grey flint. Focal striking-platform and hinged distal termination. Possibly broken off a pounder. Length 0.97, width 0.75, thickness 0.32.
9) Flake or chip. Sub-triangular flake of good-quality brown flint. Length 0.52, width 0.88, thickness 0.23.
10. Flake or chip. Sub-oval flake of brown flint with whitish blotches. Dimensions 0.68x0.54x0.19.
Area 200 Phase 0.4.

H13:34:03 Flint.

Retouched flake. Possibly utilized as scraper or punch. Sub-oval flake of light grey and dark brown, flinty chert with cortex flaws. Possible bipolar flake. Striking-platform partly reworked and difficult to identify, but appears scarred with a possibly plunging distal termination. Opposite, distal, end is also scarred. Previous strikes on the dorsal surface from the distal end and both sides. One side edge coarsely bifacially retouched. Length 2.54, width 2.05, thickness 0.70. Test Pit 1 Phase 0.3.

H13:36:03 Bitumen fragments.

Fragments of bitumen, robust, with impressions of leaf or reed on one side. Dimensions of largest piece 3.2x2.4x0.9. Test Pit 1 Phase 0.3

5: Index of Finds Arranged by Phase

6: Index of Finds Arranged by Material

BITUMEN BEAD
1780:02

**BITUMEN FRAG-
MENTS**
1504:01
1505:01
1507:02
1512:01
1513:02
1523:02
1524:01
1526:01
1527:01
1528:01
1529:06
1536:06
1538:02
1541:03
1543:04
1549:03
1550:04
1581:03
1588:02
1596:08
1597:09
1598:04
1599:06
1600:04
1604:04
1612:07
1750:02
1764:03
1772:02
1776:01
1843:02
1844:02
1906:03
1915:04
1919:03
1924:03
1928:04
1929:04
H13:05:04
H13:06:03
H13:09:05
H13:11:03
H13:12:03
H13:13:03
H13:14:03
H13:16:03
H13:20:03
H13:22:03
H13:24:03
H13:25:04
H13:29:04
H13:29:06
H13:31:04
H13:32:03
H13:33:03
H13:36:03

BITUMEN SEALINGS
1505:08
1763:04

BITUMEN STOPPER
1505:04
1597:03
1611:01
1662:01
1772:01

BITUMEN VESSEL
1599:02
1752:02
1752:03
1752:04
H13:29:01

WORKED BONE
H13:24:04
H13:24:05

CLAY FRAGMENTS
1752:11
1930:03

CLAY SEALINGS
1508:03
1539:01
1539:05
1542:01
1542:03
1542:04
1543:03
1543:06
1550:06
1581:04
1587:02
1587:05
1588:05
1593:01
1596:01
1596:02
1596:03
1597:01
1597:02
1597:05
1597:10
1598:01
1599:01
1599:07
1599:09
1599:10
1599:11
1599:12
1599:13
1600:01
1600:02
1600:05
1610:03
1612:02
1612:09

1612:10
1612:11
1750:05
1750:10
1752:06
1763:05
1763:08
1763:09
1763:10
1763:11
1785:04
1785:09
H13:12:01

COPPER FRAGMENTS
1502:02
1506:01
1510:04
1511:01
1514:01
1526:04
1528:04
1529:02
1529:07
1529:09
1533:08
1538:03
1541:02
1550:05
1587:03
1596:04
1604:05
1611:02
1612:08
1617:01
1618:03
1661:04
1750:03
1763:07
1896:03
1905:03
1911:03
1915:03
1928:03
1929:03
H13:05:01
H13:09:06
H13:12:04
H13:14:05
H13:20:04
H13:22:04
H13:27:06
H13:32:04

COPPER OBJECTS
1502:01
1505:03
1610:01
1785:01
1785:02
1785:03
1874:02

H13:09:01
H13:09:04

COPPER SLAG
1516:03
1529:08
1529:10
1597:08
1599:05

DATES
1512:02
1513:05
1516:02
1523:01
1527:05
1533:06
1536:02
1539:02
1610:05
H13:14:08

**FLINT TOOLS AND
FRAGMENTS**
1500:01
1512:03
1512:06
1513:03
1516:10
1523:04
1527:04
1527:10
1533:05
1536:04
1587:01
1596:09
1599:08
1750:04
1752:07
1843:04
1905:04
H13:09:07
H13:20:05
H13:34:03
H13:33:04

FOSSIL
1512:07

GLASS BEADS
1907:03

IVORY OBJECT
1821:01

**LATEX IMPRESSIONS
TAKEN**
1785:05
1785:06
1785:07
1785:08
1824:01

METAL FRAGMENT
1874:01

METAL ORE
1513:07
1527:07

METAL SLAG
1527:08
1543:05

NUT
1549:04

PEARLS
1516:09
1896:04

PAINTED PLASTER
1505:05
1610:04
1763:01

POTTERY JAR
1750:07
1750:08
1752:01

POTTERY OBJECT
1541:01

SHELL (WORKED)
1527:12
1610:02

**STEATITE RIM FRAG-
MENTS**
1529:03

STEATITE SEAL
1612:01

STONE BEAD
1773:01

STONE FRAGMENT
1598:05

STONE OBJECT
1529:04

STONE SOCKET
1775:01

STONE TOOLS
1512:04
1512:05
1512:10
1516:06
1750:09
1770:02
H13:27:04